The Black Struggle for
Public Schooling in Nineteenth-
Century Illinois

The Black Struggle

Southern Illinois University Press
Carbondale and Edwardsville

for Public Schooling
in Nineteenth-Century Illinois

Robert L. McCaul

To the memory of Margaret Ann McCaul

Printed in the United States of America
Designed by Loretta Vincent
Production supervised by Natalia Nadraga
90 89 88 87   4 3 2 1

Library of Congress Cataloging-in-Publication Data

McCaul, Robert L.
    The Black struggle for public schooling in nineteenth-century
Illinois.

    Bibliography: p.
    Includes index.
    1. Afro-Americans—Education—Illinois—History—
19th century.   2. Afro-Americans—Civil rights—
Illinois—History—19th century. I. Title.
LC2771.M33   1987   370'.8996073'0773   86-26004
ISBN 0-8093-1335-9

The paper used in this publication meets the minimum requirements of
American National Standard for Information Sciences
– Permanence of Paper for Printed Library Materials, ANSI Z39.48-1984.

Contents

Preface   vii

1. Coping with Exclusion   1
2. Black Efforts at the State Level   17
3. White Efforts at the State Level   33
4. Exclusion at the Local Level   44
5. Segregation in Chicago   55
6. Winning Suffrage   73
7. Participating in Mainstream Community Life   90
8. Gaining Access to Public Schools   108
9. Illinois Supreme Court Opinions in School Segregation Cases   127
10. Yesterday, Today, Tomorrow   143

References   159
Notes   171
Index   185

Preface

The larger question I have addressed is this: why, how, and with what success do disadvantaged groups within our society make use of the available sources of power in their struggles to win an equal share of the rights and benefits from which they are excluded? Within the frame set by this question the case of the nineteenth-century Illinois blacks' struggle for public-school and other rights becomes one more instance of a disadvantaged group fighting for equal treatment in the arena of American community life.

I do not claim that nineteenth-century Illinois blacks were perfectly representative of disadvantaged groups as a class or that the circumstances of their deprivation were identical to those amid which other disadvantaged groups have struggled to attain their own particular goals. Illinois blacks during the antebellum and bellum periods did not have access to the voting booth, the courts, and the schools and to occupations generating bargaining leverage to the same extent that other disadvantaged groups had then and have now or that blacks themselves have in the last decades of the twentieth century. The state of Illinois one hundred and thirty or so years ago was less developed demographically and socially than the two older states of the region, Ohio and Indiana, and the states farther east and south. Nor did the states to the west assume the same pattern of growth. Nevertheless, as will become clear, these are differences in degree. There are enough similarities in kind to permit cautious generalizations to be drawn on the basis of the experience of nineteenth-century Illinois blacks and whites and to permit other scholars studying other disadvantaged groups to find something here relevant to their own concerns and purposes. In describing how what I have called rewarding power, punishing power, and dialectical power were exercised in Illinois, my study may also have something to say to those scholars who are interested in the nature of power per se and to those activists who are now struggling to gain for blacks, Hispanics, women, and others a fuller participation in all sectors of our society.

No other study of disadvantaged groups and their efforts to improve their condition has the same focus or covers the same terrain as this one. Here central attention is given to what the blacks were trying to do for themselves, not so much on what white abolitionists and white antislavery crusaders were trying to do for them. The stage on which action takes place is the entire state. Local events are considered auxiliary to the major drama. Public schools are creatures of the state; state laws govern education down in the school districts. To win admission into public schooling, members of the aggrieved group must obtain repeal of the laws that discriminate against them. Having secured repeal, they can campaign to have the offending laws replaced by laws favorable to them. Then they can exert pressure at the local level to entice, force, or persuade the local authorities to obey the new laws, or else if repeal is not followed by favorable legislation, they can attempt to entice, force, or persuade the local authorities to act on the opportunities made available to them by the freedom from compulsion ensuing from repeal.

This study is keyed to the concepts of "bargaining power" and "community." It utilizes the concepts in presenting, explaining, and interpreting events occurring across a broad span of community living. Events within one institution are viewed as influencing those in others, and therefore the study becomes not just an account of a struggle for school rights but a study of interacting struggles for political, civil, economic, social, and, to be sure, educational rights and of the manner in which each of these struggles affected the other components within the whole. The study examines the behavior of people acting as individuals and as they were organized in associations, councils, committees, and legislative bodies. It shows how Illinois blacks devised organizations that would, they expected, impart unity and endurance to their efforts and how they tried to form supportive alliances with other organizations, black and white, to maximize the impact of their efforts beyond that which they could muster alone. Yet despite its attention to blacks and whites in official leadership roles and to collective action, the study endeavors to give due heed to the exertions of private individuals doing the best they could to win access to public schooling for their own children or for other peoples' children.

The study has been based on both quantitative and qualitative analysis of data in discussing issues, arguments, voting behaviors, organizational structuring and deployment, and strategies and tactics. Counts and analyses of petitions to a legislature and of measures introduced in a legislature (motions relating to bills, resolutions, and reports and to revisions, amendments, and repeals of these) have been used systematically in estimating the strength of a disadvantaged group's and their allies' motivation and cohesiveness. But petitions and measures are just two types of evidence among types I have studied—such as proceedings of conventions and meetings, briefs and court decisions, articles and editorials in northern, central, and southern county newspapers, letters and documents in state and local archives, and the like.

The arguments for universal, public, and free schooling uttered in nineteenth-century Illinois are still to be heard today; the issues relating to problems of appropriate instruction for the races and the institutional structures within which this instruction should be offered are as perplexing and divisive today, or nearly so, as they were a century or more ago. Although this study looks most intently at a period ending in 1875, the arrangements for the schooling of blacks in place at that time were to persist substantially unchanged until 1940 and the uses of power that established the arrangements were to be repeated in the last half of the twentieth century and would culminate in winning, at least in *de jure* authorization, racially desegregated schooling throughout the state.

Thus I have attempted within this context and by these methods to explain how and why an important victory was achieved by a disadvantaged group among us. The struggle demanded courage, intelligence, and energy at a time when Illinois blacks did not have bargaining power to the degree possessed by other disadvantaged groups that have been able to wring concessions from ascendant majorities indifferent or hostile to their cause. The black struggle for public-school rights in nineteenth-century Illinois reveals in starkest detail the predicament of a disadvantaged group in search of instrumentalities by which it can, it hopes, win an equal portion of the good things the community offers to others, not to it.

For their generous assistance I wish to thank the librarians of the Joseph Regenstein Library of the University of Chicago, the Chicago Historical Society, the Withers Public Library and Information Center, Bloomington, and the Illinois State Historical Library, Springfield. I am especially grateful to Ray Gadke, Microform Librarian, Regenstein Library, for his patient and efficient help over the years that I have been reading the microfilms and microfiches in his department. I am indebted to the late Clell L. Woods, Clerk of the Illinois Supreme Court, for briefs and documents pertaining to nineteenth-century state supreme court cases involving racial segregation in the public schools. My thanks go also to Roy Turnbaugh, Head, Information Services, Illinois State Archives, for his professional advice and cooperation in searching for the originals of the petitions to the General Assemblies and for supplying me with copies of those extant. Too, I should express my gratitude to H. Thomas James and the Spencer Foundation for funding a project dealing with a later period of Chicago racial and school history on which Professor Robert J. Havighurst and I are working and from which I have drawn financially because I have regarded this study as a preliminary to that project. Finally I must say how much I appreciate the help of my friend Professor William E. Eaton, Southern Illinois University, for sharing with me his unrivaled knowledge of Illinois educational history.

I wish to thank my wife above all others for her loyal support and help in this and all my research ventures through the many years.

The Black Struggle for
Public Schooling in Nineteenth-
Century Illinois

1

Coping with Exclusion

After the English had stacked their arms at Yorktown and the last strains of "The World Turned Upside Down" had died away, the Continental Congress would come into possession of some 170,000,000 acres of virgin forest, fertile prairies, navigable lakes and rivers, and clear and sparkling brooks and springs stretching north of the Ohio and west of the Alleghenies to the Mississippi, surely one of the richest prizes the fortunes of war had ever bestowed upon a victorious government in all the annals of mankind. What should the future of this vast territory northwest of the River Ohio be? How and by what rules should the land be sold to settlers? What structures of government should be erected there and what should the relation of those governments be to the thirteen original states and to the national government? Which institutions should be encouraged, which discouraged? What rights should the inhabitants have? The answers given by Congress to these questions would do much to condition the quality of the lives led by the human beings, red, white, and black, who would dwell there and do much to define the terms on which they would associate together.

Congress on May 20, 1785, ordained that the northwest territory would be divided for sale into townships six miles square, each township to be subdivided into lots one mile square, of 640 acres, numbered from 1 to 36. Lot number 16 of each township was to be reserved for the maintenance of public schools. When each of the states of the Old Northwest entered the Union, Congress would turn the Section 16 lots over to the states with the stipulation that the moneys arising from the rent or disposal of the lots should be used in aid of public schooling. Ultimately Illinois received 985,066 acres of Section 16 lands, and the interest from the rental and sale of the sections invested in a permanent state school fund would comprise the largest source of yearly public-school revenue until 1855 and one of importance for decades thereafter.[1]

On July 13, 1787, another congressional ordinance set forth a plan for organizing republican governments in the territory and for admitting them into the Union on an equal footing with the older states. Among its articles were one urging the new states to make provisions for education and one prohibiting slavery within their borders. Article 3 was an exhortation: "Religion, Morality, and knowledge being necessary to good government and the happiness of mankind, Schools and the means of education shall forever be encouraged." Article 6 laid down an absolute prohibition: "There shall be neither Slavery nor involuntary Servitude in the said territory."[2]

Ohio and Indiana incorporated Article 6 almost word for word into their first constitutions, and, besides, banned long indentures except for apprenticeship and forbade alterations in their constitutions that might open an avenue to slavery. But the Illinois constitution of 1818 offered a loophole by being evasive about indentures and by omitting any ban on changes in the constitution to permit slavery or a disguised form of it. This omission was deliberate. As soon as Illinois was accepted as a state of the Union, a number of its citizens began agitating for a convention to repeal or soften the nonslavery article in the state constitution. A furious battle ensued between proconvention (proslavery) and anticonvention (antislavery) parties, continuing until a referendum on August 2, 1824, resulted in 6,640 votes being cast against holding a convention and 4,972 for.

The closeness of the vote on holding a convention and the political and social attitudes of Illinoisans on other issues less extreme than enslavement of blacks yet posing questions about granting them the same rights as whites, a subject to be discussed later in this chapter, were produced in part, though only in part, by demographic and cultural factors. Toward the middle of the antebellum period the pattern of immigration into the state shifted in such wise as to lead to the sectional differences that have been features of Illinois life and politics since. At first most of the settlers came from the slave states of Virginia, North Carolina, Georgia, Tennessee, and Kentucky and from the lower reaches of Indiana. Some two-thirds of the 53,387 white inhabitants in 1820 were of southern stock, with a thin scattering of New Englanders, New Yorkers, Pennsylvanians, Englishmen, and Germans. The settlers moved up the state, planting tier upon tier of new counties above the bottom row along the Ohio River. After 1824, when the victory of the anticonvention party meant that Illinois would be a free state permanently, the direction of the flow of immigration began to deviate from its earlier channels. The vertical movement gradually slowed and in the 1830s the main flow became lateral from the eastern states into the northern and north-central counties. The rate and magnitude of the new immigration may be understood more readily (and analyses of voting in subsequent chapters of this study more easily comprehended) if the state is divided into three sections, the northern to include the 33 counties above a line drawn across the lower border of Henderson County eastward to Indiana, the central to include the 36 counties between the northern counties and a line drawn across the lower border of Montgomery County westward to the Mississippi and eastward to Indiana, and the southern to include the 33 counties below this line to the Ohio. By 1860 the total population of the northern counties had caught up with that of each of the other two, being 766,788 in the northern section, 575,305 in the central, and 369,958 in the southern. Yet the central and southern county population combined was greater than that of the northern section alone, a factor of importance in the balance of representation in the General Assemblies and in the voting behavior of the senators and House members.[3]

Differences among the sections in number of inhabitants and their origins were accompanied by differences in culture, politics, and mix of socioeconomic classes. The northern section became more and more urban, industrial, and ethnically and religiously pluralistic, while the southern section stayed rural, agricultural, and homogeneously native American and Protestant. The central section resembled the southern section more than it did the northern. Given these generalizations, it would be tempting to reduce the dynamics of the struggle for Negro public schooling to an interpretation anchored in sectional conflict and pitting problack northerners against antiblack southerners, with the inhabitants of the central counties acting as a swing section. But this would be an oversimplification, though having some semblance of validity, and would ignore much evidence to the contrary. Apart from the fact that there came to be Republicans in southern Illinois and Democrats in nothern Illinois, especially as the Irish crowded into Chicago and Cook County, it should be said that being a northern county, antislavery Republican did not mean that a voter or legislator would be for black rights, or that being problack in respect to suffrage, jury duty, or occupations would mean that the voter or legislator would favor the admission of blacks into the public schools. He might fear that access to public schooling would bring white and black children together in the classroom and on the playground and lead to that most dreaded of consequences, racial "amalgamation." Attitudes, motivations, and behaviors varied within and among the sections and were influenced by a complicated nexus of personal and situational, not just demographic and sectional, factors.

The black population of the state was 2,384 in 1830, 3,929 in 1840, 5,436 in 1850, and 7,628 in 1860. Southern county blacks far outnumbered those in the northern and central counties during the antebellum, bellum, and immediate postbellum periods. A consequence was that the northern county blacks, comprising the most militant and resourceful of their race in the state, could not speak or act for "Illinois" blacks unless they had persuaded their downstate brethren to accept their ideas and plans and join their campaigns, and this they sometimes found difficult to obtain because the downstaters did not see eye to eye with them on priorities and issues. Again, as with the whites, it is possible to exaggerate the influence of sectionalism among the blacks, though again one should recognize that sectional differences among both blacks and whites did produce divisions and conflicts within their ranks.[4]

In constitutional provisions for public education Illinois lagged behind its neighbors to the east. The 1851 constitutions of Ohio and Indiana repeated verbatim or in abridged language Article 3 of the Northwest Ordinance of 1787 exhorting the new states to encourage schools and the means of education forever. Both the Ohio and Indiana constitutions included articles on education. Not until 1870 did an Illinois constitution have an article devoted to education and the public schools. When in the

Illinois constitutional convention of 1847 an education article was proposed for the new constitution, a majority of the delegates feared that such an article might bring blacks into white schools. The proposition was voted down, and the Illinois constitution of 1848, in force until 1870, avoided the subject of public education.[5]

Nonetheless the state was willing to translate into statutes the reasoning of Article 3 of the Northwest Ordinance that knowledge along with religion and morality are "necessary to good government and the happiness of mankind." The "good government" argument was expanded into the axiom that universal schooling is essential to the preservation of republican government, depending as that government does upon the wisdom and virtue of its citizens. This idea was expressed, for example, by Newton Bateman, the third Illinois superintendent of public instruction, in his report for 1861–62 when he wrote that republican institutions cannot survive without "intelligence" and "virtue," for "in a government where all were rulers, all must be educated, or else all would be involved, sooner or later, in one common ruin." The generations after 1787 defined "happiness" within the natural rights tradition as the enjoyment and safety of life, liberty, and property. "Happiness" for the community was to be gained through schooling that would cultivate the hearts and minds of the children and direct their wills toward peace, justice, and the common good. Such were the postulates of the early nineteenth-century American political, civil, social, and economic arguments for common public-school education and common public-school taxation, arguments given currency in the older states by Horace Mann, Henry Barnard, and other crusaders for "popular" education and reiterated again and again by Illinois governors and legislators, teachers' and schoolmen's organizations, newspaper and magazine editors and journalists, and concerned clerics, laymen, and parents.[6]

These were the arguments that Ninian W. Edwards, for instance, chose to freshen in the minds of the governor, legislators, and citizens when he submitted his first report as first state superintendent of public instruction on December 10, 1854. "It is both the duty and the interest of the state to provide for the education of her children," he wrote. Children must be taught to comprehend the principles of the federal constitution as the true foundation of our civil liberties; they must learn how justice is established and domestic tranquility ensured and how they may best promote the general welfare and perpetuate our free institutions. The state must solemnly pledge itself to the education of its children, and the state's schools in a republic must diffuse virtue and knowledge. "It is cheaper to sustain schools than poorhouses, and courts, and prisons; and as certainly as education is neglected, ignorance and vice, and pauperism and prisons, must draw heavily upon our treasury." A state system of education should cooperate with the home in fixing soon in life the habits of industry, temperance, neatness, and regularity. It must improve the higher and subdue the lower passions of human nature and implant principles of thought, feeling, and action that will control the behavior and forge the character of the child and the man. "And truly there is no better investment, nor in any way can such security be given to property as by the education of the masses." To achieve these goals, the schools must be made free to rich and poor alike. Free schooling is in keeping with our republican institutions. It is predicated on the maxim "that all men are born free and equal"; it commends itself "to our common sense of justice, and must, ultimately, command the respect of all classes of the people." The free school system must be financed by a tax on property, and Edwards did not bother to put into words the obvious corollary that all property owners whether or not they had children attending the public schools should be taxed in support of public schools because everyone derives political, civil, social, and economic benefits from the existence of those schools.[7]

Pragmatic arguments of the kind offered by Edwards were reared upon a bedrock of assumptions about the nature of people and society. People, according to the natural rights philosophy Edwards had quoted and paraphrased, are endowed at birth with uniquely human potentialities of mind, body, spirit, and will. A person's right to knowledge is inalienable; every human being has a right to the means by which knowledge is gained and a right of access to those schools through which American society seeks, collectively, to develop the human potentialities of its young for their sake and for the sake of the society itself. That society in its local, ideal manifestation is a community in which all persons living together within certain geographical and social boundaries are participants and in which the actions of one member have an effect upon the happiness, prosperity, and safety of every other member and on the quality of life experienced by all members. "Our social organization, to use a familiar illustration, is a partnership, in which the affairs are generally prosperous or the reverse, according as the partners are good or ill managers," proclaimed a committee of the Illinois State School Convention in a memorial to the legislature, December 7, 1844. As in ordinary partnerships the losses in the great partnership of the community do not fall solely upon the mismanaging partner but upon all. Having one ignorant man in an intelligent community adversely affects all members, "and it is for their interest, and their just right, to get rid of him or of his ignorance."[8]

Illinois was not the only state of the Old Northwest in which the argument for universal schooling and a universal school tax was built upon the partnership concept of community. The first Ohio commissioner of common schools, Hiram H. Barney, like his counterpart Ninian W. Edwards, began his inaugural report in 1854 with a discourse on the ideology undergirding the political, civil, social, and economic reasons for providing schooling for all children. "The important fact is too often overlooked," Barney wrote of the community, "that disorder and misery in one part bring disorder and misery upon every part; that the prosperity of *one* communicates itself to *all*, and the strength, and wealth, intelligence and happiness of *each*, are entwined with the vigor, and prosperity and security of *all*." For the citizens "the State may with propriety be regarded as one great School District, and the population as constituting but one family, charged with the parental duty of educating all its youth." Continuing in his third report, he told his audience: "Wherever, in our midst, a human being exists, with capacities and faculties to be developed, improved, cultivated, and directed, the avenues of knowledge should be freely opened, and every facility afforded to their unrestricted entrance." Banish ignorance and "in its stead introduce intelligence, science, knowledge, and increasing wisdom and enlightenment, and you remove, in most cases, all those incentives to idleness, vice, and crime." Educate every child to the top of his capacities "and you not only secure the community against the depredations of the ignorant and the criminal, but you bestow upon it, instead, productive arti-

7

sans, good citizens, upright jurors and magistrates, enlightened statesmen, scientific discoverers and inventors, and dispensers of a pervading influence in favor of honesty, virtue, and true goodness."[9]

Likewise in Indiana the arguments for universal education and universal taxation for free schools were tied into the concept of community. Both of the antebellum Indiana constitutions included education articles and these beside quoting from Article 3 of the Northwest Ordinance added the term "community," not to be found in the original. To illustrate, the second Indiana constitution, 1851, Section 1, Article 8, says, "Knowledge and learning generally diffused throughout a community, being essential to the preservation of a free government, it shall be the duty of the General Assembly to encourage, by all suitable means, moral, intellectual, scientific, and agricultural improvement, and to provide by law for a general and uniform system of free schools, wherein tuition shall be without charge, and equally open to all." These ideas were at the heart of the speeches and reports of Indiana governors and superintendents of public instruction in the 1860s when they were pleading with the legislature to make provisions for the public schooling of all.[10]

Listening to the arguments of the advocates of universal, free, public schooling, one hears among the rationales several that might lead to quite different conceptions of what the primary task of the school should be. Some of the arguments tend toward a belief that the school should be a preventive institution, inculcating attitudes and behavior that would keep the children from becoming pauperized and criminalized adults who would pose a threat to the prosperity, security, efficiency, and happiness of the shared partnership of the community. Other arguments seem to regard the school as a developmental institution, cultivating the potentialities and talents of the children so that as adults they could and would lift the quality of shared community life to higher and higher levels from generation to generation.

Listening further to the language in which the ideology of community and the arguments for universal, free, public schooling were couched, one hears no attempt to circumscribe the "all." The community, as it was envisioned, included all persons within certain geographical clusters of terrain and population and all such persons were thought to be sharing and participating in the mutual interests, obligations, privileges, and joys of communal life. Nevertheless, ironically, not quite "all" was intended. One class of human beings, the blacks, were considered residents to whom the ideology and arguments did not apply. The black code and school laws and custom and prejudice isolated them in the communities in which they dwelt. In antebellum and bellum Illinois they were treated as "outlaws," said their leader, John Jones of Chicago. They were "pariahs," said the *Chicago Tribune;* they were "inhabitants and strangers," said Governor John M. Palmer. Their isolation from the community was alluded to by Governor Joel A. Matteson in his call to the General Assembly in 1855 to charter an Illinois colonization society and aid it in "colonizing [in Africa] our colored population, where they would enjoy the rights of citizens, and be considered men, and take part in all the duties in life," implying, correctly, that in Illinois the blacks did not possess citizenship rights, were not considered men, and did not take part in all the duties of communal life.[11]

Isolation from the community brought isolation from public schooling. Illinois blacks, denied the right to vote and to participate and share in mainstream decisions and responsibilities, did not, therefore, come within the frame of reference of the conventional arguments for universal education. Educating them was not necessary to "good government" and to the "happiness" of the community. This unconcern about their schooling was reflected in the state's antebellum school laws. Section 1 of the first act for establishing public schools, approved January 15, 1825, ordered the schools to be "open and free to every class of white children" of school age, and the restrictive term "white" appeared in other clauses of the law. Subsequent revisions dropped the discriminatory language of the initial section but retained or implied the term "white" in the sections controlling the organization and administration of schools and the apportionment of state, county, and township funds.[12]

The various Illinois free schools laws enacted between 1825 and 1870 provided that the state superintendent of public instruction, an office created in 1854, should be elected by the "legal voters" of the state, the county commissioners of schools by the "qualified voters" of the county, the township school trustees by the "legal voters" of the township, and the district school directors by the "legal voters" of the district. Because blacks were not "legal" or "qualified" voters before 1870, they had no voice in the election of school officers at each layer from top to bottom of the school governance hierarchy and had no suffrage means of bringing pressure to bear upon the officials who determined which children were or were not to be accepted into the public schools. Nor were black children counted within the formula used to distribute money from state, county, and township funds among the districts. These funds consisted of returns from the sale or rental of Section 16 or other lands donated by the federal government, from money parceled out to the state by the United States congressional Surplus Revenue Act of 1836, and from an annual tax raised after February 15, 1855, by a two-mill levy on each dollar's valuation of all taxable property in the state. The proceeds from the funds were, by law, apportioned according to the number of "white" children of school age. School officials, were they to admit black children into the district schools, would not be reimbursed from the funds and would in effect be penalized financially inasmuch as they would have to sustain the cost of educating the blacks without aid from the state, county, and township.

The general free schools laws permitted the individual districts to levy a school tax but did not stipulate that the tax should be devoted to the instruction of whites. For some districts, however, special acts of the legislature incorporating the school district or certain sections of town and city charters or regulations drawn up by the district itself might reserve the public schools to white children or assign the black children to a separate "colored" school. Many towns and cities of the time were not yet ghettoized, with the result that black children living outside the neighborhood in which the colored school was located might have to walk long distances to the colored school. Their parents might be reluctant to have them suffer this hardship and might keep them out of school altogether. Of course where legal and geographical impediments did not exist prejudice and custom might operate to discourage black children from going to the district schools. In the years before, during, and immediately after the war relatively few black children had access to public schooling or were attending public school. The third Illinois state convention of blacks protested in 1866 that "the colored citizens of this great State, that prides itself on its 'system of free schools,' must . . . submit to see [*sic*] their children driven from the well organized and ably conducted schools in the districts where they reside, for no other delinquency than the crime of being created with a darker skin than their neighbors." A committee of the convention estimated that less than 100 of 8,000 black children of school age in the state were in public schools.[13]

When Illinois blacks chose to engage in a struggle to win the rights to which they felt they were entitled, what kinds and sources of bargaining power did they find were available to them? Another and better way of posing the question is to broaden it and ask what kinds and sources of bargaining power exist in a community and then to ask which of these did the state's blacks possess and which did they utilize. Hence the essential attributes of "bargaining power" can be laid out, as has already been done for "community," and the reader will receive a preliminary briefing on the meaning of the two concepts used in this study to interpret and explain the events of which the Illinois blacks' struggle for public-school rights is composed.

Simply put, "bargaining power" here refers to the capacity of a person or group of persons to elicit a response favorable to his, her, or their intent from a "target" person or group of persons who are in control of the benefit being sought and yet, perhaps, hostile or indifferent to the idea of giving that benefit to or sharing it with those persons trying to get it. Bargaining power, so defined, can be subdivided into rewarding power, punishing power, and dialectical power. The exercise of rewarding and punishing power is through overt, direct action. Those exercising one or the other may vote for or against a candidate for political office, or donate money to this cause or party and not to that cause or party, or buy from certain stores or manufacturers and not from others, or rally for the support of some schools or boards of education or boycott other schools or boards, or, at the extreme of violence, resort to arson, rioting, or armed rebellion until the community bows to their demands or retaliates by employing its own rewarding or punishing power to buy off the protesting group or to subdue or destroy it.

Dialectical power is exerted in verbal forms, oral or written, and attempts by argument to elicit a desired response by appealing to logic or conscience or to acquisitiveness or fear. Illinois blacks and whites were using dialectical power when they petitioned the legislature to pass equal-rights bills or wrote letters to the newspapers basing their arguments on premises derived from the Bible, on patriotic doctrines enunciated in the Declaration of Independence or the Constitution of the United States, or on the promptings of humanitarian sympathy or a sense of justice or *noblesse oblige*. To be sure, among the oral or written arguments in the dialectical form there may be promises of rewards or threats of punishments but this is different from the behavior of rewarding or punishing.

The tripartite categorization of the different kinds of bargaining power, first arrived at from an analysis of the Illinois data, was later found to be similar to that made by John Kenneth Galbraith in his recent *The Anatomy of Power*. Galbraith dissects power into the compensatory, condign, and conditioned. Compensatory power is the ability to gain "submission" by offering something of the value to the opposition. Condign power is the ability to force "submission" by imposing or threatening to impose unpleasant consequences upon the person or group that is unwilling to bestow the concession being sought. Conditioned power is the ability to secure "submission" by changing the beliefs of opponents. Galbraith's triadic anatomization of power should lead to greater confidence in the frame of analysis utilized in this study. One's trust in a division of power into the rewarding, punishing, and dialectical becomes stronger when it receives independent corroboration from a parallel categorization from an experienced scholar like Galbraith, though the chief criterion for testing any construct has to be empirical, lying in its capacity to raise questions and exploit the possibilities of the data of human experience.[14]

Manifestly the efforts of person employing power of any variety are the more likely to be successful in proportion to their ability, among other means, to organize and unify their members and form alliances with other groups. They may create consensus mechanisms by which they are able to reach agreement among themselves on strategies, tactics, and priorities before bringing their case to the community. They can then speak with one voice about their grievances and can exercise their bargaining power in pursuit of an agreed-upon agenda of means and ends. They need not worry that some of their members will make a different set of public demands or embark on different applications of bargaining power that will fragment the impact of their drive, dissipate their energies, and reduce their credibility. By organizing they can assure themselves, too, that system and continuity will be imparted to their efforts and that they will have devised an entity that will be their spokesman and agent in negotiating with other such entities in the community.

If a deprived group is limited by an exclusive criterion of membership, as the blacks were by race, the group can try to add strength by forming coalitions and alliances. The members may employ all appropriate methods of bargaining at their disposal to attract other groups into collaboration. They can demonstrate the congruence between their objectives and those of other organizations and how others can, by yoking their objectives and efforts to the deprived group's, achieve success. Or the deprived group can offer votes or money with the expectation that it will receive support in its quest for rights and benefits. Or it can argue that the target audience from which it is seeking cooperation will fail unless that audience will join it in the struggle toward the desired goals.

The most effective of all these sources and kinds of power were closed off to Illinois blacks. Most crippling of all, they did not have suffrage rights. The state constitutions in force until 1870 gave the vote exclusively to white males above twenty-one years of age. Hence the blacks did not have command of the political rewards and punishments by which other disadvantaged groups like the Irish have been able to improve their position in the community; the blacks could not influence by votes the very legislators who would decide whether or not the laws would be changed to admit black children into the public schools. They could not cultivate symbiotic relationships with the political parties and receive the fruits of patronage. In Chicago when the Irish were filling up the fire and police departments and other branches of government, only one black, Adam Carey, a janitor in the United States courts, held a job in the public sector during the antebellum and bellum periods.[15]

Besides disabilities imposed by the state constitution, the blacks suffered handicaps and harassments inflicted by a "black code" taken over from legislation in the slave states. By law the blacks were not allowed to give evidence in court for or against a white. A Negro or mulatto was permitted to stay in the state only if he or she could show a certificate of freedom and posted bond that he or she would not become a financial burden to the state and would at all times conduct himself or herself in strict conformity to the laws. In 1853 "an act to prevent the immigration of free Negroes into this state" declared that any Negro or mulatto entering Illinois and remaining ten days with the intention of residing therein would be deemed guilty of high misdemeanor, be fined the sum of fifty dollars, and be ejected. If the fine were not paid forthwith, the justice of the peace would commit the Negro to the custody of the sheriff and the justice would advertise the black or mulatto for sale. On the day and at the time and place mentioned in the advertisement, the justice at public auction would proceed to sell the Negro to any person who would pay fine and costs, and the purchaser would have the right to compel the black to work for and serve out a certain time period. It was possible, too, for any person claiming such Negro or mulatto as a slave to take and remove him from the state, the claimant having proved his case and paid costs.[16]

The Illinois black code refused blacks the most fundamental rights of citizenship and attempted to keep them out of the state altogether by treating them as fugitive slaves unless they could prove otherwise and by offering what amounted to an invitation for slave hunters to invade Illinois and assert legal ownership of blacks in the courts, knowing that the Negroes would not be permitted to testify on the witness stand.

In the private sector of community life the blacks' occupations generated little bargaining power. Zebina Eastman, the publisher and editor of the abolitionist *Genius of Liberty* and *Free West* and the blacks' staunch friend, told them that the history of the Jews afforded them a "parallel" from which they could draw. "If you had been a rich class of citizens, like the Jews, think you, would you have been objects of that legislative insult," he asked. "Money has a wonderful charm to do away with prejudice, and endow the once lowly and despised with respectability." "Get money, get gold," he advised them. By 1865 the Chicago Jews were already prominent in banking and business, and Jews had already been elected to the city council and appointed to the board of education and to the offices of clerk to the council and chief financial agent of the public schools. No Chicago black had been elected or appointed to public office or had become a lawyer, banker, or owner or manager of a large industrial firm or business. The handful of black businessmen were mostly small barbers, restauranteurs, tailors, and saloonkeepers; 80 percent of Chicago blacks and probably more than that in the rest of the state were semiskilled and unskilled workers. Their history and condition were in few respects "parallel" to that of any other deprived group. The hard fact was that they were without the principal means by which others were able to procure a remedy for their grievances and advance their fortunes upon the Illinois scene.[17]

Yet the blacks were not barred entirely from the use of many of the mediums through which dialectical power could be exercised. They could petition for the redress of wrongs and send memorials, remonstrances, and pleas to General Assemblies, county commissioners, city and village councils, school boards, and other legislative bodies. They could lobby in person or through surrogates in the corridors of the state capitol, county seats, city and town halls, and school board chambers. They had the right peaceably to assemble in conventions and mass meetings and to organize campaigns. They had freedom of speech and press: they could establish journals and newspapers of their own and try to induce the white organs of communication to print the proceedings of their conventions and meetings and to carry editorials, articles, and letters of supplication or protest informing the community of their woes and of what could be done to ameliorate their condition. Too, if they were willing to bear the consequences, good or bad, they did not have to limit themselves to verbal persuasion. They could resort to punishing power. They could boycott, picket, and force their way into offices or into schoolhouses where their children were not wanted. They could riot and commit crimes until the community would pay attention and be intimidated into doing something to remedy injustices.

Nor did the blacks, if succeeding in their coalition tactics, have to engage in a lonely struggle. There were idealistic whites and white organizations who might be induced to help them. These were whites who did possess the elective franchise, wealth, and influence and who might be persuaded or pressured into collaboration.

The extent to which Illinois blacks capitalized on such

sources and mediums of bargaining power as were available to them (and did not stand by almost as mere spectators watching the abolitionists and antislavery whites do battle for their cause) is one of the two major themes developed in the following chapters. A second major theme concerns the degree to which the blacks came to share in the advantages and prerogatives of community life and so the degree to which the commonly accepted arguments for universal schooling came to be recognized as applying as much to them as to the whites. As, more and more, Illinois blacks might become partners in the community and therefore more and more capable of enhancing or diminishing the prosperity, safety, and happiness of the other partners and of increasing or decreasing the quality of the institutions created to serve those ends, so more and more would the incentives for providing them with access to public schooling gain in strength and more and more their bargaining power increase.

2

Black Efforts at the State Level

In the antebellum and bellum periods the principal leaders of the Illinois blacks were John Jones, James D. Bonner, Henry O. Wagoner, the Reverend Byrd Parker, Reuben H. Rollins, and William Johnson. All of these were Chicagoans. A dozen or so blacks from northern counties outside of Cook and from the central and southern downstate counties were lesser leaders.

Foremost among the black leaders was John Jones. He was acknowledged by blacks and whites alike as the man who did most to inspire and guide his people in the struggle for equal rights. Jones had been born on a plantation in Greene County, North Carolina, in November 1816, the son of a German named Bromfield and of a free mulatto mother named Jones. As the child of a white man and free woman, there should have been no ambiguity about Jones' legal status as a freeman, but his mother feared that his father or the father's family would sell him into slavery. To protect him, she had him apprenticed to be taught a trade. The indenture was transferred to several persons and the boy ended up as an apprentice to Richard Clere (or Clare), a tailor in Memphis. After some years Clere became seriously ill, and Jones, hearing that Clere's heirs planned to sell him to some persons going to Texas, rode back to North Carolina to collect documents and statements attesting to his free birth. On his return to Tennessee in January 1838, he filed a petition of *habeas corpus* and the court discharged him from Clere's custody and pronounced him at liberty to go where and when he pleased.[1]

Jones worked at his trade until he had saved enough money to move north to Alton, Illinois, and marry Mary Richardson, the daughter of a free Negro, a blacksmith, who with his family had formerly lived in Memphis. In March 1845 Jones and his wife decided to see what opportunities lay in Chicago. Arriving with only $3.50 in his pocket, he rented a cottage for his family and a shop for his business and set to work. From this meager start he built up the largest and best known tailoring and cleaning establishment in the city. His skill, reliability, and punctuality attracted a large white clientele. In his business he depended upon the patronage of whites, yet he was also active in the antislavery movement. Frederick Douglass, John Brown, and other vigorous opponents of slavery visited him, and his home was a station on the underground railroad.

Jones' labors for his people ranged beyond the boundaries of the state. Although he was not the first Illinois black to attend a national Negro convention as a delegate—Nimrod W. Jones of Chicago was the first, having attended the National Convention of Colored Citizens in Buffalo in 1843—John Jones was the first to become active in national Negro organizations. In 1848 he was an Illinois delegate to the National Convention of Colored Freemen in Cleveland. His abilities were immediately appreciated, and he was elected one of the vice-presidents of the convention and appointed to the National Central Committee. In 1853 he went to the National Convention in Rochester, New York, and was again elected a vice-president. He also served on the National Council of the Colored People and was their agent in the West for collecting funds for a Colored Manual Training School.[2]

At the state and city levels Jones was usually elected chairman or to another office at conventions and meetings, appointed to committees, and selected to be the representative of his people in dealing with whites. Opposed to black separatism and to a black go-it-alone philosophy, he constantly sought to enlist the participation of whites and their backing in the struggle for equal rights. He himself was an example of what was to be gained from the assistance of whites, for to them he owed much of his personal and business success.[3]

On his list of priorities Jones tended to place public-school rights below the rights of suffrage and of testifying and bringing suits in the courts. He had had no formal schooling; he had taught himself to read and write. He was a businessman in a large urban center and most of his customers were white. He was keenly aware of how detrimental it was to be walled off from the legislative and judicial institutions of the community. Besides in Chicago the blacks were not excluded from the public schools. During the antebellum period they were admitted without *de jure* discrimination and apparently without *de facto* discrimination either. These reasons may, in part, explain why Jones, though not ignoring the importance of public schooling, chose to stress more the advantages of relieving blacks of the disabilities that had a negative effect upon their performance as workers for themselves or for whites and that reduced their contributions to the economic sector of the community.

Other Chicagoans frequently elected as delegates to national "colored men's" conventions and to offices and committees at local and state conventions and meetings were James D. Bonner, a barber, Henry O. Wagoner, a hominy manufacturer, Byrd Parker, a minister, Reuben H. Rollins, owner of a confectionery store, and William Johnson, proprietor and owner of a barbering and shaving "saloon." Outside of Cook County in the northern, central, and southern counties some of the leaders were the Reverend Robert J. Robinson, southern Madison County, the Reverend R. H. Cain, northern Jo Daviess County, the Reverend A. W. Jackson, central Morgan County, the Reverend Henry Brown, central Edgar County, and Spencer Donegan, owner of a barber shop in Springfield.[4]

It will be noted that clergymen were more often black leaders outside of Cook County than in Cook where Byrd Parker alone among the six was a minister and where four of the six were owners of businesses. This was one of the factors causing divisions among Illinois blacks in relation to their priorities and selection of measures in meeting the problems facing them. The Chicago group dominated policy-making during the antebellum and bellum periods but not without differences between themselves and blacks in other sections of the state. Altercations over means and ends had the effect of sparking conflicts and producing contradictions in the leaders' public statements and postures that fragmented the blacks' campaigns and drives. "Why is it that we colored people do not hang together like white people," asked the Reverend Byrd Parker in a letter to Frederick Douglass. The unwillingness of Illinois blacks to "hang together" was a hindrance in their attempts to muster full leverage behind their struggle to win schooling for their children.[5]

In their struggle they depended on dialectical power, for

they had no rewarding power of heavy substance and they did not choose to resort to punishing power until late in the bellum years and then only in Chicago. The instrumentalities they used most in exerting dialectical power were speeches and resolutions in meetings and conventions, letters to the newspapers, and petitions to the General Assemblies. About the latter it should be said that for blacks the petitions had the value of conveying their grievances and desires directly into the hands of legislators—and the legislators had to operate the legislative machinery in the blacks' favor through the process of enacting, amending, and repealing if the blacks were to succeed.

For historians, the act of petitioning and the petitions per se may afford objective data on the willingness or unwillingness of a disadvantaged group to put forth effort to help themselves. The content of petitions may indicate consistencies or inconsistencies in the demands of various subelements within the disadvantaged group and so of the extent to which the group is in agreement or in disagreement on priorities and goals. The petitioning campaign and the identity of the persons participating in it may cast light on the degree to which the members of a disadvantaged group cherish the boons petitioned for and the degree to which they are capable of securing the cooperation of their brethren and the collaboration of other disadvantaged or advantaged groups. Hence petitioning and petitions can offer an enriching addition to other sources of data upon which historians may draw in estimating possibilities and probabilities. Admittedly petitions do have flaws as a species of proof. Sheer counting, for instance, attaches equal weight to each petition although a petition signed by 500 people ordinarily ought to be given more weight than one signed by 5. In any case petitioning, and petitions, used cautiously, do furnish evidence of value to the historian in performing the difficult tasks of explaining, reasoning, interpreting, and generalizing.

Thirteen petitions signed by blacks or blacks and whites together were presented in the 1st through the 24th General Assemblies, 1818–65, and the constitutional conventions of 1847 and 1862. Here the term "presented" means that in a session of the General Assembly a senator or House member would inform the legislators of his chamber that he had in hand a petition from such and such a group of Illinois residents who prayed that a certain law be repealed or a certain bill passed. Having summarized the prayer of the petition or read all of it or a key sentence from it, he would move that the petition be referred to an appropriate Senate, House, or joint committee. "Presented" does not mean "submitted." A petition might be sent by blacks or whites to the clerk of the Senate or House or to a legislator from the district in which the signers lived, but the clerk might not transmit it to a senator or House member. Or the senator or House member, receiving it from the clerk or from a group of residents of his district, might not present it.

Not many petitions were submitted but not presented, for the legislators seem to have been conscientious about meeting responsibilities of this kind. Submitted petitions are not mentioned in the printed journals of the Assemblies. Even in the case of petitions presented and of which notice is entered in the printed journals problems may arise because the complete prayer and all the names of the signatories are never given in the journals, and the journals' brief notice may lack any clear information about what the prayer was, who the signers were, and where they were from. When, for example, the race of the petitioners is not divulged in the printed journals, the historian must hope that fortune will smile upon him or her and that the manuscript original of the petition has been preserved in the State Archives. If not, he or she must turn to newspaper accounts of the proceedings and see what can be gleaned from them and from similar sources.

Four of the thirteen petitions from blacks or blacks and whites together presented between 1818 and 1865 dealt with colonizing Illinois blacks in Africa, three with public schooling for blacks, two with repealing the black laws, one with granting suffrage rights to blacks, one with repealing the laws disqualifying blacks from giving testimony in the courts, and one, an omnibus petition, with granting the rights of equal schooling, voting, giving testimony in the courts, and repealing the law prohibiting the immigration and settlement of blacks in the state. The remaining petition of the thirteen came from "Free Frank," a farmer in Pike County who had been born a slave in North Carolina, had purchased his freedom and moved to Illinois, and now asked the legislature to give him the surname of "McWorter." [6]

The four procolonization of blacks petitions were the result of urging from the Illinois State Colonization Society and from blacks cooperating with it. Apprehension over colonization and other concerns provided the motives for calling and holding the first Illinois state convention of blacks. The blacks met in Chicago on October 6, 7, and 8, 1853, with John Jones presiding and chairing the committee on colonization. The report of the committee, approved by a convention dominated by Chicago delegates, announced that "we will plant our trees in American soil, and repose in the shade thereof," and castigated colonization schemes as having the purpose of fomenting a spirit of disunity among blacks and of depressing their willingness to devote their energies to elevating their condition within their home state.[7]

Procolonization evangelizing by both whites and blacks continued, and anticolonization blacks remained deeply worried—especially since Governor Matteson put the prestige of his high office behind state aid by proposing that the General Assembly supply funds for transporting Illinois blacks to Africa. But the emotions displayed by one side or the other in the controversy quickly simmered down after 1855 and it disappeared as a significant issue in the years just before the war.[8]

Judged by any standard of accomplishment, the colonization movement in Illinois would not rate very high. But if the movement was short on accomplishments, it was long as an issue igniting disputes and spawning factions among the blacks that would impede their struggle for equal rights—and this during the years when their white friends were coming into a position in the legislature where they could be of assistance. From one camp petitions favorable to colonization signed by central or southern county blacks were being sent to the General Assembly and lectures and sermons were being given by black advocates. And a few Illinois blacks were actually emigrating to Liberia. From the other camp speeches and letters vehemently attacking colonization were being written to the newspapers by black leaders and resolutions denouncing colonization were being adopted by national and Illinois state conventions of blacks.

It was in the years from 1849 through 1855 that Illinois blacks exhibited sharp disagreement over the crucial question of whether they desired to stay and strive in Illinois or depart for the promised land across the sea. Yet those six years offered the best opportunity up until that time of repealing the disabling

state laws inflicted upon them: when Liberty party men, abolitionists, and Free Soilers were being elected to the General Assemblies and when in 1855 the hard-line Democrats lost their
majority in the legislature. But after 1855 the white friends of the
blacks became distracted from state affairs and fixed their attention instead upon national issues relating to the extension of
slavery, the needs of the newly founded Republican party, and
the task of winning the election of 1860. As the interests of the
white antislavery people of Illinois turned away from colonization and from the condition of blacks in the state, so did the
hopes or fears of Illinois blacks over colonization subside and so
did their interests turn elsewhere too.

Similar divisions within the ranks of the blacks occurred on
the issues of whether they should pay a school tax and, if so,
whether the tax should be returned to them and for what purpose it should be used. Three schooling petitions from blacks or
blacks and whites were presented in the General Assemblies of
1853 and 1855. The first, from Presley L. Donegan and other
blacks of Springfield, presented on January 11, 1853, prayed that
the blacks be exempted from the school tax and assured the legislators that the blacks would then "sustain" their own schools.
The second, from 52 persons of color, presented on January 14,
1853, avowed that the blacks did not wish to be exempted from
the school tax but rather wanted the school tax paid by black
property owners to be "set aside" for the education of their children. The third, from blacks and whites in Madison County,
presented on January 11, 1855, requested that a sum of money
from the school fund be appropriated for the education of blacks.
All three of these petitions asked for different boons from the
legislature.

Another petition, an omnibus petition, was also different.
Whereas none of the first three sought the admisson of black
children into the public schools, the fourth did. Presented on
February 9, 1857, it was from 300 citizens (whites) and inhabitants (blacks) and requested that the blacks have "equal participation" with whites in being admitted to public schooling. All four
petitions plainly reflected divergencies among the blacks on the
issues of school taxes and of educating black children inside or
outside of the public system. Even the white members of the
General Assembly who were sympathetic toward the blacks

might become confused about what the blacks wanted them to do. Such confusion as well as other obstacles may account for why the first three of the petitions were not acted upon by the committees to which they were referred and the fourth rejected by a vote of 50 to 17 in the House.

Donegan and the Springfield black signatories of the first of the petitions argued against what they perceived to be the injustice of the school law. Imposing school taxes on blacks and then refusing to allocate to them any portion of the school fund into which the taxes were fed was manifestly "unjust." The blacks ought to be exempted from the school tax.[9]

But the members of the 18th General Assembly were not about to amend the free schools law by passing a clause that would excuse the blacks from the school tax. This was an issue that had already been thrashed out in the 15th General Assembly in 1847 when a petition from sundry white citizens of Pike County had asked that the blacks be given the benefit of the school fund or that the law be amended. A majority of the committee to which the petition was referred approved the introduction of a bill for "An act to exempt the property of persons of color from taxation for school purposes." The bill did not reach a second reading because a member of the committee, Samuel Snowden Hayes, submitted a minority report that convinced the General Assembly of the dangers of changing the tax sections of the school law for the purpose of making exceptions on account of race.[10]

Everyone, Hayes had argued, would acknowledge that the policy of taxing all property owners for defraying the cost of institutions benefiting all persons in the community was a just policy and a just tax. A school tax was such a general welfare tax. Prosperity and schooling were linked. The erection of schoolhouses and the provision of education for the young increased the value of property. All property owners, even those who were childless and those whose children did not attend the public schools, were recipients of benefits, direct or indirect, flowing from the presence of public schools. Black property owners, though their children might be barred from public schooling, likewise benefited. Their property also increased in value; they should not be exempted from paying school taxes. Probably it was the Hayes' argument that influenced the members of the

18th General Assembly in 1853 when they were considering what action to take on the Donegan petition and in the end let it die by taking none.

The second of the blacks' schooling petitions coming into an antebellum General Assembly was from "52 colored persons" and was presented in the Senate of the 18th General Assembly on January 14, 1853. It was part of a complex plan by the state's blacks to establish a network of schools for their children that would be separate from the public school system. "We do not desire to be released from School Taxes," the petitioners insisted, but prayed the legislature "to set aside the portion of the School Tax arrising [*sic*] from the Property of colored citizens for the education of colored persons in the state."[11]

The identity of the persons signing the petition, the phrasing and content, and other clues reveal that it originated with the Wood River Colored Baptist Association of Illinois, a group of ministers and laymen of the African Baptist churches along the Wood River, near Alton, southern Madison County. The officers of the Association, who were among the 52 blacks signing the petition, had issued in the preceding August "An Appeal to the Christian—to the Patriot—and the Philanthropist," a document that the petition was to imitate in wording, reasoning, and ultimate purpose. Both the "Appeal" and the petition assumed that the blacks would have to go the separate route and found their own schools and finance these out of such money as they could garner from private sources. The Association, seemingly aware that complete dependence on private giving was risky, had now turned to the legislature and petitioned for the refunding of the blacks' school taxes and hence assurance of an annual, reliable source of income for black schools. In this they were to be disappointed. The petition of the 52 blacks met the same fate as the Donegan petition, being bottled up in the Senate committee on school lands and education for the rest of the legislative session.[12]

Frustrated in petitioning, the Wood River Colored Baptist Association and its agent, the Reverend Robert J. Robinson, sought other methods of pursuing its plan and campaign. When the first state convention of blacks was held, in October 1853, Robinson attended and as chairman of the committee on education recommended that the delegates form a School Fund Association with a board of nine trustees, a treasurer, secretary, and agents. The delegates, however, betrayed some misgivings about a Fund drive to establish independent black schools, apparently fearing that this might be interpreted as a surrender of all their claims to the right of public schooling for their children. Frederick Douglass, a guest of the convention, offered a motion asserting that the delegates wanted it distinctly understood that they were adopting Robinson's recommendation from "necessity," that they protested and would continue to protest against the proscriptive school laws, and that they believed the whites' sense of justice and magnanimity would prompt the whites to acknowledge the blacks' equal right to the advantages of public education. Douglass' resolution and Robinson's recommendation, which he now labeled an answer to an "emergency" taken until more "liberal" and "humane" sentiments prevailed in the legislature, were adopted by the convention, as was another resolution urging the blacks of the state and their white friends to petition the General Assembly to repeal the laws they alleged were denying them the right of sending their children to the public schools.[13]

Presumably the School Fund Association would be able to mount a stronger campaign than the Wood River Colored Baptist Association had, for its broader base would include blacks of all denominations from all regions of the state, not just Baptists from the Wood River area. The School Fund Association would also, the delegates to the convention hoped, draw strength from being a component of a larger structure they were creating to organize the efforts of the blacks throughout the state. This was a State Council that would act as a State Central Committee and be composed of twenty members elected statewide, with a state commissioner as executive officer and with auxiliary committees in each of the counties.

When the State Council held its first meeting in Chicago on January 2 and 3, 1854, only nine of its twenty members came to the first day's session. Three more appeared later, but two of these arrived on the evening of the last day. The Council members that did attend spent their time wrangling over whether members of the National Council should be permitted to be honorary members of the State Council and over whether women should be allowed to vote in their state elections. The bickering in the meetings and the failure to produce results led an anonymous black Illinoisan, "Brick," to write a letter to *Frederick Douglass' Paper* sarcastically accusing the Council of "old fogyism" and predicting that unless the members changed their ways the people would become disgusted and refuse to give it their support.

In a rejoinder Henry O. Wagoner ended up admitting that the Council's meeting had been a bungled affair. He was bothered by the dissension and he wished the blacks to become more "fraternal" in their relations with each other and not suffer themselves to be "crippled" by internal conflict "just at a time all our union and strength is needed." The same fears were voiced by the Reverend Byrd Parker. His diagnosis of the problem was that the blacks had been taught from infancy by those who would keep them in bondage to "look with a suspicious and envious eye at each other" and to do all in their power to "destroy the character and standing" of persons of their own race. Despite the warnings of Wagoner and Parker, the Council remained ineffective and was never able to harness the energies of the blacks of the state or become a source of strength for the School Fund Association.[14]

Nor were all Illinois blacks ready to make a total commitment to the Association. As the doubts expressed in the state convention proved, the delegates were divided on the issue of whether their efforts should be concentrated on establishing independent schools or getting their children into the public schools. Critical was the resistance of the Chicago blacks to the idea of making either independent school support or public school admission a major goal. The Chicagoans, the most prosperous, influential, and vigorous group of blacks in the state, placed school rights lower in their listing of priorities than they did the repeal of the black laws, especially those denying suffrage and prohibiting them from offering testimony in court cases involving whites.

At a mass meeting in Chicago on December 27, 1852, they had elected a committee to canvass blacks and whites for signatures to a petition praying the General Assembly to repeal the section of the laws excluding them from the courts. A petition with this intent from 3,000 persons, black and white, headed by John Wentworth, lawyer, former congressman, owner and editor of the *Chicago Democrat*, and soon to be mayor of Chicago and a member of the school board, was presented in the Senate of the 18th General Assembly on January 21, 1853. Referred to the committee on the judiciary, the petition was returned to the floor in the form of a bill for repeal, which the Senate tabled.[15]

Three and a half years later at the second state convention of blacks, again under the domination of the Chicagoans, the *coup de grâce* was given to the School Fund Association and to the idea of establishing a chain of black schools independent of the public school system. On the final day the report that the delegates heard from the secretary of the Association, William Johnson of Chicago, was a confession of defeat. At fault, he said, was the voluntary nature of the plan for financing the schools: it was a "fallacy" to depend on free-will subscriptions and donations for founding and maintaining black schools. His suggestion was that the activities of the Association be suspended until a more permanent and practicable method of support could be discovered. The delegates accepted Johnson's proposal and resolved to advise the blacks of the state to keep up schools "in some other way." This resolution in effect killed the School Fund Association and the ambitions connected with it. Thereafter such endeavors as were initiated to establish and operate nonpublic schools for blacks were locally sponsored and locally financed out of tuition, donations, and, be it noted, out of school taxes returned to black property owners by local school boards.[16]

The return of the blacks' school taxes was rendered possible by legislation passed by the 19th General Assembly in 1855. It was the only change in the school law and indeed in any Illinois law remotely favorable to blacks in the antebellum period. And if it was, as it seems to have been, a delayed answer to the petition of the 52 blacks praying for setting aside their school taxes for schooling for their children, it was the only legislation passed in the years before the war that was responsive to petitions from blacks or blacks and whites.

The shift in the attitude of the General Assembly between 1853 when the 52 blacks' petition had remained stalled in committee and 1855 when a law containing a section rebating school taxes to blacks had been enacted must be seen in the context of state history. In the 1840s and 1850s the existing school laws proved incapable of providing a system of public education that would satisfy the needs of a school-age cohort drawn from a population of 155,715 under twenty years of age in 1846 that had risen to 361,954 under twenty-one years of age in 1852, and this within a state undergoing rapid transformation from frontier conditions to more complex political, economic, and social arrangements. Most of the citizens clamoring for revision of the school law agreed that an office of state government headed by a superintendent should be created for supervising and improving the schools. A bill for "an act to provide for the election of a state superintendent of public instruction" was passed by the General Assembly and approved by the governor on February 28, 1854.[17]

Ninian W. Edwards was appointed interim superintendent until the November elections should come around on the regular schedule. His first report to the governor and Assembly contained the draft of a bill for a revised school law. The bill kept the discriminatory "white" that in prior laws had been an obstacle to the public schooling of blacks but added a new section enabling school boards to allot to "schools for the education of persons of color" the portion of the school taxes paid by blacks. The bill, amended in some minor respects, was passed by the 19th General Assembly, and in the final version approved by the governor on February 15, 1855, Section 84 read:

> *Schools of Persons of Color.* In townships in which there shall be persons of color, the board of education shall allow such persons a portion of the school fund, equal to the amount of taxes collected for school purposes from such persons of color in their respective townships.

Section 84, becoming Section 80 later but continuing largely unchanged, remained in the free-school laws until dropped in the revision of April 1, 1872.[18]

Section 84 (80) was unique. Other states had exempted blacks from the school tax or applied their taxes to the support of public "colored" schools. None had returned school taxes to blacks to use for educating their children, if they wished, apart from the public-school system. Section 80 seems to have been tailored to the particular set of circumstances reflected in the petition of the 52 blacks, the "Appeal" of the Wood River Colored Baptist Association, and the efforts to establish a network of independent black schools. A changed climate of opinion that had brought into the General Assembly a greater number of legislators sympathetic to the black cause had helped as well. Whereas the 18th General Assembly of 1853–54 had been composed of 20 Democrats and 5 Whigs in the Senate and of 59 Democrats, 16 Whigs, and 1 Free Soiler in the House, the 19th General Assembly of 1855–56 was composed of 11 Anti-Nebraska and 14 Democratic senators and 41 Anti-Nebraska and 34 Democratic House members. The 19th General Assembly would be more likely than the previous Assembly to vote passage of a Section 84 because it was, as a contemporary said, a measure yielding "justice" to the blacks, "very scant" though it was.

The blacks did not treat Section 84 (80) as if it were a victory. They criticized the section because it would return to them only the amount of school taxes they paid in and not, as the rule was for whites, in proportion to the number of their children of school age. They complained, too, that the section did not allot them money from the part of the school fund derived from sources other than taxes or grant them funds for schoolhouses, school management, and anything else necessary for schooling. The section "under the specious pretence of 'establishing schools for persons of color'" in reality, they charged, cut them off from the public-school privileges available to whites. Their dissatisfaction was warranted. Statistics on the return of the blacks' school taxes were given in only one of the state superintendent's biennial reports, the ninth for 1871–72, where the table shows $43.30 returned in southern Gallatin County and $7.66 in southern Lawrence County.

In all of the published reports of the county superintendents of schools to the state superintendent there is only one mention of Section 84 (80). Thomas W. Hynes, southern Bond County superintendent, remarked in 1867–68 that Section 80 had been "practically a dead letter" in his county: the blacks "paid school taxes on their property, and, while excluded from the schools, they have never, as I suppose, drawn a cent from the funds they have aided to raise." Testimony from Newton Bateman, the state superintendent of public instruction, in his sixth biennial report, 1865–66, reveals that what was true of Bond County was true of nearly all others.

According to Bateman, who was in a better position than anyone else to know the full extent to which the blacks took advantage of Section 80, the purpose of the section was to furnish funds for separate schools for black children and this purpose had not been attained except in a few instances. The reasons, he said, were two. First, the school taxes paid by blacks were generally not returned to them, and, second, even when returned the amount was so small as to be of no help in enabling them to support their own schools, especially as most of the blacks were scattered through the counties and school districts in clusters of one, two, or three families, not numerous enough to sustain independent schools for their children despite the "pittance" that would be remitted to them from the school taxes of the property owners among them.[19]

The evidence shows that Section 84 (80) was enacted in the expectation that the blacks would found independent nonpublic schools and that the return of their school taxes to them would furnish a helpful supplement to the money they would raise privately. But the collapse of the School Fund Association and of the blacks' all-state effort to establish and maintain their own schools had made Section 84 (80) virtually a nullity. Apparently most blacks were unwilling to seek a return of taxes that would be of very little assistance in providing schooling for their children and that, in addition, might be read as a signal that they were relinquishing all of their claims for public-school rights.

So in antebellum Illinois the blacks had won nothing but the dubious victory of seeing legislation passed that would permit an amount of school-fund money equal to their school taxes returned to them. They had tried to take advantage of many of the means of persuasion and pressure at their disposal; they had attempted to apply such bargaining power as they did have to the task of acquiring the rights and benefits they did not have. But their efforts had been weakened by fragmentation, by conflicting petitions and public quarrels on colonization and on whether their highest priority should be repeal of the black laws or whether they should ask for exemption from the school tax, have it remitted to them in aid of their own independent network of private schools, or have their children accepted into the public schools.

A second weakening factor had been their inability to marshal and concentrate their efforts through organizations like councils, societies, and committees. Their voluntary associations for ameliorating their condition had not succeeded in holding the support and interest of their northern, central, and southern county brethren. As a consequence their organizations had weakened to the point of losing the will and energy needed for achieving the goals originally set for them.

A third factor that had operated against blacks' success had been the limitations confining their exercise of bargaining power. Because blacks did not have the vote or wealth they could not make effective use of rewarding power; because they were a peaceful, law-abiding people they would not use punishing power. They had to do the best they could with dialectical power. They had petitioned, written letters to their own and to white journals and newspapers, made speeches, lectured, sermonized, met in black conventions and mass meetings, and had tried to organize their people in the School Fund Association, State Council, and Illinois State Repeal Association.

But the arguments they had communicated through these mediums had failed to win for them school, suffrage, or other rights. They had appealed to religious, ethical, and patriotic beliefs and sentiments. In their "Address of the Colored State Convention to the People of the State of Illinois" in the printed proceedings of their convention in 1853, their most elaborately argued statement in the antebellum period, they had, for instance, built their reasoning on the precepts of the biblical Golden Rule ("Do unto others as you would that all men would do unto you"), the postulates of the Declaration of Independence ("All men are created free and equal and life, liberty, and the pursuit of happiness are the rights of all"), the promises of the Constitution of the United States ("The Union was formed to establish justice, promote the general welfare, and secure the blessings of liberty to all the people of this country"), and the lessons of past American history ("Taxation without representation is tyranny"). Arguments consisting of these exhortations and principles had not conquered the prejudice of the persons arrayed against them.

Clearly one of the ways for Illinois blacks to improve their chances would be for them to attract the steadfast, undivided collaboration and support of white humanitarian, religious, or political organizations.

3

White Efforts at the State Level

During the early years of the antebellum period the chief, nonpolitical, white organization lending some assistance to the black cause was the Illinois State Antislavery Society. Founded on October 28, 1837, the Society established auxiliary societies, sent its agents and lecturers out into the state, sponsored campaigns for petitioning the legislature, and published the antislavery newspapers, the *Genius of Liberty* and the *Western Citizen*. The mission of the Society was the extirpation of slavery, but in seeking to put an end to slavery in the South it found that its reasoning led it into attacking the antiblack policies and practices existing in its own state. Its arguments, like those of the blacks, were erected on religious and patriotic premises: to deprive a human being of freedom and rights is to disobey God's and Nature's laws and to depart from the pronouncements of Holy Scripture and the ideals of the Declaration of Independence and the Constitution of the United States.[1]

The Society was especially active in mounting petitioning drives from 1842 through 1847. It was during those years that the greatest number of problack petitions from white allies of the blacks were presented in the General Assemblies convening in the antebellum and bellum periods. Eighty-eight petitions, 75 problack and 13 antiblack, from whites were presented in the 3rd through the 24th General Assemblies. Of the 75 problack, 49 came into the 13th, 14th, and 15th General Assemblies in 1842–43, 1844–45, and 1846–47. Almost all of the 49 originated in vigorous petitioning campaigns by the Illinois State Antislavery Society and its auxiliaries. In the middle 1840s it exhorted its members and all citizens of like mind to loose upon the General Assemblies a "tremendous onset" of petitions against Illinois laws "oppressive" to the blacks and making a "distinction" on account of race. These petitions stressed first the repeal of the black laws, hence subordinating school rights to relief from the harassments that the black laws were inflicting upon the Negroes of the state. An example is the petition the Society's propaganda organ, the *Western Citizen*, circulated through the state in 1844 for citizens to duplicate and sign.

To the Honorable, the Legislature of Illinois.

Your memorialists, citizens of   County, would respectfully represent to your honorable body, that there are numerous laws upon our Statute Book, many of them long since enacted, which are oppressive in their bearing upon particular classes of our inhabitants, inconsistent with the rights of man, and disgraceful to us as a people; such as the laws regulating the introduction and residence of colored persons, visiting with fines and imprisonment the feeding of the hungry, and the clothing of the naked, permitting the holding of persons, under certain circumstances, in a state of slavery, debarring them from the privileges of Common Schools granted to white persons under twenty years of age.

We do most respectfully request of your honorable body a careful examination of these laws, and would pray that they be repealed or so amended as to secure the blessings of Liberty to all our citizens.

And your memorialists, as in duty bound, will ever pray.[2]

Despite the receipt of some 49 similar petitions with hundreds, perhaps thousands, of signatures, the General Assemblies stood fast against repealing the black laws and the racially restrictive sections of the school laws. The leaders of the antislavery movement, thwarted in their efforts from outside of the legislature, decided to go inside. They changed their emphasis from moral suasion to political power; they created new political parties and assumed the task of electing their own members or persons sympathetic to their cause to the General Assemblies. As the antislavery movement became politicized, the old antislavery organizations went into a decline and the Illinois State Antislavery Society and its auxiliaries played a role minor to that of the Liberty, Anti-Nebraska, and finally Republican parties in the great drama unfolding in the 1850s.

While the Society busied itself with submitting petitions, some of which also mentioned public-school privileges for blacks, the female branch of the Society was trying in a practical way to expand educational opportunities for them. At meetings on May 23 and 24, 1844, during which the Illinois Female Antislavery Society was organized, a resolution to assist black children to obtain schooling was adopted. The author of the resolution, Mrs. Irene B. Allan, the secretary-treasurer of the Female Society and wife of the Reverend William T. Allan, pastor of the Presbyterian Church of Peoria and agent of the Illinois State Antislavery Society, took the doctrines espoused by the parent society and applied them to the field of education. She explained that schooling for blacks would be in obedience to "one of the principles of God's universal government—the equality and brotherhood of his children" and to the American principle that " 'all men are by nature equal,'—and that the color of the skin is not an index to the quality of the mind." Educating the blacks would enable them to become a living refutation of the slander that they were an inferior race.[3]

To make a start on clearing away this thick underbrush of prejudices, Mrs. Allan proposed that the women go out into their neighborhoods and search for ambitious black children and help them acquire an education. If no schools open to blacks were located in the district, the women should encourage blacks to found one. The Female Antislavery Society had no money, but the ladies might donate clothing and form sewing circles to prepare articles that could be given to black schools.

Nothing said by Mrs. Allan then or later or by other members of the Female Society at their meetings or in their correspondence indicates that they were willing to launch a drive to persuade or pressure the General Assembly into repealing the racially discriminatory language in the free-schools law or into enacting legislation granting blacks access to the public schools. The ladies of the Society seem to have been satisfied with abiding by state school policy as it was. Were a particular public school, as at Galesburg, open to black children, well and good. Should the district school be closed to blacks, the women would do what they could to help the blacks establish and maintain a school of their own. As individuals or as a local ad hoc group the women of the Society might try to get the neighborhood school board to admit black children, but this the women would not do at the official behest of the State Society or with its official support.

In the absence of relevant documentation it is impossible to assess with any great accuracy what the Female Society accomplished. There is evidence to show that some black children who were eager to go to school were found and that at least one girl had her way paid to a school at Galesburg and returned home to Bloomington to teach in the blacks' school there. How many other blacks were aided, how much assistance was rendered to the blacks' schools at Bloomington, Alton, and Springfield, and how many schools for blacks were founded with the cooperation of the Female Society are questions that cannot be answered definitively. Not many and not much, probably, for the activity of the Female Society in education was short-lived. The Female Society suspended operations in 1846, and when it resumed meetings in the next year it turned its attention to the repeal of the black laws. In the following decades the reform-minded women of the state became less and less active in the antislavery and black rights causes and more and more absorbed in the struggle to gain rights for their own sex and to win passage of an Illinois version of the Maine temperance law.

It is doubtful that either the State Society or the Female Antislavery Society was responsible for the whites' one antebellum problack petition specifically and solely concerned with schooling. That petition, referred to the 15th General Assembly's House committee on education on January 5, 1847, came from "sundry" citizens of central Pike County and prayed the legislators to amend the free-schools law in order that "the black and colored children of our State may have an equal benefit of the money appropriated by law to school purposes, or so amend the law as to exempt the property of blacks."

The word "sundry" implies that the signers were not representing an organization but had banded together on a single-issue basis. Furthermore, the object of the petition was quite different from that of the sample petition circulated by the Illinois State Antislavery Society for submission to the 15th General Assembly; the sample petition was directed against the black laws and asked for the repeal of laws making a "distinction" on account of color. But the original Pike County petition does not survive in the State Archives and the exact identity of the signers as well as the meaning they attached to "equal benefit" must remain uncertain.

Their meaning may have been the same as that placed on the two words by the House committee to which the petition was referred: that black and colored children would have the right of attending public schools with whites. The committee, having so defined the words, then unanimously opposed such "equal benefit." A majority of the committee was, however, in favor of the exemption alternative and they reported to the House a bill for "An act to exempt the property of persons of color from taxation for school purposes." This was the bill that Samuel Snowden Hayes was instrumental in having scuttled, contending that blacks should not be excused from paying school taxes inasmuch as taxation for schools promotes the general welfare by enhancing the value of property, blacks' as well as whites'.[4]

The assistance lent to blacks by the Illinois Antislavery Society and the Female Antislavery Society, sparse and limited though it may have been, was more than the blacks received from any other of the state's nonpolitical organizations. Illinois blacks did not have the advantage of strong, persevering support from the Societies and from white religious and social organizations that their brethren in the two states to the east had. In Ohio the antislavery women were the most helpful of any citizens in procuring schooling for black children before the Ohio law of March 14, 1853, ordered township boards of education to establish black public schools. In Indiana the Quaker antislavery women were the most helpful before the war. In both states the efforts of the women were well organized, in Ohio through the Ohio Ladies Society for the Education of Free People of Color and in Indiana through the Committee on People of Color of the Antislavery Friends. The women raised money, recruited teachers, encouraged blacks to start schools, and did all those things that the Illinois antislavery societies and other white Illinois nonpolitical organizations were far from doing as adequately.

Among the reasons for the difference was the earlier origin of the Ohio and Indiana antislavery societies, giving them a longer span of time in which to grow and flourish before being distracted by competing reform causes and the demands of the new antislavery political parties. In 1837 there were already 200 antislavery societies in Ohio and no more than 8 or 10 in Illinois, and the total in Illinois never got much higher. In 1860 there were 93 Quaker "churches" accommodating 41,330 persons in Indiana, while in Illinois there were 8 Quaker churches accommodating 1,650 people. The only three Illinois petitions relating to blacks in the antebellum and bellum periods that were identified as being from Quakers were presented in the Illinois General Assembly in 1865 and were signed by members of the Western Yearly Meeting of Friends of Southern and Western Indiana and Eastern Illinois, a group in which the Indiana Quakers were surely in the majority. But comparisons with other states aside, the extant data suggest that the Illinois State Antislavery Society, the Illinois Female Antislavery Society, the Quakers and the religious denominations, and other Illinois voluntary nonpolitical organizations did not furnish the blacks with effective assistance in their struggle for equal rights and schooling for their children.[5]

Did the antislavery people furnish more effective assistance after the movement had become politicized? Did the Anti-Nebraska and Republican members of the Illinois General Assemblies introduce measures favorable to blacks and vote for such measures?

In pursuing answers to these questions, "measures" can be used as petitions were to supply a quantitative and qualitative kind of guidance along the way. Here "measures" include motions introducing bills, resolutions, and reports, substitute bills, resolutions, and reports, and amendments to bills, resolutions, and reports made by senators and House members of the General Assemblies meeting from 1818 through 1875 and by delegates to the constitutional convention of 1847 or 1862 or 1869–70. The term does not appertain to procedural actions like presenting petitions and/or referring them to committee or actions ordering to a second or third reading or demanding yeas and nays.

In the antebellum and bellum General Assemblies and constitutional conventions thirteen problack schooling measures and seventeen antiblack were introduced. The object of four of the problack measures was to strike the discriminatory word "white" from free-schools bills or laws, of four (including here the Swan proposal of August 23, 1847) to have school funds distributed according to population or number of school-age children regardless of race, of three to exempt blacks from the school tax or allow them the benefit of their school taxes, of one to return to blacks a portion of the school fund equal to their school taxes, and of one to apply part of a black's estate, G. Washington's, to the education of black children. Twelve of the antiblack measures were intended to preserve the distribution of school funds exclusively to whites. One antiblack measure attempted to prevent the elimination of "white" from a free-schools bill, one to resist the exemption of blacks from the school tax, one to keep them from having an "equal participation" with whites in the public schools, one to prevent them from attending the same schools as whites, and one to appropriate their school taxes for use in "separate" schools for their children.[6]

Least ambiguous of the problack schooling measures are those calling for the elimination of "white" from the free-schools laws. If "white" were excised, the financial obstacle to the public education of the blacks would be removed. Removal would not guarantee admission to the district schools. But a vote for or against the measure would demonstrate whether a legislator might be willing to take a minimal first step toward providing access to public schooling for the black children of the state.

During the antebellum and bellum periods four measures proposing to strike "white" from the free-schools laws were introduced in the General Assemblies. The first was offered in the House of the 4th General Assembly, 1st session, by David McGahey, a Democrat from southern Crawford County, on January 7, 1825. His motion was defeated, 13 to 22. Since at that very early time in the history of Illinois biographical facts about most of the legislators are missing, there are more "unknowns" than "knowns" for political party affiliation. The facts, for what they are worth, are these: 2 Whigs, 1 Democrat, and 10 legislators whose political party is unknown voted for McGahey's motion. Four Whigs, 6 Democrats, and 12 of unknown political party voted against. A second motion to strike "white" from the free-schools law was made in the Senate of the 16th General Assembly by Alfred E. Ames, a Democrat from northern Winnebago County, on January 29, 1849. His motion lost, 5 to 16. All 5 legislators voting for the motion were Democrats; 10 voting against were Democrats, 6 were Whigs.[7]

It is in and after 1855, when the third and fourth measures to drop "white" were introduced, that the voting behavior of the political parties becomes significant. On February 9, 1855, Senator Wait Talcott moved to strike "white" from every clause in which the word occurred in the revised free-schools bill before the Senate of the 19th General Assembly. Talcott, formerly a leading light of the Liberty party, now an Anti-Nebraska man and soon to be an ardent Republican, had been elected from northern Winnebago County. He and 4 other senators voted for his motion; 18 voted against. All 5 senators voting for were of the Anti-Nebraska party; of the 18 voting against, 5 were Anti-Nebraska and 13 were Democrats. This record of dividing antislavery party legislators and unanimously opposing Democrats was repeated in the voting on the fourth and last of the prewar and war motions to eliminate the discriminatory "white" from the free-schools laws.

On February 5, 1857, Rollin Wheeler, a Republican member of the House of the 20th General Assembly from northern Carroll County, submitted a motion to drop "white." Immediately Samuel W. Moulton, Democrat from central Shelby County, moved to table. His motion was sustained, 55 to 19. All 19 members against tabling were Republicans. Seventeen of the 55 members voting for tabling were Republicans or Free Soilers; 38 were Democrats.[8]

On the 1855 and 1857 measures the Republicans had divided while the Democrats had remained perfectly united. Just as divisions among the blacks had reduced their chances of effecting a repeal of the laws discriminating against the public schooling of their children, so had divisions among their white allies or potential allies. Two measures, fundamental to the blacks' acquisition of public school rights, had not attracted the votes of nearly half of the legislators from whom the blacks and their white friends might reasonably expect support. If instead of splitting 5 to 5 the 10 Anti-Nebraska senators in the 19th General Assembly had all voted for Talcott's motion to strike "white" from the free-schools law and if they had been joined by two Democrats, the motion would have passed in the Senate. Again, if in the 20th General Assembly all 36 Republicans and Free Soilers had voted against tabling Wheeler's motion and if they had been joined by 2 Democratic defectors, Wheeler's motion might have been acted on and eventually passed. As it was, on both occasions the Republicans had divided and the Democrats had held together, and in consequence Illinois law would not be purged of the principal statutory hindrances to the public schooling of blacks during the antebellum and bellum periods. The struggles were not to go for naught. Lessons had been learned. Many of the conditions that had produced the weaknesses plaguing black and white efforts would be neutralized and Illinois blacks with the aid of antislavery and Republican whites would succeed in repealing the black laws in February 1865. The attack on the state's black laws was led by the most capable and influential black emerging from the battles of the 1840s and fifties. John Jones was chosen to lead the campaign. He began by writing an eloquent essay, *The Black Laws of Illinois and a Few Reasons Why They Should Be Repealed,* a long and carefully reasoned pamphlet of 16 pages. He repeated the familiar arguments about the inhumane, un-Christian, un-American nature of the black laws; he also put forward new arguments based on the blacks' entrance into the military and economic spheres of community life during the war. He spoke of the Illinois blacks' service in the Union army and he emphasized how much it was in the financial self-interest of the whites to have the black laws stamped out. "The interest of one, is the interest of all," he told the whites. "You ought to, and must, repeal those Black Laws for the sake of your own interest, to mention no higher motive. . . . You ought, therefore, to look well to your own interests, and see that no legislative enactments cripple your legitimate business relations with the community at large." This was reasoning based on the partnership concept of community, and Jones was directing his appeal not just to humanitarian, religious, and patriotic motives but also to practical, self-benefiting ones.[9]

The plan for the campaign called for money to be raised from balls, festivities, and sales of Jones' tract—as well as the hiring of agents to canvass the entire state for signatures to petitions. Assisting would be organizations like the Chicago Repeal Association and perhaps other of the black voluntary associations surviving from the 1850s. As the campaign was planned, so it came about. Jones spearheaded the drive for petitions and he lobbied in person in the corridors of the capitol at Springfield. The legislature—acting in that deliberative forum devised to protect and promote the exercise of dialectical power in framing the rules of human association, although in the real world of law-making and lawmakers the practice of rewarding and punishing power is certainly not unknown—was inunduated with petitions from the northern, central, and southern counties. Governor Yates instructed the senators and House members to sweep the black laws from the statute books "with a swift, relentless hand," and the Senate judiciary committee, to which the petitions were referred, recommended that the General Assembly quickly act to "let the oppressed go free."[10]

In their report the committee did not neglect the old arguments relating to the injustice and inhumanity of Illinois' treatment of blacks, but the report was weighted more toward the motive of restoring the honor of the state. The senators on the committee made the recommendation they did "because urged to do so by the earnest petitions and solemn resolves of thousands and tens of thousands of their fellow-citizens, as well as by their own convictions of justice, humanity, and a sound State and national policy." Should Illinois "foremost in her efforts to save our common country from destruction—foremost in the number, gallantry, and undying patriotism of her troops; foremost in the just and universal fame of her Generals, and also foremost in the development of educational, agricultural and commerical interests" be the last to accept the great and sublime teachings of the age, that "all men are created free and equal"? The former slave states were freeing their slaves, "yet true it is (though hell-born the fact) that not a slave freed in Maryland or Missouri, or to be freed elsewhere, can enter our state under the present insidious, accursed and accursing 'black laws.'" Now that the darkest hour "of our terrible national adversity has gone by; the fears which once crowded thick upon us have been dissipated by the glorious sun light of the new born day; let us then wipe out forever the deepest stain upon the history of our beloved State, and all will be well; we shall be greeted with the acclamation of our country and of the world, and our constituents will say of us 'Well done, good and faithful servants.'"

Jones', Governor Yates', and the Senate judiciary committee's display of dialectical power drew cogency from a climate of opinion much changed by the war years. The drive for repeal had gained from past experience and present circumstance. For the occasion, at least, the blacks had learned the lessons of unified effort and singleness of purpose. Collaboration had been secured from a white organization, the Republican party, possessing power for transcending that of any other within the political sphere. And as the Democratic party came to be viewed as treasonable and Democrats as treasonous and as emancipating the Negro had become an objective equal to that of preserving the Union, two purposes for which enormous amounts of blood were being shed and treasure spent, the Republicans had shown less and less inclination to join the Democrats in opposing problack measures and petitions. In the triumph of the Union armies, too, the service of the Illinois Negro volunteers and their willingness to share the dangers of the battlefield had produced gratitude on the part of whites and expectations on the part of blacks. Jones' tract urging the repeal of the black laws had acted as a culminating summary, presenting within a dialectical, rhetorical framework a statement that had accelerated the momentum for repeal.

These were among the factors combining to influence the General Assembly when the issue of rescinding the black laws came to a vote. The repeal bill passed 13 to 10 in the Senate and 49 to 30 in the House. All 13 senators and 49 House members voting for repeal were Republicans; all 10 senators and 30 House members voting against repeal were Democrats. The governor signed the repeal bill into law on February 7, 1865. This time the Republicans had not divided. This time they had not let the blacks down.[11]

4

Exclusion at the Local Level

In any consideration of the interplay between statewide imposition by General Assemblies and local freedom of decision-making by district officials, it should be remembered that the Illinois school laws applying to the entire state did not prescribe or proscribe public schooling for blacks or require either racially integrated or segregated public schools. What the state school laws did do was use the restrictive word "white" to link the amount of state school tax apportionments for a district to a count of the number of "white" children of school age residing there. A district could, if it wished, incur the financial expense of admitting black children into its public schools provided that its freedom of choice on the matter were not narrowed or eliminated altogether by local injunctions. Clauses in town or city charters, ordinances passed by municipal councils, and rules and regulations by school boards might forbid the admission of black children or admit them to "colored schools" only or admit them generally according to formal directives making no mention of race at all.

Rather naturally a question arises as to how many school districts did admit black children into the local public schools on a segregated or nonsegregated basis during the antebellum and bellum years. Quantitative data are lacking for the early period, but statistics bearing on the issue were offered by the blacks themselves at their third state convention, held at Galesburg on October 16, 17, and 18, 1866. The call for delegates had announced that the object of the convention was to lay plans for securing the rights of suffrage, access to the courts, and a share of public-school "privileges." In connection with the latter the convention's committee on education told the delegates that it had found in the state 8,000 black boys and girls eager for learning but that less than 100 were "in" the public schools.[1]

State Superintendent of Public Instruction Newton Bateman was more optimistic in his biennial report for 1865–66. The information he collected from the county superintendents of schools in 1865 showed 743,226 white children and 4,444 black six to twenty-one years of age in the state. Dissatisfied with gaps in the returns on black children, Bateman in his next year's inquiry ordered the county superintendents to be sure to have the township treasurers answer the question about the number of blacks of school age in their districts. For 1866 the figure was 4,931. Still dissatisfied, Bateman made some calculations that he thought would yield a more accurate statistic. He assumed that the percent of black children between six and twenty-one years of age to the total state population of blacks would be the same as that for whites, or 35 percent. Taking 35 percent of 17,340, the total state population of blacks in 1865, he arrived at the sum of 6,069 blacks of school age. Of these, he estimated that at least one-half were, as he ambiguously phrased it, without the "means" of a public-school education.[2]

The convention's judgment that less than 100 black children were in public schools was certainly too low. Bateman's calculations were literally correct but convey an impression that black public-school enrollment or attendance was far higher than it truly was. Various reliable sources reveal that in the mid-1860s black children were being admitted to public schools in Alton, Chicago, Decatur, Galesburg, Jacksonville, Peoria, Quincy, and Springfield. In Chicago 97 blacks were attending public school in 1865; in Galesburg 87 were attending in 1867; in Peoria 23 were attending in 1862; in Springfield 60 were attending in 1866. If 33 more were being taught in the schools on the preceding list and in others accepting blacks for which no quantitative records are available, the total number of black children attending public school during those years would be 300 (5 percent) out of some 6,000 blacks of school age.

Bateman's returns for 1866 indicated that the total number of pupils "in attendance" at all public schools was 614,659. To be on the generous side, double the number of 300 black pupils and add 59 and say that 659 were attending Illinois public schools in

1865–66. Then the percent of blacks "in attendance" at public schools would be approximately 10 percent, whereas the number of whites attending would be 614,000 or 80 percent of 759,987 school-age whites in 1866. Hence, although the estimate of the Galesburg convention's committee may have minimized the number of blacks attending (or enrolled if that is what the committee meant by "in public schools"), the committee's distress and alarm were fully justified. Measured by any standard, whether against the percent of whites in public schools, the number of school-age blacks, or the expectations and aspirations generated by living in a sovereign free state and under a republican government in the sixth and seventh decades of the nineteenth century, public-school opportunities for Illinois black children were deplorably meager.[3]

With the few schools hospitably disposed toward the admission of blacks scattered thinly here and there in the state, parents ambitious for their children or adults ambitious for themselves would have to hunt around for districts in which they could settle and satisfy residence requirements for schools that would accept blacks as pupils. Take Dennis Williams of Springfield, James Henry Magee of Madison County, and George Brown of the town of Normal, McLean County, as examples.

Williams had been born of slave parents in Mississippi. His earliest memories were of riding behind his mother on a mule out into the cotton fields in the morning and back late at night, and he was put to work picking cotton when he was six or seven years old. As soon as Grant's army invaded the state, the Williams family made a run for the shelter of the Union lines. They stayed in Vicksburg for several years, but Dennis's mother was eager to have her son obtain formal schooling and the family moved northward to Springfield, Illinois. Here there was a colored school that Dennis could attend. The crude pictures of dogs, cats, and other animals in his primers fascinated him and he decided that he would be an artist. Despite later rejections and disappointments he persisted in his resolve and, self-taught, became an honored and popular "portrait artist" with a studio in downtown Springfield.[4]

James Henry Magee in his autobiography, *Night of Afflication*, has left the most detailed account of what the search for an education was like for a highly motivated young Illinois black hungry for knowledge. He had been born in southern Madison County on June 23, 1839, one of the children of a free Kentucky black who had worked as a pork packer and saved enough money to purchase the freedom of the slave woman he loved. They were married and moved north to the Illinois farm on which James was born. He attended the district school, apparently along with the white children of the neighborhood, and then a colored school, and next the Brooklyn district school just across the line in St. Clair County.

Some of the Brooklyn whites objected to his presence, and as "the trustees thought it best, for peace sake, to have my parents withdraw me from school," his parents sent him to a colored school taught by a white woman until they decided he should stay home and help on the farm. Shortly afterward he was stricken with a mysterious illness about which he is vague in his autobiography except to say that it left him ailing for the rest of his life. While he was recovering, his brother Samuel, visiting from Wisconsin where he, Samuel, had settled, told James about the opportunities for schooling afforded in Racine. James, "having an insatiable desire for knowledge," as he says, accompanied Samuel and their younger brother, Alfred, to Wisconsin, and James and Alfred enrolled in Racine High School.

After several years in Racine James returned to Illinois, becoming the teacher of a school in the African Baptist church in Jerseyville, central Jersey County. While he was teaching school, he also studied Latin with a "professor" and walked for his lessons three times a week to his tutor's home a mile away. In 1861 he took a teaching position in what seems to have been a racially mixed school in Ridge Prairie, a village in Madison County, remaining there until January 1863, when a measles epidemic caused the school to be shut down. (If the Ridge Prairie school was a public school, Magee was probably the first black public-school teacher in the state, his service antedating that of Mary E. Mann of Chicago in that city's colored school by some two years.)

In August he applied for ordination to the Wood River Colored Baptist Association and, receiving his credentials, he served as a minister for congregations in Piasa and Wood River. His craving for education undiminished, he transferred to the ministry of a Baptist church in Toronto, Canada, so that he could attend school there. Along with the responsibilities of his pastorship he carried courses in the Toronto Grammar School. After two years he sailed for England to study in the Pastor's College of the Metropolitan Tabernacle College in London.

In 1868 he returned to the United States and became the principal of the African Baptist College in Nashville. He next moved north to Alton, Illinois, where the city board of education appointed him the teacher of the colored public school. His schoolroom was damp and poorly outfitted for instruction and his pupils were crowded together in a single room, with groups ranging from children who were learning their ABCs to students who were studying Latin, but he was praised for his teaching and he himself felt he had accomplished much under such conditions. Magee left Alton in 1871, having been called to the pulpit of the Union Baptist Church of Cincinnati, the oldest black church in Ohio, a position he held at the time he wrote his autobiography.

Some readers of Magee's autobiography will be reminded of the wandering scholars of the Middle Ages, traversing the Continent from Oxford or Paris to Salerno or Salamanca in search of a *studium generale* having a celebrated program of studies or renowned lecturer in their field. Magee was spurred on in his travels by the same passion for learning that inspired his medieval predecessors.

Magee was exceptional. Yet there were other Illinois blacks who were highly motivated although by a desire for more rudimentary skills. Some were like George Brown, adult blacks ambitious to acquire a mastery of the tools of literacy and willing to go to school no matter where instruction was to be found or what humiliations they might suffer. Brown, a black thirty to thirty-five years old, wishing to learn to read, applied for admission to the model school of the State Normal University in the town of Normal, central McLean County.

The model school was conducted under a contract between the university and the town and enrolled pupils who were taught by university and town teachers and by students in the university who were preparing to become teachers and needed classroom practice before embarking on their careers. The principal, John Williston Cook, assigned Brown to the primary class. The teacher refused to admit him. She would not seat him in the same room with six- or seven-year-old boys and girls. Cook insisted and declared that if no one else would teach Brown he would even if the parents took their children out of the school. Brown apparently stayed, whether in the primary class or elsewhere in the school the records do not tell, and some parents did withdraw their children. The university policy of nonsegregated schooling for blacks displayed in the Brown and other cases came under criticism, and it was accused of being a miscegenating, tax-squandering institution run for the benefit of the radicals and "niggers." Cancelling the contract with the university, the town school board organized for itself a system of separate schools for the races. But the university did not depart from its policy.[5]

That the Brown incident of an adult black being motivated to apply for admission to a school for literacy instruction was not unique is shown by events occurring in Galesburg, northern Knox County, during the war. The city was first settled by a colony of Presbyterians who had as one of their objectives the founding of a college to educate ministers who would go out among the frontier folk and preach the austere doctrines of John Knox. Many of the settlers were abolitionists, and the public schools mixed blacks and whites from the beginning. With the railroad in 1850 a new element arrived, Irish and Germans considerably less friendly in their attitude toward the blacks. But integrated public schooling continued, for the old residents were more accepting of the blacks than they were of the newcomers—a feeling reflected in the comment by a member of the school board that black children "would be better associates for our little children than the Irish and Dutch now attending the schools."

Galesburg's reputation for racial tolerance attracted to it large numbers of contrabands. As the southern states had laws that prohibited teaching slaves to read and write, the contrabands were often illiterate. If any of the adults desired to learn to read once they had settled in a city like Galesburg, they might face the prospect, as George Brown did in Normal, of obtaining instruction in the lowest grades of the district public school and of suffering the embarrassment and awkwardness of being in a class with small children.

Shrinking from this prospect, the Galesburg blacks petitioned the school board to establish a school for blacks alone. The school board complied and passed a rule that "the colored children in the district are expected to attend the school provided for them, and no other." A room was set aside in the black church for the school, and a white woman volunteered to be the teacher. She was Mary Allen West, the daughter of one of the founding colonists, a graduate of Knox Seminary, and later to become superintendent of the Knox County public schools and a nationally prominent journalist, editor, and social reformer. In September 1863, the Galesburg colored school opened, the children attending in the morning and the adults in the afternoon. All of this explains how and why segregated schooling for blacks came to exist in a community in which the ruling elite was on the whole very problack in sentiment.[6]

The experiences of Dennis Williams, James Henry Magee, George Brown, and the Galesburg blacks supplement other evidence (to be presented in this and later chapters) of the strength of the motivation some blacks had for educating their children and themselves. This account also suggests how complex the intentions and actions were that produced "colored" schools in various districts within the state. Even where racially mixed or racially separate schools were established, however, their life was precarious and the blacks might find that a school to which they were admitted today might be closed against them tomorrow or have vanished altogether. Changes in the personnel of boards of education, committees of county commissioners, panels of village and town trustees, and councils of city aldermen could bring to an end the blacks' chances of securing an education arranged for and paid for by local governmental agencies. And when a school was provided and was a colored school, it might be far from the homes of many of the children and be held in a dank, unhygienic room into which might be shunted a heterogeneous collection of pupils across the school-age years of five or six to eighteen or twenty and be taught by a person without adequate training or sufficient previous practice.

Under such detrimental circumstances pupils coming motivated to school might lose much of their desire for instruction and begin to exhibit severe disciplinary and learning problems. Their parents might lose their ambitiousness for their children and let them go to school, stay home, or roam the streets as whim and impulse might lead them. Some of these conditions and results are to be observed in the histories of a sampling of schools open to blacks in smaller and larger communities, including the city of Chicago, in the 1850s and 1860s. It should not be forgotten, of course, that in most districts during the period the blacks were barred entirely from public schooling. To cite an especially heartless example, out on the prairies of southern Edwards County a group of farmers living in proximity decided to build a schoolhouse for the children. They chopped down trees, hauled logs with their ox teams, laid the timber, and caulked the chinks in the walls. One of the farmers was a black, "powerful and dextrous in the use of the axe," who cheerfully did his share. But when the schoolhouse was ready for the children, he was "politely informed that he must not think of sending one of his children to the school, because they were not of the right complexion." Nothing seems to have been said about helping him erect a school for his children.[7]

In those districts in which preparations were made for teaching blacks, harsh treatment was sometimes meted out to idealistic whites who dared to instruct them. In Shawneetown, southern Gallatin County, one Sarah Curtis began teaching a school for blacks, but she was ostracized by the whites and after a few months she gave up "in utter disgust." In Galena, northern Jo Daviess County, the blacks' taxes were put aside until enough money had accumulated to defray the expenses of a school for their children. For several years the money lay idle because no white had the courage to teach the school, and when at last Hannah Christopher, the daughter of the Congregational minister, volunteered, she became, in the words of an old history of the county, a target of malice and contempt: "Slander, abuse, traduction—everything that prejudice could suggest or hatred of the blacks invent—were hurled at her with such merciless virulence that she was compelled to abandon the undertaking."[8]

When schools for blacks were actually put into operation, their existence might be erratic, their housing makeshift, and their teachers the most poorly paid in the system. In 1854 in Quincy, central Adams County, the city council began to appropriate $25 a quarter for a colored school conducted in a one-story, single-room "hovel" by a teacher who was paid a wage below what the female teachers in the white schools were earning.

Some years later the authorities ordered the school to be closed because the average attendance amounted to less than twenty pupils. It was reopened, closed, reopened, and reclosed. Finally it was reopened in better surroundings in 1864 and was continued in various locations without interruption into the next century.[9]

The capital city lagged in providing public schooling for its black children and when that schooling came it was of poor quality. On December 21, 1858, the Springfield board of school inspectors adopted a resolution to have the superintendent organize a colored school and to hire a teacher and select a room. The room chosen was a "shanty" at the rear of St. Paul's African Methodist Episcopal Church, and the teacher and principal hired was Thomas York. He began teaching on January 10, 1859, going about his duties in a "dilapidated" room where he had to instruct forty to sixty pupils divided into nine age and achievement levels.

His salary for doing this was $900 a year as contrasted with the $1,250 a year all the other male principles were making. York's feelings about this disparity could hardly have been soothed if he read in the superintendent's report that the teachers' and principals' salaries were being published to show how much their labors were "appreciated by our citizens." When the size of salaries was used as the criterion by which citizen appreciation was measured, York's labors would not have been highly appreciated, obviously.

In 1863 the "shanty" was repaired, but the school board believed that new quarters were needed and referred to the city council a report in which "the cruel neglect that this portion of our population has been subjected to, ever since the school was opened seven years ago, was fully exhibited." The school was moved to a larger building with well-ventilated rooms and school furniture equal to the best in the white schools and York was given a teacher to assist him. For the first time, confessed the superintendent, the colored school was to be conducted "with advantages that will bear some comparison with those long enjoyed by a more favored race."[10]

Of the towns and cities having public schools for blacks that were mentioned at the beginning of this chapter as supplying a basis for recalculating the number of black children "in" public schools during the 1860s, only Decatur, Bloomington, Jacksonville, Peoria, and Chicago remain to be profiled. On April 12, 1865, the Decatur school board responded to a request from the congregation of St. Peter's African Methodist Episcopal Church by establishing a public colored school in the basement of the church. A public colored school in Bloomington was opened in 1860 under a Mrs. Howard who had been a missionary in Burma. In Jacksonville in the 1850s a private school for black children was taught by a "pious female," and in the 1860s a separate public colored school was housed in the Mt. Emery African Baptist Church. The board of school inspectors in Peoria began financial support of a colored school in 1860 by allotting $15 a quarter toward the salary of a teacher, a Miss Rebecca Elliott, the rest of her salary being paid by the parents of her pupils. The school was in an African church. Two years later the whole of her salary was absorbed by the board and the colored school became a part of the public system.[11]

As this montage of snapshots reveals, there were public schools open to blacks in a few districts during the antebellum and bellum periods. Nevertheless even if the number of pupils enrolled or attending those schools exceeded the "less than one hundred of our colored children in public schools" reckoned by the committee of the third Illinois state convention of blacks, the education made available to them was often as minimal as public-school officialdom could contrive to make it. The children were usually taught in separate colored schools in one-room "hovels," "shanties," and African churches designed for religious services and ill-suited for teaching and learning. Their teachers, no matter how idealistic and courageous, were frequently lacking in the training and experience that would enable them to cope with the difficulties they would encounter every school day in a room full of children of widely varying levels of maturity, motivation, and achievement.

Chicago was different. Its treatment of the black children in the public schools was responsive to national, state, and municipal influences and the bargaining tactics employed by the city's blacks and whites were dissimilar in certain respects from those pursued in other districts. Dissimilar too was the issue over which conflict arose in Chicago. Whereas in most of the districts of the state the major issue was whether black children should be allowed any public schooling at all, in Chicago the major issue of the antebellum and bellum periods was whether the blacks, already having access, should be taught separately.

From the creation of the city's public school system in 1837 until the Civil War the black children were taught with white children in the same classrooms of public schoolhouses or in the same rooms rented and outfitted by the school board. Blacks and whites shared the very same instructional environments. None of the Chicago city charters or ordinances or regulations of the board of education contained any school restrictions as to race. Children went to the public schools in their neighborhoods. All this changed in June 1863.

By order of the city charter and rules of the board of education the black children were obliged to attend the Colored School and forbidden to enroll in any of the public schools in which white children were taught. The interval between June 1863 and April 1865 has been the only period in the long history of public education in Chicago in which *de jure* racial segregation has existed in the schools. After decades of nonsegregated public schooling, during a war being fought for Negro freedoms by an army in which blacks were serving loyally, the policy and practice of racially segregated schooling were put in force. Why so constitutes an intriguing problem that deserves more extensive analysis. It is, moreover, a problem of a kind that has been and is being faced by black and white Illinoisans and Chicagoans in the last half of the twentieth century. Perhaps the Chicago of the 1860s has something to say to the Chicago of the 1980s.

5

Segregation in Chicago

The appearance of racially segregated schooling in Chicago in 1863 was the result of forces boiling up within a city undergoing the urbanizing process with a speed and on a scale with which Americans had had no previous experience. Strain to the breaking point was exerted on municipal institutions, including the public-school system, by an extraordinary increase in population, by the heterogeneity of that population, by bitter competition for jobs during alternating peaks and troughs of prosperity and depression, and by fierce strife between the political parties. Emotions were inflamed by racial, ethnic, and political prejudices and fanned by the irresponsible mudslinging of the newspapers. All of these phenomena were occurring in a city wrought up to a high pitch of nervous irritability and suspiciousness by an exhausting ideologically divisive war, the outcome of which was long shrouded in doubt.

The population of the city spurted upward from 29,963 in 1850, to 109,260 in 1860, and to 298,977 in 1870. The Negro segment was 323 in 1850, 955 in 1860, and 3,691 in 1870. Of the foreign-born, numbering 52 percent of the total population in 1850, 50 percent in 1860, and 48 percent in 1870, 32 percent were of German birth and 39 percent of Irish birth in 1850, 41 percent and 36 percent in 1860, and 41 percent and 28 percent in 1870. The large percentage of Irish-born in the population posed special difficulties for the blacks because the lowest class of the Irish competed with them on the unskilled labor market, for housing in the most blighted, crowded sections of the city, and, before the Catholic parish school network had matured, for seats in the public schools in the South Division, between the main and south branches of the Chicago River, 16th street, and the lake-front, where the Jones and Dearborn schools were located.

Antagonisms provoked by the jostling of the blacks and Irish against each other were further exacerbated by the scare-mongering of the two most widely read Illinois newspapers, the *Chicago Times* and the *Chicago Tribune.* The Democratic *Times* under its editor and owner, the notorious Wilbur F. Storey, attacked the blacks and the nonsegregation policy of the public schools with scurrilities that projected a diseased kind of hatred. On the other side the Republican *Tribune* was almost as bad. It denounced the Irish as drunken, unruly captives of an ecclesiastical despotism that was at heart violently anti-Negro and treasonably prosecessionist. "It is not forgotten," wrote James W. Sheahan, the prominent Irish-Catholic editor of the *Chicago Post,* that the *Tribune's* "abuse and vilification of the Irish was made in behalf of the cause of the Negro."[1]

All the while, the Chicago school board was trying to solve the formidable school housing problems brought by rapid demographic changes in the city. In 1850 the number of school-age children was 9,097 whites and 81 blacks; in 1860, 40,891 whites and 243 blacks; in 1870, 79,342 whites and 938 blacks. (In 1860 the statistics for whites and blacks of school age are for Cook County; for other years the statistics are for the city of Chicago.) The board frantically built schools and rented rooms, but despite its efforts, at least 1,000 more children would have attended the public schools in 1858 if seats had been available for them, according to the Chicago superintendent of schools, William H. Wells, in his annual report.

In his next report he complained that Chicago had the smallest number of classrooms and smallest teaching staff in proportion to number of pupils of any major city in the United States "simply because the population of our city has increased faster than that of any other." Two years later he had much the same to say, estimating that 15,159 children were enrolled in the public schools, 7,750 in private schools, and 4,091 in no schools at all. It was from this soil of racial and ethnic competition and hostility, of overcrowding in the schools, and of desperate effort by the board to furnish accommodations for all school-age children in the city that controversies sprang up over its policy of racially unsegregated public schooling.[2]

The first formal attempt to change this policy was made by George M. Higginson, a wealthy businessman, probably a Republican, and a Protestant born in Massachusetts who had come to Chicago in 1843 and been appointed to the school board in 1855. (Here and later I give the religious affiliation, place of birth, and political party of the protagonists so as to test out one of the beliefs current at the time: that antiblack actions by the Chicago school board were instigated by Democrats, Irish, and Catholics.) At the board's meeting on January 30, 1858, Higginson proposed that a separate school for black children be organized. He asserted that about one hundred and thirty "colored persons" were enrolled in the Dearborn and Jones schools, "whereas many white children are excluded from attendance in said schools by reason of the great number who seek admission." So as to accommodate the white children the board should "recommend to the Common Council [of the city] that they provide suitable separate accommodations for the colored children." The resolution was adopted by a vote of seven to five.

A motion to reconsider was offered by Dr. John H. Foster, of New Hampshire birth, a Protestant, and probably a Republican, and this motion passed six to four with two members abstaining. An additional motion was made by John C. Dore, also of New Hampshire birth, a Protestant, and a Republican, to direct the principals of the Dearborn and Jones schools to seat Negro children by themselves. Dore's motion was voted down, but a motion by Foster to table the Higginson resolution until the next meeting of the board was approved. At the next meeting, after the Higginson resolution had been taken from the table, Perkins Bass, a Vermonter, Protestant, and Republican, moved to table. His motion lost eight to six, but after further discussion Higginson withdrew his resolution and the subject was postponed indefinitely. Unfortunately the published accounts of the meeting offer no clues about what was said in the discussion or what Higginson's motives were for withdrawal.[3]

At the meetings on January 30 and February 27 the debates over the issue of racial segregation in the public schools were probably the first within official Chicago school board sessions in the history of the city. Overcrowding was the ostensible reason for the emergence of the issue: the purpose of segregating the black children was alleged to be that of making vacancies for the whites. Hence the earliest attempt to separate the races in the Chicago public schools displayed on the part of some members an attitude that was to surface again and again in the nineteenth and twentieth centuries: white school rights should take precedence over black school rights.

In this the Chicago school board's first series of votes on the segregation issue, the variables of political affiliation, ethnicity, and religion did not come into play. The four protagonists, Higginson and Dore for segregation and Foster and Bass against, were all Republicans or probably Republicans and were all of old New England stock and Protestants. On the Chicago school board, just as in the General Assembly in Springfield, there were members from whom the blacks might reasonably expect support but who failed them at crucial moments.

The next racial issue dividing the board was precipitated by events occurring in July 1861. A public high school had been opened in Chicago in 1856, with a three-year Classical program preparing for college, a three-year General program preparing for "life," and a two-year Normal program preparing girls for teaching in the city's schools. Mary E. Mann, a black, had graduated from the Dearborn elementary school, had earned the necessary 55 percent or better mark on the high school entrance examination, and had applied for the Normal program. Yet when the board's committee on the appointment of teachers reported the names of the candidates for admission to the Normal program, Mary E. Mann's name was not on the list. She had been rejected, said the committee, because she was of Negro birth. Immediately John Wentworth introduced a resolution that her name be added to the list. A motion to amend the resolution by substituting the words "That no person of African blood be admitted to the Normal department of the High School" was made by James W. Sheahan. His substitute was defeated six to three, and the original Wentworth resolution prevailed by the same number of votes. A majority of the board then approved the list, and the candidates, including Mary E. Mann, were accepted into the Normal program.[4]

Whereas all the leading protagonists in the 1858 controversy were Republicans, Yankees, and Protestants, the two principals in the Mary E. Mann issue were opposites in certain important social variables. John Wentworth had been born in New Hampshire, was a Protestant and a Republican, while James W. Sheahan was of Irish descent, a Catholic and Democrat, and born in Maryland. Otherwise the voting pattern was that of a division among members of a board predominantly of New England origin, Protestant, and Republican. Of the six members voting against Sheahan's substitute and for Wentworth's resolution, four had been born in a New England state, one in New York, and one in Germany. All were Protestants and Republicans. Joining Sheahan in voting for his substitute and against Wentworth's resolution were two members of New England birth, Protestants, and Republicans. It was a voting situation in which there was some splintering of a New England, Protestant, and Republican coterie on the board. But although there had been two defectors, the majority of the coterie had held together in favoring Mary E. Mann's admission to the Normal program and in opposing a rule that would have prevented blacks from entering that program.[5]

Mary E. Mann began her studies in the high school at the beginning of the school year in September 1861. She was the first black to attend a Chicago and perhaps an Illinois high school in the history of the city and the state. She was a good student. She earned a scholastic average of 97, ranking her tenth among the twenty-two Normal graduates. Nonetheless at the graduation ceremonies she was not allowed to sit with her classmates on the stage at Bryan Hall or march forward with them to be awarded her diploma by Philo Carpenter, the acting president of the school board. She sat in the audience, and her diploma was handed to her by John Wentworth. Whatever the reason or reasons for her being isolated, she did receive a teaching assignment for the school year 1863–64, and was appointed teacher and principal of the city's new "colored" school. To her other "firsts" she now added the honor of being the first black to graduate from a Chicago and Illinois public high school, albeit from a two-year instead of a three- or four-year program, and when she started teaching and performing the duties of a principal in September, the first black to teach and hold an administrative position in the city's and perhaps the state's public schools.[6]

The colored school to which Miss Mann was appointed had opened on June 15, 1863, although the series of events that had culminated in this break with the Chicago tradition of racially unsegregated public schooling had begun some fourteen months earlier. Frustration over Union defeats in the eastern theater of war and fears of an inundation of contraband blacks from plantations liberated by Union victories along the lower Mississippi had weakened the Republican party in the city elections of April 1862. A Democrat was elected mayor and Democrats were elected to the city council from seven of the ten wards, changing the composition of the council from twelve Republicans and eight Democrats to ten from each party. On June 2 the Irish-born, Catholic, Democratic alderman from the tenth ward, Redmond Sheridan, introduced an ordinance in relation to public schools. Section 1 ordered the board of education from and after the summer term, 1862, to make provisions "whereby the several children of color attending the public schools shall be educated separate and apart from the white children, in such school-houses, school-rooms and classes as the Board of Education may direct." The proposed ordinance was referred by the council to its committee on schools, a committee consisting of two Republicans and a Democrat.[7]

Summer, autumn, and winter passed without anything being heard from the committee on the subject. The committee's failure to report may have been due, in part, to Sheridan's absence from the council and his inability to put pressure on the committee. In September he had enlisted in the 90th Infantry Regiment of Illinois Volunteers and would not be mustered out until the war had been won. His proposed ordinance did get support in December, however, from Samuel Snowden Hayes, the city's school agent and comptroller.

Born in Tennessee and a Protestant, Hayes, who as a member of the House representing White County in the 15th General Assembly had blocked the bill to exempt Negroes from school taxes, had moved to Chicago and become a powerful personage in the Democratic ranks. With the success of his party in the municipal election of 1862, he had been appointed school agent and comptroller and in that capacity he had transmitted information to the council in December showing that the number of blacks in the city was 1,614 and that 1,391 of these lived in the South Division.

He had indulged his chronic bias against the blacks by editorializing on his statistics and telling the council that "it is thus proven that the separation of the colored children from the schools attended by our white children, which justice to the white race requires should be made, can be carried into effect without inconvenience, or necessarily depriving the colored children of instruction, which can be given them in a school of their own, situated in the South Division, so as to be accessible to their entire numbers."

This conclusion simply ignored the fact that some black children lived outside the South Division and that some living in the Division, which extended over a large section of the central city, would have to walk long and dangerous distances to a colored school, no matter where in the Division it might be located. Hayes' report, applauded by the *Chicago Times* as "a most unanswerable argument in favor of the exclusion of colored children from the schools attended by white children," was referred by the council to its committee on schools. The committee maintained as deep a silence on the Hayes report as it had and continued to have on Sheridan's proposed ordinance.[8]

The stalling by the committee had the effect of permitting the initiative on the issue of racial segregation in the Chicago public schools to slip away from local hands into those of the 23rd General Assembly convening in Springfield on January 5, 1863. In that Assembly the Republicans, who had enjoyed a majority of 1 in the Senate and of 7 in the House of the previous General Assembly, were in a minority of 1 in the Senate and of 28 in the House. A leading Democratic member of the House was Melville Weston Fuller of Chicago.

Twenty-five years later when he was nominated as chief justice of the United States Supreme Court by President Cleveland, those persons who objected to the appointment cited his voting record in the "unpatriotic" Illinois 23rd General Assembly and denounced him as a former "Copperhead." Fuller was no Copperhead, but he had joined his Democratic colleagues in advocating a negotiated peace with the Confederates, in protesting the "usurpations" of the Lincoln administration, in criticizing the Emancipation Proclamation, and in re-enacting the Illinois law forbidding the immigration of blacks into the state. He had also been the sponsor of a bill containing an article forcing racial segregation upon the Chicago schools.

On January 19 he introduced a bill for "An Act to reduce the charter of the city of Chicago and the several acts amendatory thereof into one act, and to revise the same." The bill was passed in the Senate and House and signed by the governor on February 13. In the revised charter the last part of Section 16, Chapter 13, "Schools and the School Fund," read:

> It shall be the duty of the common council and board of education to provide one or more schools for the instruction of negro and mulatto children, to be kept in a separate building to be provided for that purpose, at which colored pupils, between the ages of five and twenty-one years, residing in any school district in said city, shall be allowed to attend; and hereafter it shall not be lawful for such pupils to attend any public schools in the city of Chicago, at which white children are taught, after a school for the instruction of negro and mulatto children has been provided.[9]

The changes in the charter's educational provisions the *Tribune* saw as elements of a Catholic plot to capture the Chicago public schools. "Zeta," the newspaper's Springfield correspondent, accused Fuller of acting at the behest of a prominent Chicago Irish Catholic. According to Zeta the Catholics' intention was to exclude the Bible and the blacks from the public schools and reserve certain public schools only for Catholics so that these schools could be controlled by the priesthood. The literature of Protestantism and freedom would be eliminated, and the literature of Catholicism, despotism, and slavery would be substituted.[10]

To a degree Zeta's interpretation was plausible. Chicago Catholics would have liked to obtain more power on the school board and over the public schools. Excerpts from the King James Version of the Bible were read every morning at the beginning of the school day; anti-Catholic materials were present in the textbooks; and a Protestant minister, the Reverend William H. Ryder, pastor of St. Paul's Universalist Church, was serving on the school board. No Catholic priest had been (or was ever to be) a member of the school board and the few Catholics that had been appointed were always an ineffectual minority.

The Right Reverend James Duggan, bishop of Chicago, the clergy, and the laity did nourish some hopes of exercising more influence over public school policy and practice. But beyond this point Zeta's analysis is not convincing. No Irish Catholic from Chicago was serving in the 23rd General Assembly; the two Chicago senators and seven House members, four of the nine of whom had voted for the revised charter, were probably all Protestants and three had been born in New England, three in New York, two in Germany, and one probably in Germany. Melville W. Fuller, a devout Episcopalian, born in Maine and a descendant of Yankee forebears, would not be inclined to act as an accomplice or as an agent for the Catholics of Chicago. That the Catholics would put textbooks slanted toward slavery and the Confederacy into the curriculum was a patent absurdity, given the many Irish Catholic enlistments in the Illinois volunteer regiments and Bishop Duggan's ardent support of the Union cause and the war effort.

More probable is the interpretation offered by the other Chicago Republican newspaper, the *Evening Journal:* it believed that racial prejudice and political intrigue were at the root of the matter. Still a political explanation is not altogether satisfactory either. The five Chicago Republicans in the House of the General Assembly had voted against the bill to revise the charter, but the two Chicagoans in the Senate, William B. Ogden and Jasper D. Ward, the former a Protestant and the latter almost certainly one, and both born in New York state and Republicans, had been appointed by their colleagues to advise them on the bill, had recommended passage, and had so voted themselves. Racial prejudice had certainly been a motive. Otherwise, despite the various suppositions, as the *Evening Journal* in an unusual burst of candor had admitted, the motives, the intentions, and the persons responsible for the changes in the schools chapter of the charter were something of a "mystery." [11]

The General Assembly's revision jolted the committee on schools of the city council into action on March 23. One member of the committee had died, but the two remaining members, John Q. Hoyt, Republican, and William T. Shufeldt, Democrat (for neither of whom is there information about place of birth or religion) urged the council to obey the injunction embodied in Section 16, Chapter 13, of the new charter and to direct and authorize the board of education to rent a building or rooms in the South Division and hire teachers "for a school for the instruction of colored children." The council concurred, the votes for or against, if called for, not being placed upon the record. [12]

The board of education met on May 8, two months and two

days before the end of the school term. On the board were twelve Republicans and three Democrats. If such a thoroughly Republican-dominated board had been genuinely committed to a racially unsegregated policy, it could have procrastinated through the few remaining weeks of the school term and into the next school year and waited to see whether the city council would do anything to enforce the directive in the charter. John Wentworth did try to get his fellow members on the board to engage in delaying tactics, but of the eleven board members attending the meeting only four Republicans voted for his motion while six Republicans and one Democrat voted against.

In the debate the six Republican defectors spoke of the board's sworn duty to obey the charter and the directive from the Common Council of the city. Paired with this argument was the old relief-from-overcrowding rationalization about the many white children being refused admission to schools "overflowing" with blacks. Were a separate school founded for blacks, "there would be room enough for the white children or, at any rate, none of them would be deprived of the benefits of our free schools, while the children of negroes enjoy them to their fullest extent, even to the advantages of the High School." To gather evidence, Charles N. Holden, a Republican, born in New York and a Protestant, moved to have the board ask its committee on buildings and grounds to ascertain how many black children were attending each of the public schools and to determine where a separate school for them might best be located. This the board agreed to unanimously.[13]

At a meeting on June 9, with all fifteen members present, James Ward, a Democrat and Irish Catholic, the chairman of the board's committee on buildings and grounds, reported that 123 blacks were attending the public schools: 70 in the Jones school, 25 in the Dearborn, 4 in the Scammon, 2 in the Washington, 1 in the Moseley, 2 in the Brown, 5 in the Foster, 2 in the Ogden, 7 in the Skinner, and 5 in the Haven. None attended the Kinzie, Franklin, Newberry, and No. 12 schools. The best schoolhouse obtainable for a colored school was, said Ward, the Mission Sabbath School, owned by the Second Presbyterian Church, in the Jones school district.

What Ward's report proved, although neither he nor any other board member admitted as much, was that the argument for putting all the black children in a separate school to relieve the shortage of places for whites was as impractical in 1863 as it had been in 1858 and 1862 when it had been advocated by George M. Higginson and Samuel Snowden Hayes. At the Foster school where overcrowding was particularly acute only 5 blacks were in attendance. No blacks were attending the Kinzie, Franklin, and No. 12 schools where serious overcrowding also existed. In only one school, the Jones school, would the ousting of blacks make such difference and the vacating of 70 places there would help relatively few of the thousands of white children who, Superintendent Wells had said, were vainly striving for admission to the schools. As for the Mission Sabbath School being in the "best" location for blacks, it might have been for the 70 black children attending the Jones school but it was not for the 53 attending public schools elsewhere in the city.[14]

Nonetheless the board did not hesitate. Flavel Moseley, born in Connecticut, a Protestant, and a Republican, moved that the committee's report be adopted, and Levi B. Taft, born in Massachusetts, also a Protestant and Republican, moved that Superintendent Wells "proceed immediately to organize a school for colored children in the building designated in accordance with the provision of the new city charter and the recent action of the Common Council on the subject." Both motions were concurred in without a recorded vote. Six days later, on June 15, the "Colored School" opened in the Mission Sabbath School building, with Laura A. Kellogg, a white woman, as principal and teacher. Only four more weeks of the regular school term remained before the long summer vacation would begin.

The unhappy life of the Colored School lasted only twenty-two months, until April 14, 1865. During its existence it encountered much trouble. A series of rapid turnovers on the teaching staff was not conducive to consistency in instruction or to a peaceful learning environment. The first principal and teacher, Laura A. Kellogg, stayed only two months, June and July 1863; Mary E. Mann stayed three months, September, October, and November 1863, before resigning because she could not control the obstreperous pupils; Roxanna F. Beecher stayed fourteen months, from November 1863 through December 1864; Nellie S. Phillips stayed three months, December 1863 and January and February 1864; Emily C. Stevens stayed thirteen months, from

March 1864 to April 14, 1865; Thomas E. Anis stayed three months, from the end of January 1865 to April 14, 1865.

These teachers, especially in the early months, were laboring against very disturbing pupil behavior. The Mission Sabbath School building proved to be ill-suited for teaching and did not have a yard in which the children could play. The pupils were disobedient and resisted discipline and instruction. This was understandable, for many of them were in school for the first time and others had been pulled out of classrooms and schools where they had been with children of about their own age and level of achievement and were now herded together in a single building with a wider age and achievement span than any other in the system. From September through December 1863, the number of pupils "belonging" to the Colored School was 57. Of these, 32 were between 5 and 6 years old, 20 were between 6 and 15 years of age, and 5 were over 15 years old. Other statistics for the period showed that the school's average enrollment was 88, the smallest of any school, that the average daily attendance was 48, the lowest of any school but one, and the percent of daily attendance was 85.1, the worst in the system. Cost of instruction was $10.79 per pupil, making it the most expensive of all schools except the high school.[15]

Furthermore the school was not fulfilling the purpose for which it had been established. The average attendance in the autumn of 1863 had been 48, whereas in the preceding June the Ward committee had counted 123 black children attending the district schools. Where were the missing 75 black children? Kept at home by their parents? Or, despite the board's regulation, attending the district schools? Eventually the board's curiosity was sufficiently piqued by the discrepancy to impel it on motion of James W. Sheahan to request Josiah L. Pickard, who had followed Wells as Chicago superintendent of schools, to investigate. On October 4, 1864, Pickard told the board the 36 blacks were attending schools other than the Colored School. Two were in the high school; the other 34 were in the district schools, their parents having affirmed them to be of less than one-fourth Negro blood. (Illinois law defined a "Negro" as a person having one-fourth or more of Negro blood.)

A later report by Pickard revealed that the average daily attendance at the Colored School for November was 107, which with 36 in other schools added up to a total of 143 black children attending the public schools, only 20 more than James Ward had counted a year and a half earlier, though the black population of the city had increased from 1,614 in 1862 to 2,196 in 1864 and probably the number of black children of school age in a like ratio. The Colored School was not attended "very numerously," acknowledged James W. Sheahan, the board member who over the years had supported the idea and then the actuality of separate schooling for the races, and he attributed their poor attendance to the fact that "they [the blacks] insist on attending the public schools from which the law excludes them." [16]

For these and, no doubt, other reasons a decision was made by someone with the concurrence of others (by whom the extant documents do not reveal) to shut the school down. On January 24, 1865, Jasper D. Ward, born in New York, a Republican, almost certainly a Protestant, and a state senator from Cook County and Chicago, introduced in the Assembly a bill for amending the 1863 Chicago charter. The bill was referred to the Senate committee on banks and corporations and reported out favorably. On February 11 the Senate voted for it, 23 to 0; on February 14 the House voted 72 to 0 for it; on February 16 the governor signed the bill into law. The new charter repealed Chapter 13, Section 16, of the charter of 1863 containing the decree that the blacks were to attend a separate school.

In the 1865 charter the equivalent section said nothing about race or a colored school, merely authorizing the board to establish at least one school in each of the city's school districts and to provide free instruction within their respective districts to "all children, residing within the limits of the city, who are over the age of six years, and who may be sent to or attend such school, subject to such rules and regulations as may be established by the common council or board of education." Presumably the clause subjecting attendance to the new rules would have enabled the council or board of education or both bodies to continue the Colored School, but neither chose to do so and the school was terminated on April 14, the last day of the winter term. [17]

The circumstances surrounding the demise of the Colored School were as mysterious to contemporaries as the circumstances of its birth had been in 1863. To a man the Democrats had

67

voted for a charter without the separate school requirement. This the *Times* found perfectly bewildering. It theorized that a "swindle" and a "gross fraud" had been used to dupe trusting Democrats by deceitful Republicans, but it offered no explanation and no proof.[18]

Unmistakably the movement to establish a racially separate school in Chicago had been started and sustained by persons born in diverse places, by Protestants and Catholics, and by Republicans and Democrats. If the reader will go back over this chapter and count the persons who have been named as introducing antiblack schooling measures, he or she will find the total to be 13. Five were born in the New England states, 2 in New York, 2 in southern states, 2 in Ireland, and 2 in a place unknown. Seven were Protestants, 1 probably a Protestant, 3 were Catholics, and 2 were of an unknown denomination. Six were Republicans, 1 probably a Republican, and 6 were Democrats. The board of education that implemented the separate school article in the charter was composed of 12 Republicans and 3 Democrats. A conclusion about Chicago whites similar to that reached about Illinois whites in the previous chapter is clearly warranted: the black cause of nonsegregated schooling had suffered because of divisions and defections within white groups and organizations from which the blacks might logically have expected support.

On the other hand the events occurring in the city had proved that the exercise of power by the blacks could have been one of the factors persuading the Republicans to unite on relieving them of the ignominy of separate schooling. In their battling against the Colored School the city's blacks had used both dialectical and punishing power. They wrote letters of protest to the newspapers and held mass meetings publicizing their objections to segregation and their reasons for fighting against it.

An example will show the kinds of arguments they used toward the end of the year 1864. On September 29 a meeting of black inhabitants of the city adopted nine resolutions. First, that Sheahan's resolution at the school board's September 17 session to have the superintendent inquire into whether the black children were attending the district schools and not the Colored School might be a prelude to action barring black children from the public schools completely. Second, that Sheahan's resolution was gross in its tendency, uncharitable in its purpose, and calculated to retard the moral and intellectual progress of black children and youth and brand them with degredation. Third, as Negroes paid taxes in common with whites, they claimed equal school privileges. Fourth, Sheahan's resolution was impractical because it was impossible for the board to determine the proportion of white to black blood a child might have. Fifth, the blacks were bitterly opposed to segregated schools because such schools fostered "a prejudice in the mind of the [white] child which is difficult to eradicate." Sixth, they requested the board to dispense with the Colored School and admit black children into the district schools without distinctions on account of race. Seventh, the blacks were now with whites fighting as soldiers in the Union army to preserve the rights blacks were denied. Eighth, they would petition the state legislature at its next session to repeal the black laws. Ninth, the daily papers were asked to publish the proceedings of this meeting.[19]

These in some respects were arguments annointed by long usage, but some were novel and would be heard in the next century as well. Thus the blacks at the meeting had recognized that segregation had injurious emotional effects, that it was harmful to white children because it instilled attitudes of prejudice and to black children because it infected them with feelings of degredation and inferiority.

To be observed, too, is the fact that the blacks capitalized on service in the Union forces as an argument for full rights of citizenship. In September 1863, Governor Yates had received authorization from the War Department for Illinois to "raise one regiment of infantry, to be composed of colored men, to be mustered into the United States service for three years, or during the war." Energetic recruiting by John Jones, Joseph Stanley, H. Ford Douglass, and Lewis Isbell, and exhortations by the *Tribune* enabled the Chicago companies of the 1st Regiment Illinois Colored Volunteers to fill up by April. The unit, as the 29th Regiment United States Colored Infantry, fought in the East until Appomattox, was posted to Texas after Lee's surrender, and was stationed near the Mexican border until disbanded on November 6, 1865. Of 1,811 Illinois blacks in the Union army, some 1,400 were in the Illinois regiment and the rest scattered among other federal and state contingents.

To induce Illinois blacks to enlist, certain promises had been made. Here at last, cried the *Tribune*, was a chance for Illinois blacks to demonstrate that they possessed the qualities needed for citizenship: "Prove now that you are men, that you possess the noblest elements of humanity—exalted aspiration and the spirit of self-sacrifice in the attainment of liberty and the public weal." The reward would be full citizenship, for "there is no nobler way that he [the black] can earn a place among citizens than by ranking himself among the defenders of the land." If black men enlisted, "they would be made like ourselves by the uniforms they wore." These were promises that built up obligations for white Republicans and expectations for the blacks. As a *Chicago Times* correspondent who mingled with the Negro recruits from Chicago wrote, "they are elated with the hope held out to them of being elevated to a political and social equality with the white citizen," and were looking forward to the day when "they can vote and 'help make de laws.'"[20]

Fighting in the army against a common foe marked the first time that Illinois blacks in large numbers were permitted to participate in a white community enterprise of an important sort. True the occasion was transitory, but it deposited some residue of rights; never again in the state were questions raised about blacks serving in the military. But, as important, service in the Union army provided one more "piece," so to speak, that the blacks could add to the dialectical ordnance that they would train on the bastions of white privilege. Granted that such service in a day of technologically unsophisticated warfare for the foot soldier and common seaman would not function directly as a motive for bestowing school rights on blacks, still it should not be discounted. It did lead to promises and expectations that suffrage rights would be forthcoming for blacks, and historically the necessity of having a virtuous and educated voting electorate had been the major premise of those persons who advocated universal, public, and free schooling.

In addition to dialectical power the Chicago blacks had applied punishing power. James W. Sheahan had hinted at black disobedience in his diagnosis of the reasons for the poor attendance record of the Colored School. He had emphasized the fact that many blacks had insisted on sending their children to the district schools and staying away from the Colored School. More specific was an answer made later by Chicago Superintendent of Schools Josiah Pickard when he was asked by an Indiana school official about the city's provisions for the education of blacks. Pickard replied that the experiment of a colored school had been tried but that the school had been "disorderly," that "much trouble" had existed in the vicinity of the school, and that desegregated "we certainly have less frequent complaints than in the separate system." Most specific of all is the testimony of an "Old Settler" who gave Drake and Cayton, the authors of *Black Metropolis,* an account of the blacks' campaign against the Colored School, as told to her by her mother:

> The parents—most of them—objecting to segregation sent their children right on to the nearest schools as before. The teachers declined to assign them to classes or studies.
>
> The children, however, attended daily, taking their seats in an orderly fashion throughout the controversy that ensued. The school board then determined that any child with no more than an eighth of Negro blood could attend the usual schools; but here again was trouble, for the wide range of complexions in the colored families soon demonstrated the impossibility of such a division. After a short time and a determined fight on the part of the colored citizens who invaded the offices of the Board of Education and the Mayor, the inglorious career of the Black School was done away with and never resumed.[21]

No matter how much this story may have been embroidered as it was told down through the years, what is clear is that the Chicago blacks did employ punishing as well as dialectical power against segregated schooling and that in the opinion of contemporaries this was a factor bringing about the Colored School's demise. It should be pointed out, too, that the blacks' bargaining power had been directed at a white audience that had become increasingly receptive to black pleas and to the black cause. The rationale for fighting the war, the triumph of a Union army enlisting blacks, the defeat of a foe defending slavery and inflexibly opposed to black rights, and the ascendancy of the Republican party had all worked in the blacks' favor.

In the antebellum period Illinois blacks had exercised dialectical power via a series of petitions that seem to have persuaded Ninian W. Edwards and the General Assembly to include

Section 84 (80) in the free-schools law. It was at best a minor victory. But toward the end of the bellum period the blacks had scored two genuine, major victories. By their exercise of dialectical power in the form of John Jones' *Black Laws of Illinois* and his petitioning drives and lobbying they had played an important role in gaining the repeal of the black laws. By exerting dialectical and punishing power through protests and argumentation and disobedience and "invasions" the Chicago blacks had helped kill the policy of segregating the races in the city's public schools. Would the momentum thus generated carry forward into the postbellum period and enable the blacks to have the discriminatory "white" purged from all sections of the free-schools law? Would they be able to secure, besides, an addition to that law of a clause guaranteeing them access to public schooling in whatever district they might reside throughout the entire state?

6

Winning Suffrage

Despite the collaboration between Illinois blacks and whites that had brought about the repeal of the black laws and revision of the Chicago charter, there still remained a question of whether that cooperation would continue into the years immediately following the war. Would blacks and whites, having got rid of the extreme discriminations embodied in law, unite on expunging from the statutes less offensive discriminations and on enacting into law positive rights for the state's blacks?

The report of the members of the Senate judiciary committee recommending repeal of the black laws would not be a source of comfort on this score. Their arguments had been directed mostly at repealing the black code for the sake of the honor of the state, that is for the sake of the whites, not for the sake of the blacks. Indeed the committee had been careful to point out that its recommendation did not contemplate the bestowal of positive rights. Questions of black rights, said the committee, should be entrusted "to the lapse of time and the influence of events, controlled by the hand of a wise Providence." Neither the committee nor Republicans in common had anything to propose about shortening the lapse of time, hastening the influence of events, or reinforcing the hand of a wise Providence. Sympathies created by the war and the power possessed by triumphant Republicanism might induce the majority party to unite in eliminating the black code but that did not mean that those same legislators would vote together for bills yielding to blacks such fundamental rights as suffrage, testifying in the courts, and access to public schooling.[1]

From 1867 through 1875 seven petitions relating to blacks were presented in the 25th, 26th, 27th, 28th, and 29th General

Assemblies and in the state constitutional convention, meeting December 13, 1869, to May 13, 1870. Five of the petitions dealt with schooling; three of these were problack and two antiblack if petitions for racially segregated schooling are classified as antiblack. In the same General Assemblies and in the state constitutional convention, twenty-nine black schooling measures, thirteen problack and sixteen antiblack, were introduced.

The earliest postwar test of Republican unity on the issue of school rights for blacks came in the 25th General Assembly. Five such measures were introduced. Of these, the fourth, submitted in the Senate on February 16, 1867, by James Strain, a Republican from northern Warren County, was a straightforward attempt to amend the free-schools law by striking from it all language discriminating against race. During its travel in the Senate the Strain bill was voted on, pass or fail, with ten Republicans voting for and six Republicans and seven Democrats voting against. The Republican unity that had been achieved in revoking the black laws had not been repeated when the issue was one of dropping racially discriminatory language from the school laws. Just as in antebellum days the Republicans had divided and the Democrats had held fast in opposition: defecting Republicans had joined Democrats in refusing to make changes that would render blacks eligible for school rights.[2]

A somewhat similar chain of events had occurred in the legislature on the issue of political rights for blacks. A State Convention of Colored Men, the third since 1853 and the first after the war, had been held at Galesburg on October 16, 17, and 18, 1866. Once more the convention had been dominated by Chicagoans, and once more public-school rights were relegated to a secondary place. Topping the docket of priorities was the attainment of suffrage rights. The delegates elected a State Central Suffrage Committee of thirteen members, three from Chicago and one from each of ten other Illinois cities, and a General Agent who was to travel through the state collecting money, promoting the creation of local suffrage societies, and circulating petitions to be signed and transmitted to the 25th General Assembly. For their General Agent they again chose John Jones and again Jones did the job well.

Jones' conduit into the 25th General Assembly was Francis A. Eastman, Republican senator from Cook County, who had acted in the same capacity for Jones in shepherding petitions for the repeal of the black laws into the legislature two years earlier. On January 11, 14, 15, 16, 22, 23, and 29, 1867, Eastman presented petitions, some signed by thousands of persons, praying for amending the constitution so as to confer impartial suffrage or abolish all political distinctions on account of race or color. The petitions were referred to the Senate judiciary committee. Before the committee reported, the House acted. By a vote of 81 to 0 the House adopted a resolution to have the people at the next general election vote for or against calling a convention to revise, alter, or amend the constitution of 1848. The Senate voted concurrence, 19 to 3. Whites and blacks in the state were thus treated to the spectacle of an Assembly, with a Republican majority in the Senate of 17 to 8 and in the House of 60 to 25, engaging in evasive maneuvers to put into the lap of a constitutional convention, if the people voted to call one, the decisions on voting and other political rights for blacks.

By their resolution the members of the Assembly were also postponing these decisions until, at best, three years into the future. Twenty months would go by before the next general election, and should the convention be then approved, the delegates could not be elected until November 1869, and the soonest they could meet in convention would be in December 1869 or January 1870. The General Assembly, if it had been concerned enough, could have brought the process much nearer in time by authorizing an autumn 1867 referendum on holding a constitutional convention and scheduling it for a year later after an election of delegates in the spring of 1868.[3]

In the debates on the resolutions and bills presented in the 25th General Assembly were to be heard not only the old arguments for black rights but also new ones emerging from changes in the postwar world. The problack legislators drew their premises, of course, from the familiar sources in the Bible, Declaration of Independence, Constitution of the United States, and past American history. Additionally they offered fresh arguments that were to become staples in the dialectic of blacks and friendly whites. These were what might be called the "unfinished agenda of the war" and "mission of the Republican party" arguments. The war had been fought to free the blacks, so it was alleged, and from that it followed that the war had been fought to make the Negro a wholly free man in the northern and western states as well as in the southern. The Negro could not be free until he possessed the entire complement of human rights included within the American concept of what free men should be able to do and say. For this the blood had been shed and the money poured out. All would be wasted unless the Republican party continued to dedicate itself to the great crusade for full rights for blacks.[4]

This series of arguments was brushed aside by opposing Republicans and by all Democrats. They insisted that the war had been fought for no other reason than to preserve the Union. Saving the Union had been the cause for which the men had died and the taxes levied. If the slaves had been freed, that was merely incidental to the main object of the war. Bestowal of rights upon the Negro was not a necessary consequence. In the postwar world the obligations of the Republican party should be concentrated on restoring the Union and not on rights for blacks.

Behind this facade of antiblack logic can be glimpsed every now and then the old terrors: schooling concessions of any sort to blacks would ultimately lead to the association of black and white children in classrooms and on playgrounds. Under the surface of rational discourse expected of legislators lurked the fear of "amalgamation."

The antiblack forces had emerged the victors in 1867, but the outcome of the next state election on November 3, 1868, gave the blacks and their white allies some grounds for optimism about the future. John McAuley Palmer, the Republican candidate for governor, who had often spoken for black rights, was elected by a margin of 50,000 votes, and the Republicans won 18 seats in the Senate to the Democrats 7 and 58 in the House to the Democrats 27. By a vote of 223,124 out of 444,860 the people had instructed the 26th General Assembly convening on January 4, 1869, to call a convention for revamping the state constitution. (Later in the election of delegates to the convention, 44 of the winners were Republicans and 41 Democrats, 7 of the latter being "Progressive" or "Independent" Democrats, less rigid on racial issues than the old hard-line "Bourbon" Democrats.) Continuing in the office of state superintendent of public instruction was Newton Bateman, who had urged schooling for blacks in his biennial reports.

Palmer had been born in Kentucky on September 13, 1817. His father, Louis, a descendant of an old Virginia family, had moved to Kentucky where farmland was cheap. Despite his Virginia heritage, Louis was a stern foe of slavery and intoxicating liquors, convictions that did not exactly endear him to his slave-holding, whiskey-drinking Kentucky neighbors. When John was twelve years old, the whites in the vicinity became agitated over rumors of a Negro uprising, and patrols were appointed to watch the movements of the blacks and interrogate those off their proper plantations. These patrols were usually manned by wild, reckless young fellows, who would break into any house or room where they thought a black might be hiding and whip those without a "pass." The Palmer family had a black servant, America, whose husband, Abram, was a slave on a nearby plantation. One Saturday night as Abram was visiting America a patrol rode up, surrounded the Palmer house, and prepared to force open the door of the room into which America and Abram had retired. Mr. Palmer came out and ordered the patrol off his land; they were insolent and threatened him; he defied them and eventually they went away. The next morning Mr. Palmer announced to his family that they would no longer live in a state where events of the kind they had experienced on the previous night could happen. He had made up his mind that the family would move to the free state of Illinois.[5]

They went to Illinois in 1831, settling on a farm in southern Madison County about ten miles from Alton. John, who had attended the common schools in Kentucky, enrolled in Alton (Shurtleff) College, a Baptist manual training institution. After eighteen months he quit college and tried coopering, peddling clocks, and teaching school, finally reading law with a lawyer and passing the bar in 1839 with help and encouragement from Stephen A. Douglas. Palmer, a Democrat, was elected probate judge of Macoupin County, a delegate to the state constitutional convention of 1847, and senator to the 17th, 18th, and 19th General Assemblies. Parting from Douglas, his hero, Palmer helped found the Republican party of Illinois, presiding over the first Republican convention in 1856 and serving as a Republican presidential elector in 1860.

During the war he rose from colonel to major general, saw heavy fighting, was wounded, and in February 1865 was appointed by Lincoln commander of the department of Kentucky. He had been stunned when Lincoln had proclaimed emancipation, but he himself had theatrically set the Negroes of Kentucky free. For the occasion he borrowed a gilded chariot and four piebald horses from a circus in Louisville and drove up to a high platform before twenty thousand blacks chanting "Dar he comes, in the golden chariot and the hosses of salvation!" Ascending the platform, he shouted, "My countrymen, you are substantially free!" Then swept away by the emotions of his audience, he cried, "My countrymen, *you are free*," and afterwards boasted that he had driven the "last nail" in the coffin of slavery in Kentucky. He returned to Illinois, to his law practice, and to state politics and was successful in his campaign for governor in 1868.

(After the expiration of his term as governor in 1873, Palmer became uneasy about the centralization of power in Washington and about the actions of the Grant administration. He rejoined the Democrat party, unsuccessfully running for United States senator three times and for governor once. On his fourth try for senator in 1891 he was elected. When his term was up, he came home to Springfield and lived on until September 25, 1900.)

In the constitutional convention of 1847 Palmer, as secretary of the committee on education, had introduced an article requiring the public schools to be "equally free" to "all" the children of the state, a proposal rejected by the delegates because a majority supposed the article would open the public schools to blacks. Again in the Senate of the 18th and 19th General Assemblies he had offered resolutions asking that bills be framed to give "every child" and "all children" an adequate education in Illinois public schools.

But in his first two years as governor Palmer stressed suffrage rights more than school rights for blacks. An example: in a remarkable speech on September 22, 1869, before a large audience of blacks celebrating the anniversary of the preliminary emancipation proclamation, he told his enthusiastic listeners that he was certain that the 15th Amendment to the Constitution of the United States would be ratified and that they would have the right to vote and hold public office, and, he promised, should any Negro be recommended to him "as the most suitable person to fill any office that comes within the limits of my power of appointment, I should not doubt his eligibility, and would not hesitate to acceding to their wishes." Proof that this was not empty verbiage was forthcoming a few weeks later on November 12 when Palmer appointed John Jones a notary public, said by contemporary newspapers to be the first appointment of a black to public office in the whole history of the state.

Other portions of Palmer's September 22 speech dwelt on the importance of education and suffrage in elevating the blacks' condition. He reminded them that they must gather their children about them because "the family is the foundation of society." They must educate their children: they must avail themselves of the public schools. But the larger part of his speech he devoted to counsel on how the blacks' vote, when they had gained suffrage rights, could be most effectively utilized to extract concessions from the whites. "Suffrage is the most powerful and most valuable weapon of defense," was his theme. If they took advantage of their eligibility to vote and then were astute in casting it, they would be able to secure election and appointment to public office for themselves and favors from white officeholders. Ruling over the blacks now were officials who thought them of little account. All would change when they began to use their vote to advance their own interests. They could hold office themselves and reap the fruits of patronage; they could make sure that those who held office would respect their needs and desires. In other words, to interpret Palmer's reasoning within the conceptual structure employed in this study, he was telling the blacks that having voting rights would gain for them an immense increase in rewarding and punishing power.

With a sympathetic governor and state superintendent of public instruction in office the blacks would have good reason to suppose that the 26th General Assembly, convening on January 4 and adjourning on April 20, 1869, might act favorably on such problack bills as were introduced. They were to be frustrated again, however, partly because the Republicans bestirred themselves just to the extent of introducing a single problack bill and partly because the blacks themselves were divided and did not muster unified strength behind the one petition they submitted.

Opening the session Governor Palmer in his message to the Senate and House said that the public schools of the state offered "equal facilities" for "all" children, implying that black children should have equal access to public schooling and should be included in the "all." Bateman, too, transmitted to the governor and the Assembly a report in which he urged the enactment of legislation that would strike racial discrimination from the school law by removing "white" and Section 80. Another plea for the public schooling of blacks was contained in a memorial from the "colored citizens of Illinois" presented on January 8 by Republican senator Willard C. Flagg from southern Madison County. The memorial, praying for suffrage and public-school rights, had been sponsored by the fourth state convention of colored men meeting in Springfield on January 4, 5, 6, and 7, 1869. The convention of blacks had been dissimilar to the three that had gone before in that no black from Chicago or Cook County had attended or, apparently, signed the memorial.[6]

The memorial was referred to the Senate education committee and on January 27 Daniel J. Pinckney, a Republican from northern Ogle County, reported the petition back by way of a bill to secure a free education and an equitable distribution of school funds to all persons and districts in the state and to accomplish this by eliminating "white" from all sections of the school law. After debate the Pinckney bill was referred, without vote, to the judiciary committee, from which it did not return to the floor.

The failure of Chicagoans to attend the fourth colored men's convention would seem to have been the result of a division on the issue of strategy and tactics. Central and southern county blacks had decided to memorialize the 26th General Assembly; Chicago blacks had decided to delay action and to concentrate on face-to-face lobbying at the state constitutional convention gathering in Springfield on December 13, 1869. Three months earlier, on September 27, the blacks of Chicago at a mass meeting had chosen John Jones and Lewis B. White, an old resident of the city and a clerk in the United States Post Office, as lobbyists. To buttress their case, the meeting adopted resolutions reminding whites of blacks' contributions during the war and pointing out that they expected to acquire suffrage rights and participate in the political sector of community life. As the qualities needed for useful and capable citizenship were "possessed in a greater degree as people are educated and intelligent," they asked for school privileges equal to those enjoyed by whites, "believing that thereby the interests of the citizens at large will be benefited, and we, as a class, rendered more valuable as citizens." It was a clear statement of the "partnership in community life" argument for universal schooling.[7]

The September 27th meeting had been marred by quarreling and abusiveness. In the past Jones and a combination of black owners had run the meetings in a fashion that had imparted to the proceedings a certain decorum. But their leadership began to be challenged, first at a meeting in November 1868, at which representatives of black Chicago were picked to go to a National Convention of Colored People in Washington, and then more fiercely at the September 27th meeting. The two most vocal of the critics were Elam C. Freeman, a porter, and Harrison D. King, a janitor. Freeman was insulting, accusing John Jones of, as the *Chicago Times* phrased it, "shootin' his mouf off too much."

He and King leveled the more serious charge that the election of the lobbyists had been rigged to insure victory for Jones and his cronies. The "bloated aristocrats" and "big guns with their long title deeds and immense wealth" were trying to squeeze out the "rag pickers, express drivers, common sort of people." Scheduling the meeting at two o'clock in the afternoon was an artifice for keeping the "masses" away and of making certain that the Jones' "clique" could manipulate things as it wanted. Diatribes and accusations had not blocked the election of Jones and White, but even so Freeman and those siding with him were not ready to desist from efforts to hamper the lobbyists.

On January 17 Jones and White departed for Springfield and the state constitutional convention; on January 18 they had retreated back to Chicago. They had abandoned the lobbying task for which they had been chosen because the Chicago newspapers arriving in Springfield on the morning of the 18th had carried an account of a meeting of the "colored citizens of Chicago" in which resolutions had been passed proclaiming that nothing was to be accomplished by lobbying at the constitutional convention. These resolutions Jones condemned as a "squib in the rear, loaded with offal," "a cold blanket," "a fire in the rear, a shot in the back, a thrust in the dark," stirring up doubts among the constitutional convention delegates about whether he and White could truly represent the opinions of their people. Feeling betrayed and believing that their credibility had been destroyed, he and White had immediately returned to Chicago.[8]

Jones dubbed the blacks signing the offending resolutions as "carpet-baggers," and he was correct in that a number of them had recently arrived in town. Although Freeman and some of the others were longtime residents, the presiding officer at the meeting had been Lloyd G. Wheeler, who had come to the city in 1867 or '68, read law with a white lawyer, and had been admitted to the Illinois bar on April 20, 1869, the first black to have succeeded in doing so in the history of the state. The meeting's committee on resolutions, whose critical polemic had been adopted, consisted of William C. Phillips, new to Chicago, Joseph G. Johnson, a barber, recently from Baltimore, and John P. Jones, from Washington where he had been a teacher in the public schools.

When a post mortem was conducted on the lobbying failure, a majority of the persons attending censured the Freeman-Wheeler group for "most disgracefully" compromising "the efforts of regularly selected representatives of our people, appointed to secure measures favorable to our political welfare." Angry at being castigated publicly, Freeman and other dissidents wrote to the *Chicago Evening Post,* asking it to refrain from publishing the resolutions of censure because these were "infamous, and detrimental to the interests and advancement of our people in this city." A similar letter to the *Chicago Times* spoke of the authors of the motions of censure and of those supporting censure as "enemies to the cause of our people."

Among the signers of both letters had been Richard A. Dawson, a law school student and son of John B. Dawson, the owner of a downtown barbershop, and Jacob F. Platt, Jr., a bookkeeper in the office of his father's lumber business. Here were children of veterans of the black-rights movement signing letters branding their fathers' comrades in the battles waged in the 1850s and sixties as "enemies," guilty of actions "detrimental" to the progress of the city's blacks. And for circulating one of these disparaging letters they had sought space in, of all places, the columns of that inveterate enemy of black rights, the *Chicago Times.* Combined with socioeconomic antagonisms and of differences in the views of newcomers, there may have been a factor of generational conflict as the children of the old guard were reaching adulthood and rebelling against the established black leadership.[9]

Whatever the sources of dissension among the Chicago blacks, had this dissension been damaging to their cause in the constitutional convention? Had the failure of Jones and White to lobby for no more than half a day hurt the blacks' chances of gaining school and voting rights? If the questions are regarded as an opportunity to give free rein to reasonable speculation, then the answer for damage to school rights would be "perhaps yes," for damage to suffrage rights "perhaps no."

During the constitutional convention one petition and twenty-nine measures relating to blacks had been introduced. Most dealt with suffrage but five were schooling measures. Two of the five, one by James M. Washburn, Democrat from southern Jackson and Williamson counties, and one by Charles E. Mc-Dowell, Democrat from southern Edwards and White counties, would have incorporated into the constitution an article opening up the possibility of mandating separate schools for blacks and whites. Both resolutions were tabled, Washburn's by a vote of 42 to 27 (35 Republicans and 7 Democrats voting for tabling and 26 Democrats and one Republican voting against) and McDowell's 36 to 18 (34 Republicans and 2 Democrats voting for tabling and 18 Democrats voting against). The pattern of unified Republican voting first displayed in repealing the black code in 1865, in abeyance since, had now reappeared in rallying against measures going to the extreme of imposing racially segregated schooling upon the districts.[10]

But would this unity be maintained in facing the harder question of voting for measures taking actual steps toward guaranteeing school rights for blacks? The answer is that some Republicans were not yet ready to vote for such a guarantee. David C. Wagner, a Republican from northern Jo Daviess and Carroll counties, introduced into the convention a resolution explicit on the subject of schooling for blacks: "Resolved, that this Convention should incorporate in its Constitution a provision requiring the General Assembly to provide for a complete and thorough common school education of every susceptible child, within its limits, without regard to color or previous condition." His resolution was referred to the committee on education, a committee with a Republican majority.

What came out of this Republican-dominated committee was a recommended article shorn of a specific commitment to the schooling of blacks: "The General Assembly shall provide a thorough and efficient system of free schools, whereby all minor children of this State may receive a good common school education." ("Minor" referred to age, not race or ethnicity.) This with "minor" scratched as redundant was adopted by the convention, without a call for yeas and nays, and was to be Section 1, Article 8, "Education," of the constitution as later ratified by the people:

> The General Assembly shall provide a thorough and efficient system of free schools, whereby all children of this State may receive a good common school education.[11]

(Some versions of Section 1, Article 8, have "all children," some "all the children." I have reproduced the text of the article and section as it actually was when adopted by the convention delegates on May 9, 1870.)

Evidently the Republican majority on the education committee had not rallied unanimously to support an article reflecting the explicit guarantee of black school rights contained in the Wagner resolution. Republicans must have defected to the Democrats in recommending an article devoid of all mention of race. The committee and the convention could have inserted language defining "all children" to include black children as specifically as Wagner's resolution had or the delegates could have taken the 15th Amendment to the United States Constitution as a model and added to Section 1 some such sentence as "The right of children to receive this education shall not be denied or abridged on account of race or color." Instead the "all children" was left without referents although, as frequently noted in this study, in the school laws the noun "children" was modified by the adjective "white," indicating that "all children" could be assumed at the district's pleasure to refer only to whites.

This timid (insofar as black school rights were at stake) article may have come out of the education committee and into adoption for many reasons, one of which may have been Jones' and White's lobbying only an evening and a morning in Springfield before hurrying back to Chicago. The linkage between antecedent and consequence here is through a resolution from Elijah M. Haines, a Republican from northern Lake County. Haines asked the convention to instruct the education committee to report an article "securing the advantages of the school fund to all inhabitants of the State." He explained the intent of his resolution to be that of doing nothing more than propose incorporating into the constitution the principle of Section 80 of the free-schools law empowering the districts to rebate to persons of color a portion of the school fund equal to their school tax.

He had been, he told the convention, waited on by an Illinois citizen of "African descent" who had been chosen by several thousands of the race in the southern part of the state to come to the convention to inquire into what the convention would do about suffrage and school rights for blacks. Haines had replied that the convention would act favorably on suffrage but that the law already afforded the blacks equal advantages with other Illinoisans in the common school fund. To this the citizen of African descent had demurred. Thereupon he, Haines, had drawn up his resolution affirming "the naked principle of the right of all citizens or inhabitants of the State of Illinois to partake of and enjoy a civil right—that of deriving from the common school fund a share thereof, for the purpose of education." [12]

Haines' explanation sheds some light on the question of whether dissension among Chicago blacks had hurt their cause in the constitutional convention. He had drawn up his resolution in response to opinions expressed by the person of African descent from the southern counties. If he had had a similar exposure to the views of John Jones and Lewis B. White he would not have heard from them a conception of school rights as narrow as those embodied in his resolution and intended by it. Jones and White had received from the Chicago mass meeting the assignment of lobbying for "equal school privileges throughout the State, in common with our white fellow-citizens."

Had Jones and White not been demoralized by the "squib in the rear" from the Freeman dissidents and fled back to Chicago and had they remained on during the sessions at which school rights had been discussed, they might have put pressure on Haines and other delegates to introduce a resolution granting "equal school privileges" to blacks. The resolution might have been referred to the education committee and tended to reinforce Wagner's and other measures in persuading the committee to report out a section with "all" defined so as to include black children. This had not happened, and one among the complex of factors keeping it from happening may have been Jones' and White's premature departure from Springfield, allowing the spokesman for the southern county blacks, whose ambitions were more limited than those of the northerners, to be the only member of the race to lobby intensively for black school rights at the convention.

The story on suffrage had a happier denouement for blacks. Back in the 26th General Assembly on March 5, 1869, Governor Palmer had communicated to the Senate and House his recommendation that the members ratify the proposed 15th Amendment to the United States Constitution forbidding the denial or abridgment of the right to vote on account of race, color, or previous condition of servitude. The state Senate and House did ratify the amendment by votes of 18 to 7 and 54 to 28. In the Senate all 18 yeas were cast by Republicans and all 7 nays by Democrats; in the House 54 of 55 Republicans had voted yea and all 27 Democrats had voted nay. Now in the Illinois constitutional convention the question was whether the Republicans would retain their unity when confronting the issue of translating a national, remote federal prohibition into an immediate, positive bestowal of voting rights that would be exercised in their own state and communities and among their next-door neighbors.[13]

John Jones and Lewis B. White, who had been charged by their fellow blacks with the task of lobbying for this objective as well as for school rights, had managed to fit into their short stay in Springfield several conferences on voting rights with Governor Palmer and Daniel Cameron, a "Progressive" Democrat from Cook County. Palmer had given them assurances of his support and Cameron had promised that the Democrats would stand by the 15th Amendment to the United States Constitution "without the erasure of the dot of an i." True to his word, a week into the convention session when the subject of black suffrage rights was under discussion, Cameron announced to the delegates that the Democrats would "meet" with the Republicans in doing what was "just" and "right," in keeping with the "requirements" of the times.

Nevertheless, while Cameron could make promises for himself and the 6 other "Progressive" Democrats, he could not speak for the 34 remaining Democrats, especially those who were

"Bourbon" or "Irreconcilable" Democrats. These latter attempted to have the section of the state constitution of 1848 restricting suffrage to "every white male citizen above the age of 21 years" repeated in the new constitution or, failing that, to have a proposition to the same effect submitted separately to the people for their approval or disapproval.[14]

Pro and con motions were brought in by the convention's committee on suffrage. Its majority report, signed by 4 Republicans and "Independent," "Progressive" Democrats Daniel Cameron and John Dement, the latter the chairman of the committee and a delegate from northern Lee County, recommended an article declaring that "every male citizen of the United States above the age of twenty-one years, who shall have resided in the State one year and in the election district sixty days next preceding any election, shall be entitled to vote at such election." A minority report by the three "Bourbon" Democrats on the committee put forward an article restricting suffrage to white male citizens possessing the age and residency qualifications and proposing that this change be submitted to the vote of the people separately from the rest of the constitution.[15]

When the majority report was taken up for discussion by the convention, James M. Washburn, the Democratic delegate who had earlier introduced the resolution for the segregated schooling of the races, again exhibited hostility toward the blacks. He moved to substitute for the majority report's "every male citizen" the words "every white male citizen." A motion to table Washburn's substitute was made by William Cary, a Republican from northern Jo Daviess County, and his motion passed 39 to 19, with 32 Republicans and 7 Democrats voting for and 19 Democrats voting against. Then the delegates voted 39 to 19 to adopt the majority report. Thirty-three Republicans and 6 Democrats cast yea votes and 19 Democrats voted nay.

In final form Article 7, Section 1, "Suffrage," of the Illinois constitution of 1870, ratified by the people on July 2 and in force on August 8, read:

> Every person having resided in this State one year, in the county ninety days, and in the election district thirty days next preceding any election therein, who was an elector in this State on the first day of April, in the year of our Lord

one thousand eight hundred and forty-eight, or obtained a certificate of naturalization before any court of record in this State prior to the first day of January, in the year of our Lord one thousand eight hundred and seventy, or who shall be a male citizen of the United States, above the age of twenty-one years, shall be entitled to vote at such election.[16]

So the Republicans had been united in voting for an article that like the education article made no mention of race and made no commitment to bestow a right upon the blacks. Nevertheless for interpreting the suffrage article in the Illinois constitution of 1870 there was available a text of higher authority, the 15th Amendment of the United States Constitution, that was specific in its application to race and color. No such sovereign canon existed at the federal level for interpreting Article 8, Section 1, "Education," of the new state constitution. Thus a question remained about whether the Republicans would hold ranks in voting for measures that particularized the referents of the "all children" in that article and section. The human behaviors authorized by suffrage and schooling rights were not equivalents, obviously. Voting rights were exercised through delivery systems that were simpler and involved persons of greater maturity. The Republicans, on reflection, might decide that mixing adult blacks and whites for fiteen or twenty minutes on biennial or quadrennial election days would be much less threatening than the prospect of mixing children and adolescents of both races for 300 or more minutes a day in classrooms and on playgrounds, 180 days a year, over six, eight, or twelve years.

Still as matters turned out it was the acquisition of suffrage that was the key unlocking the doors of the public schools to Illinois blacks, and this was because voting rights produced, potentially, a large increase in the dialectical and punishing power blacks already possessed and gave them for the first time the crucial rewarding power of the vote. Now they could dangle in front of a candidate's or a party's eyes the promise of casting votes one way or another for quid pro quo concessions within the various spheres of community life. As Governor Palmer said, if they used their voting power adroitly, the politicians and parties would "become polite to your person and thoughtful of your interests," and would inquire "as to your health, and that of the lady, your wife, or after the prosperity of your interesting children." Why all this attention and courtesy? "They will want your good will and your vote." [17]

The same idea was couched more colloquially a hundred years later by Andrew Young, who was to become the first black mayor of Atlanta. He told the blacks of his generation and region to register and get out and vote: "It used to be, Southern politics was just 'nigger' politics—who could 'outnigger' the other— then you registered 10 to 15 per cent in the community and folk would start saying 'nigra' and then you get 35 to 40 per cent registered and it's amazing how quick they learned to say 'Neegrow' and now that we've got 50, 60, 70 per cent of the black voters registered in the South, everybody's proud to be associated with their black brothers and sisters" (*Tribune*, Sept. 5, 1976).

7

Participating in Mainstream Community Life

The assurance of receiving suffrage rights now that the 15th Amendment of the federal constitution had been ratified and Article 7, Section 1, of the proposed state constitution favorably introduced in the convention was celebrated in April by Illinois blacks from Rockford in the north to Cairo in the south. Artillery salutes, brass bands, parades, and oratory almost everywhere highlighted the occasion.[1]

In Springfield a twelve-pounder fired a hundred rounds beginning probably, as at Galesburg, just after five o'clock in the morning. Later the blacks assembled downtown, marching to Lincoln's home and then to the city rink where Governor Palmer, who had shocked the more staid of the white citizenry by riding in the parade with two Negroes in his carriage, addressed the multitude. Palmer gave them his usual advice. They must work hard so as to buy the homes and the property that would win them respect and influence in the community. They must educate their children, and if the public schools shut them out, they possessed the power of the elective franchise and ought to use it to pressure the schools to open to them.[2]

In Chicago the celebration started at dawn with the roar of cannon and ended at night with speeches and song. The morning parade, over two miles in length, had been in a sense a Grand Review, a parade down Wabash Avenue by the victorious veterans of the battles for black rights waged in the 1850s and sixties, with leaders of the dissident black factions also in the ranks. The black organizations, those that were helping to bind individuals together in ties of cultural association and brotherly and sisterly feeling despite cleavages, had stepped along, too, behind their commanders, generalissimos, and captains-general. On view had been the black ministers, the blacks' one dentist, their one lawyer, their one employee in a department of government, and their one foreman in a large industry. Joining them had been the owners of black businesses in cleaning, tailoring, lumber supplies, carpentry, building, barbering, and hairdressing and the black employees of the white hotels, restaurants, stores, office buildings, railroad stations, and other conveniences tending to the needs and comforts of the white residents of the city. Some five thousand persons had marched, and as they were mostly black males who would have the vote, it had been a display of potential power that the Republican and Democratic parties could not with impunity ignore.[3]

That night in the finale at Farwell Hall the orators jubilantly pictured what their present was now that they had the ballot, and they painted in glowing sentences a future in which, as the caption on the side of a float in the morning's parade had emblazoned it, the American nationality would be "composite." But this vision of the future, they recognized, could not be achieved without education in the present. Through the speeches and resolutions of the evening ran two themes. Having "fought right," they must "vote right"; they must vote as they "shot" and be loyal to the Republican party. Besides being faithful to Republicanism, they must apply themselves to the task of education and schooling. Voting rights had put into their possession the greatest of all political powers available to Americans. Blacks must make sure that this new power was exerted responsibly; they must prepare themselves for a "higher station" in the community. They were fully cognizant, so they declared in one of their evening's resolutions, that their voting power could be used in a way detrimental to the general welfare and subversive to good order or in a way that would be of benefit to the community and the society. Which it would be depended on education, agreed the speakers.

The connection between the blacks' attainment of voting rights and the resulting necessity of providing education and schooling for them was also the theme of white political party analyses of the meaning and effects of the 15th Amendment and the state's Article 7. In Washington President Grant in his promulgation of federal adoption of the amendment had called upon Congress to "promote and encourage popular education" and upon the people to "see to it that all who possess and exercise political rights shall have the opportunity to acquire the knowledge which will make their share in the Government a blessing and not a danger." A republican government cannot "endure without intelligence and education generally diffused among the people." Only by such means could "the benefits contemplated by this amendment to the Constitution be secured." In Springfield, as mentioned earlier in this chapter, Governor Palmer told the blacks that they were now obliged to educate their children and he prophesied, accurately, that suffrage could be the key that would unlock the doors of the public school for them. In Chicago ex-Lieutenant Governor William Bross informed an audience of blacks that they had become "part and parcel" of the nation and warned that "we must educate all our children, black and white, so that demagogues may not lead them astray, that corruption and venality in high places may not abound."[4]

These were blacks and white Republicans moralizing. But many of the Democrats were of the same mind, believing that the blacks' victory in winning voting power prompted a rethinking of the Democratic party's traditional position on issues of rights and public schooling for the Negro. Thus "A Progressive Democrat," writing to the *Chicago Times* of the divisions appearing in party ranks and of the urgency of educating the Negro, discussed the reasons why the Democrats in the southern counties had split into two rival wings. To "Irreconcilable" or "Bourbon" Democrats the Negro was still the focus of their political thinking, "A Progressive Democrat" averred, a figure that must "still be battled against; must still be warred on; must always be the issue." It was the "imbecility" of the Irreconcilables that had caused the party to lose the postbellum elections.

The young Progressive Democrats, on the contrary, deemed it flagrant folly to make a stand primarily on the Negro issue, an issue "as dead, in truth, for the present political success, as the traditional door-nail." In the judgment of the Progressives the Democratic party should abandon the Negro issue and concentrate on the tariff, finance, corruption, and other vital problems of the day. "Progressive Democrats, recognizing the fact that slavery has been abolished and the freedmen a powerful element in society, believe that every effort should be made to educate these men, and prepare them to wisely exercise the power they possess." "A Progressive Democrat's" observations and sentiments were echoed by "John Emerald" from southern Jackson County and by "Another Progressive Democrat" from northern Stephenson County in letters to the *Chicago Times.*

The *Times* itself, that historic enemy of the blacks and of black rights, did an about-face and was now resigned to the prospect of suffrage and the sequel of public-school rights. If suffrage rights were bestowed upon the blacks, "all which in that case remains to be done is to so educate the newly enfranchised Negro that his vote shall be a benefit, or at least no injury, to himself or to the body of the people."

After the state constitution had been ratified and the blacks were voting in elections and their isolation from the community breaking down, the *Times* in an editorial referring to southern Negroes but by implication to Illinois blacks repeated its earlier statement about the necessity of schooling them. The Negro was becoming "an industrial, social, and political force." If he were left in ignorance and treated with injustice, he would be "a very troublesome, not to say a dangerous, factor." But if instructed and fairly dealt with, he would probably become "not only a safe, but a very useful, factor." The blacks' "usefulness," the "peace of society," and its "material interests" would be "best promoted, . . . by education, in the best sense of the word, and by perfectly fair, honorable, and lawful treatment."[5]

Arguments of this tenor were to supply motives for blacks and whites to begin the process of breaking down the blacks' traditional isolation from mainstream institutions and of enabling them to participate in community life to an extent not previously allowed. The result was that the argument that their schooling was essential on political grounds had added to it the argument that their schooling was essential on social and economic grounds.

Naturally the doors unbarred for them at the start were those closing off the political institutions of society. In April 1870, a few weeks after the promulgation of the 15th Amendment by President Grant, Illinois blacks voted for the first time, going to the polls to elect township, city, village, or school officers in Edwardsville, Princeton, Metropolis, Morris, Bloomington, Quincy, Pekin, Jacksonville, Springfield, and Ottawa where a photograph as a "historical picture" was taken of the first Negro voter. Chicago blacks voted first on July 2 when the ballot asked for a decision on the adoption of the proposed state constitution. On the eve of the election they held an enthusiastic rally at which John Jones reminded them to vote Republican, and in the morning they repaired to a prayer meeting to invoke divine guidance in casting their ballots. They then trooped to the polls and marked the Republican ticket, without, according to the *Tribune,* heads being broken or the world coming to an end though they voted side by side with Irish Democrats. In November the blacks of the state for the first time voted in a presidential election and for candidates for the General Assembly.[6]

They were welcomed into the game of politics as it was played by the Republican party in the 1870s. Forming Republican clubs of their own or joining clubs hitherto reserved for whites, they marched in torchlight parades, cheered at rallies, and applauded partisan speeches intended to whip up enthusiasm and loyalty among the faithful. They acted as Republican judges, inspectors, and clerks at polling places; they were selected as delegates to city, town, county, and state conventions. Some were nominated to local, county, and state Republican tickets. Probably the first black to be elected to local office was James I. (or T.) Jackson of Centralia who was voted in as a ward alderman on May 26, 1870. In Monmouth a black barber was elected a justice of the peace in April 1872, and in Cairo John J. Bird, a Pullman sleeping car conductor and the leader of southern Illinois blacks, was elected a police magistrate on April 15, 1873, and John Gladney, a teamster, elected a city constable on November 4 of the same year. The Reverend Andrew W. Jackson, pastor of the Jacksonville African Baptist Church, was voted to the board of aldermen to serve for 1873–74.

At the county level the first black to win public office was Chicago's John Jones, who on November 7, 1871, received 17,893 votes to his white opponent's 8,175, in the race for one of the Cook County commissionerships. Jones was re-elected on November 5, 1872, amassing 30,811 votes to rank him third among sixteen candidates. At the state level the first black to be elected to the legislature was John W. E. Thomas, a private-school teacher in Chicago, who on November 7, 1876, was chosen by the voters of the second district of Cook County to represent them in the House of the 30th General Assembly. He was not elected to the 31st and 32nd General Assemblies but was to the 33rd meeting in 1883 and the 34th meeting in 1885, and from that time forward there have been blacks, one or more, in the Senate or House of every Illinois General Assembly.[7]

Blacks were also awarded honorific accolades. For example, it was the custom to open each morning's session of the General Assembly with an invocation by a clergyman. In the past only white ministers were invited, but on January 26, 1871, the Senate Republicans introduced and passed a resolution that clergymen "without distinction of race, color, or previous condition of servitude" would give the opening prayer. Two days later the Reverend Edward C. Joiner, pastor of St. Paul's Colored Methodist Church in Springfield, offered the invocation in the Senate. He did so again on February 15, March 8, and March 29 and in the House on February 4, 25, and March 18. Another Negro minister of Springfield, the Reverend George Brents [or Brentz], pastor of the Zion Colored Baptist Church, gave the prayer in the House on March 8.[8]

The black receiving the highest kind of honor from the state was John J. Bird of Cairo, appointed by Governor Beveridge to the boad of trustees of the University of Illinois on July 1, 1873. Bird had been born in Cincinnati in 1844. Apparently he had attended the public colored schools of the city, for he was later to praise the racially separate public-school system existing there and to recommend that Cairo and Illinois imitate it. He was well educated and according to the Democratic *Cairo Bulletin* possessed more "learning" than most white candidates for office and more intelligence than any half-dozen white Republicans "rolled into one." The war years he spent in Canada and was criticized for having gone there, it was alleged, to evade fighting for his country.

Coming to Cairo after the war, he quickly emerged as the leader of his people in southern Illinois, like John Jones in the north chosen more often than anyone else as chairman of committees and principal speaker and held in most respect by whites. In April 1873 he was a Republican candidate for police magistrate, getting 496 votes to his Democratic white rival's 431, an astounding performance for a person of his race and political party in that city and region of the state. In July the governor appointed him a trustee of Illinois Industrial University (University of Illinois) and on February 12, 1874, the Senate did advise and consent. Probably this was the first appointment of a black to the board of trustees of any non-Negro college or university, public or private, in the United States.[9]

Bird was the first black to give an address at the formal dedication ceremonies of a state of Illinois educational institution. On July 1, 1874, he was one of the chief speakers at the dedication of the new Southern Illinois Normal University at Carbondale, taking as his subject "The Education of the Colored Race." On the speakers' platform with him were Governor Beveridge, the Reverend Charles H. Fowler, president of Northwestern University, Richard Edwards, president of Illinois State Normal University at Bloomington, Robert Allyn, president of Southern Illinois Normal, William Torrey Harris, superintendent of the St. Louis public schools and the most renowned American public-school administrator of the period, Andrew D. Duff, judge of the 26th circuit court, and Thomas S. Ridgway, merchant and banker of Shawneetown and president of the Southern Illinois Normal University board of trustees.

Yet Bird was subjected to personal humiliation on a day when he had shared the podium with some of the most eminent men of the state. No welcoming committee such as those greeting all other invited speakers met him at the railroad station; no "runners" for the Carbondale hotels carried his valise; no hotel or citizen furnished him with a meal. He had to walk two miles out into the country to be fed at the table of a Negro friend.[10]

One of the advantages of having the vote and having a voice in political party affairs was that it opened up a field of new, better paying, higher status occupations for blacks. The Republicans were willing to cut them in for a slice of the patronage pie and appoint them to jobs in the departments of government. In Springfield they were given employment as janitors, porters, messengers, and ushers in state buildings and offices. More rarely, but still on occasion, they received less lowly positions. In the spring or summer of 1870 W. H. Thomas, a black from Pittsburgh who had lost an arm fighting in the Union army, seems to have been appointed state commissioner of deeds by Governor

Palmer. When the 27th General Assembly convened in January 1871, the speaker of the House, William M. Smith, made the Reverend James W. H. Jackson, pastor of the African Methodist Episcopal Church in Springfield, keeper of the outer door of the House chamber. Objections were raised on grounds of economy that the position was not needed and the appointment was revoked. A few years later, nevertheless, when William Baker, a black who had been in the calcimining business in Chicago, was appointed a doorkeeper of the House of the 30th General Assembly convening on January 3, 1877, no opposition was encountered and Baker served through the session.[11]

Blacks appointed to patronage positions in Cook County, where documentary evidence is more plentiful than for other counties, included Samuel Walter Scott, William C. Phillips, George Beard, Leroy Hayes (Hays), Robert M. Mitchell, and Robert C. Waring. Scott, a porter in downtown buildings, became a bailiff in the county court in 1873; Phillips, a carpenter, a clerk in the county records office and ultimately the superintendent of his section; Beard, former occupation unknown, a bailiff in the superior court; Hayes, a porter, a clerk in the probate court; and Mitchell, a steward, a clerk in the criminal court. Waring, a jeweler, was appointed a clerk in the office of the county clerk and treasurer and then promoted to the position of deputy county clerk.[12]

In the municipalities, blacks in Cairo were hired as laborers in the city's street repair gangs in September 1871. At Cairo, too, Warren Weims and Reuben Smith were employed as janitors in the 13th Street public school, David Ross as janitor of the public high school, and John Gladney as city teamster. Thomas Lindsay, whitewasher, became city marketmaster of Peoria, while in Chicago Andrew F. Bradley, editor of the *Chicago Observer*, a weekly family newspaper devoted "to the general interest of the colored race," was appointed one of the city sanitary inspectors, and Julia LaBough, daughter of Mrs. Mary J. LaBough, widow of Louis, a porter, was employed as a clerk on the staff of the public library.[13]

Places in the municipal departments of police and fire were also being filled by blacks in the 1870s. The first black to receive an appointment to any branch of Chicago city government was James P. Shelton, a carpenter, who was made a detective on the police force in the spring of 1870. He was assigned to Central Station and told to keep an eye on the colored district in the South Division. But Shelton was dismissed or compelled to resign on September 4, 1872, after having been accused of accepting bribes and of drunkenness and disorderly conduct. Other blacks hired as policemen and with much better records were John Ender, a porter, Martin V. (or F., or M.) French, a calciminer, Joseph H. Shreve, a blacksmith, William F. Smith, a baker, and Frank S. Terry, a porter. By 1885 out of a total of 954 policemen and detectives on the Chicago police force 6 or 7 perhaps were blacks. In 1882 in Springfield there was 1 colored policeman, Henry Vantrece, previously a laborer, in a department of 21 officers, and there may have been several other black policemen elsewhere in the state.[14]

Blacks were first examined for employment in the Chicago fire department in 1872. The board of police and fire commissioners had been requested by a "colored person" (John Jones?) to organize a fire company of blacks, and at a meeting on October 24 the board pronounced 8 of "Afric's sable sons" fit for duty. These were David Easley, a porter, Thomas Sutphon, a porter, Isaiah Washington, a worker on the streetcars, Larkhill Richardson, a blacksmith, James E. Porter, a painter, John Scott, a whitewasher, Jerry M. Smith, a cook, and Henry C. Williams, a waiter. Their company, Engine Company Number 21, under a white captain, went into service on December 23, 1872. Over the following years it was to have commendations for its efficiency and appearance from fire department chiefs, the city administration, and the newspapers, and it was, naturally, the pride of the Negro citizens of the city. In 1885 there were 10 black fireman in a total Chicago force of 451. Outside of Chicago, the blacks of Champaign seem to have been the first, sometime in the summer of 1873, to organize or be organized into a fire company, although it is not clear whether this company was volunteer or, as Chicago's was, paid.[15]

Among the federal departments of government the local units of the postal service were most disposed toward the employment of blacks. In May 1869 Lewis B. White, the janitor of the Hartford Fire Insurance building and with John Jones a leader in the campaigns for black rights, was appointed a mail clerk by Francis A. Eastman, the Grant administration's postmaster in the city. The horrified *Chicago Times* saw the appointment as the first mile down the road to a tragic future in which blacks would supplant better qualified whites in postal jobs and, worse still, would marry white daughters and America would wind up "a nation of human mongrels." Yet Eastman broke the color line in the mail carriers division as well by appointing J. Theodore Lee in June 1870. Lee had married John Jones' daughter, Lavinia, and had been working in his father-in-law's tailor shop before entering the postal service. By 1885 there were at least 5 blacks employed in one capacity or another in the Chicago postoffice. As the number of Chicago postal clerks was 482 and of carriers 321, the blacks were only a tiny percentage of the total. But they and the blacks employed in the other branches of the federal, state, county, and local governments had made a beginning and were harbingers of the thousands to come.[16]

The new opportunities brought by the vote and participation in political party affairs were generally higher on the occupational scale, demanding more sophisticated skills and carrying more respect than those the blacks had filled before. A glance back at the previous paragraphs will reveal that the positions or jobs in government to which blacks were appointed were in the main a notch or several notches farther up the hierarchy of occupations than the ones they had left behind.

For the first time elective and appointive governmental positions were becoming available to Illinois blacks after 1870 and these positions were involving blacks in more crucial and complex relations with whites than in the past. Perhaps the new positions did not increase the frequency or intimacy of their contacts with whites: the waiter in the Palmer House in Chicago, Leland Hotel in Springfield, and Planter's House in Cairo or the barber with a shop on Randolph Street, 4th Street, or Washington Avenue might encounter as many whites in the course of a day as the black police magistrate, county commissioner, clerk in the probate court, bailiff, policeman, fireman, or letter carrier. But there was a vast difference in the importance to the community at large of the service rendered and the skills required for successful performance of duty.

To the degree that the new positions entailed more of the knowledge and disciplines taught in schools and affected more the life of the white community, by so much more might the whites' recognition of the necessity of guaranteeing legal access to public schooling for blacks be fostered. For the black people themselves the prospect of obtaining positions in government might inspire hope and ambition and might motivate them the more to continue their struggle for public-school rights. Imagine the thoughts and feelings of blacks as they saw Henry Vantrece patrolling the streets of Springfield in his policeman's uniform, or John J. Bird freeing or sentencing whites and blacks in the court at Cairo, or John Jones presiding as acting chairman at a meeting of the Cook County board of commissioners, or John W. E. Thomas sitting at a legislator's desk in the House of Representatives of the General Assembly!

New opportunities within the political and governmental structures were not the only avenues opening up to blacks in the late 1860s and early seventies. They now began to give evidence in courts, to sue and be parties in suits, and to serve on juries. In June 1869, James Washington, a black resident of Quincy, sued the St. Louis and Keokuk Packet Company because he had not been allowed to eat with white passengers at a table in the dining room of the riverboat *Andy Johnson*. When he resisted, he was forcibly ejected from the dining room and put ashore at the next landing. A jury rendered a verdict in his favor of $2,000 in personal damages. In July Mrs. Teney Dunn, wife of Edmund Dunn, Negro residents of Moline, charged Dr. Morris Hale, white, with conduct toward her "not of a character suitable for publication" as he examined her for a "delicate complaint." The first blacks to sit upon a jury in the state were impaneled in Chicago in April 1870, when three Negroes, two Irishmen, and a German were sworn in to hear a suit for damages for injuries to a horse hired from a livery stable. One month later John Jones, trailblazer in this as in much else, became the first Negro to serve on a grand jury in a court of record in the state. During the same year black jurors were impaneled in Edwardsville, southern Madison County, and in Morrison, northern Whiteside County.[17]

Realizing that political and courts rights would bring a demand for lawyers of their own race, some of the younger blacks began training for the profession. Lloyd G. Wheeler, as was noted in the last chapter, read law with George W. Bellows, the eminent white lawyer, and passed the state bar examination on April 20, 1869, the first black to do so in the history of the state.

He moved to Arkansas where he became attorney for Pulaski County and returning to Chicago married John Jones' adopted daughter, worked as a mail carrier in the Chicago post office, and took over the management of Jones' tailoring business after Jones' death. Richard A. Dawson on July 11, 1870, and Ferdinand L. Barnett, Jr., on June 11, 1878, were the next blacks admitted to the state bar. Dawson, who had signed the dissidents' letter to the *Chicago Times* criticizing the veterans of the black-rights movement, helped in his father's barber shop as he was studying law at the University of Chicago. He graduated in 1870, the first Illinois black to qualify for a bachelor's degree, in his case a bachelor of laws, from an Illinois college or university.

Ferdinand L. Barnett, Jr., perhaps the most famous and influential of all nineteenth-century Illinois black lawyers, was the child of a Tennessee slave who had purchased freedom, gone to Canada, and had come to Chicago where he was employed as a janitor. The son graduated from Chicago public high school in 1874 and was the first male of his race to graduate from a four-year Illinois public high school. He taught for several years in the South; returning to Chicago he earned an LL.B. from the Union College of Law (Northwestern University) in 1878. In the same year that he graduated and was admitted to the state bar he founded the *Conservator*, the first Illinois Negro newspaper. He started a prosperous law business, served as assistant state's attorney of Cook County, and became the acknowledged leader of Chicago blacks in the last decades of the century. By example and by words he was an exponent of education, social uplift, and personal virtue. He and his wife, Ida Wells-Barnett, believed in racial solidarity as the central base for black action.[18]

In the social sphere, where the whites were most fearful of intrusions by the blacks and most resistant to black participation, the progress was slight compared to what the Negroes were winning in the political, courts, and economic sectors. Social mingling of the races, as both whites and blacks were wont to affirm when the subject was brought up, could not be compelled by law: it depended, they said, on freely offered, mutual acceptance by individuals and was contingent upon the extent to which blacks were worthy of the company of whites. This was to confuse social relations in private settings like the home with social relations in public institutional settings like theatres, hotels, lecture halls, and restaurants. Within the latter relations between the races could be governed by legislation as they were to be by the federal civil rights law of March 1, 1875. But in the period being discussed here, 1870–74, mingling between respectable whites and respectable blacks in both private and public settings was rare. Occasionally, as at the celebration in John Jones' home of the thirtieth anniversary of his arrival in Chicago, black and white guests would be invited and attend, but this was not very common.[19]

Greater progress was made in the entertainment phase of community life, in the arts, music, and sports where the blacks' talents had a better chance of being displayed and where their performance was more likely to be evaluated by a criterion of pure merit. Dennis Williams, "crayon portrait artist," is a case in point. As described in chapter 4, he had been born a slave in Mississippi, been brought north to Springfield by his family, and been intrigued by the pictures of animals in his schoolbooks. He resolved to become an artist and did as his first portrait that of the notorious Jim Fisk, then much in the limelight because of stock and railroad manipulations. The portrait was exhibited in the window of Simmons' Bookstore on South Sixth Street and was thought to be a good likeness. But the idea "of a 'little nigger' becoming an artist—it was preposterous" and disheartened he abandoned drawing for a while. Unable to resist the urge, he began sketching again and supported himself by shining shoes, retiring to his room at the end of the day and copying pictures he had scavenged from trash heaps or cheap lithographs he had bought from his slim savings. Frequently he would go to the studios of some of the Springfield artists in an effort to see how they did their work, but he was driven away and got no help from them.

In the autumn of 1874, he placed some of his pictures on exhibition at the Sangamon county fair and won three premiums, two for his portraits and one for a landscape scene. Standing by, he listened to the remarks people made as they looked at his pictures and, though some persons believed it incredible that the pictures were the work of a "nigger," the reactions were generally favorable and encouraging. The first of his pictures to be sold was a portrait of General Grant, purchased by Colonel Robert Andrews, superintendent of the Wabash Railroad. Subsequently he painted portraits of many prominent men in the state, among them Lieutenant Governor John M. Hamilton and speaker of the House Horace H. Thomas of the 32nd General Assembly whose portraits were commissioned by the Senate and House of Representatives. At the Sangamon county fairs of 1874, 1875, 1876, and 1877 he won diplomas for the best portrait in crayon and in pastel and a medal for the best crayon picture.[20] Negro semimilitary companies with their brass bands marched in parades and gave concerts and serenades. Among these were the Hannibal Zouaves of Chicago, the Capital City Guards, Zouaves, and Rogers Cornet Band of Springfield, the McLean County Guards of Bloomington, and the Phoenix Band of Cairo. It was even rumored that the Irish committee had invited the Hannibal Zouaves to march in the Chicago St. Patrick's Day parade, which, if true, would have been a gesture of acceptance bordering on the miraculous. In music, the Hyers sisters, the "California Musical Wonders," sang before full houses of whites and blacks in Chicago in 1871, and "Blind Tom," the self-taught pianist who had been born a slave, triumphantly toured southern Illinois in 1872 and 1875.

Before the war white audiences had heard white men with cork-blackened faces singing plantation songs written by whites. In the seventies they heard real blacks singing genuine Negro spirituals. For the first time white Illinoisans were treated to what the *Chicago Times* called the most thoroughly original music in the world: "the spontaneous outburst of the fervid, emotional nature of the African race," melodies of "almost unearthly sadness." The Jubilee Singers, the Tennesseeans, and the Hampton Singers were all praised and applauded and all successful in collecting funds for Fisk University and Hampton Institute. Away from the concert hall and the stage their reception was sometimes not as warm. Thus the Hampton Singers were not permitted into the main parlor of the Merchants' Hotel where they were staying but had to meet white visitors in the hotel's dingy, little second-class dining room. At least they had accomplished the unusual in obtaining accommodations at one of the largest hotels in downtown Chicago.[21]

Blacks, like whites, were infected by the baseball craze that swept the state in the 1870s. They formed teams in Bloomington (the Dexters and Crusaders), Rockford (the Pink Stockings),

Cairo (the Quicksteps), Jacksonville (the Homes), and Chicago (the Blue Stockings). Such evidence as there is indicates that no blacks played on white teams and no whites on black teams. Black teams did play white teams, though, and they played before crowds of white and black spectators.

In Chicago the Blue Stockings, "the stalwart youths of the blue hose and dusky faces," were a team of young black waiters from the hotels and restaurants. White "rowdies" chased them away from the lakefront park, considered a white man's preserve, but they managed to find practice grounds and compiled a good record in 1870. Yet they were not allowed to enter the amateur tournament for the championship of the city because, the tournament officials alleged, they were not good enough to compete with the white teams. The *Chicago Evening Journal* and the *Chicago Times* scoffed at this excuse, saying that in reality the whites were afraid that the Blue Stockings would win the prize as the best team in Chicago. Over the winter the club reorganized and changed its name to the "Uniques." It played well in the Illinois state tournament in 1874, placing second and beating all teams except the champion Chicago Socials.

Games played by the Uniques and other colored teams brought whites and blacks together to watch the fun and root for the home players. And the performance of the blacks disproved some of the theories held by prejudiced whites. According to the *Tribune* there were whites who insisted that victories won in the field of political rights and victories won on the baseball diamond were very different: the blacks' right to vote had been bestowed on them by white legislators whereas the blacks' victories in baseball would have to be earned by the exertion of their own individual and team skills. Many whites thought the blacks incapable of developing those skills. But, announced the *Tribune* in an article about a game between the Blue Stockings and the Rockford Pink Stockings, the play of the teams had proved that belief a fallacy: "Our colored brethren *can* play baseball and do it well into the bargain." The game had been an "unusually interesting one throughout, besides being extremely creditable to the Chicago lads, whose general play in the field and at the bat was fully equal to that of any amateur club in the city."[22]

Other events might be taken as signs by the people of the era that social barriers between the races were crumbling. In

Cairo the prize for the best dressed gentleman at a ball went to a Negro. At the lower end of the age scale, a colored baby at the Kendall County fair won the prize as the best looking, prompting the *Chicago Times* to inquire in jest, "What is there left to do for the Negro, now that a darkey baby has been awarded the premium as the best looking of all those exhibited at a county fair?"

In Edwardsville, southern Madison County, a white man paid off a bet with a black by wheeling him in a barrow the length of Main Street. Black men and white women were observed walking together on the central streets and sitting together on streetcars; black men took white girls to dances in Chicago and Bloomington; black and white marriages occurred in Chicago, Springfield, and Princeton. These were instances of association, still very rare, between respectable blacks and whites.

In the past the demimonde of both races had mingled in low dives and the slums and now this sort of fraternizing seems to have become more blatant. Or the newspapers more open about headlining it. Notice was taken of "Black Delilahs" walking the streets, and when the police raided "houses of iniquity" and "dens of infamy," whites along with blacks were mentioned as purchasers of "carnal merchandise." The newspapers held up their hands in horror or laughed grimly, but publicity about association of blacks and whites under these circumstances might well lead to some serious thinking about the need to provide public schooling for both races as a means of social and moral cultivation and of protection for the community.[23]

"Our people are to be seen in all the relations of life," exulted John Jones, and he told a reporter for the *Chicago Times* that "the colored people now represent a large part of the voting population, and as such will be looked to by politicians, and will have no trouble securing any just rights they may be entitled to." He was, if the hyperbole is overlooked, quite accurate in his evaluation of the blacks' new status. They had won the vote and were entering those sectors of society from which they had hitherto been excluded. Their acquisition of voting rights and the consequent enhancement of their rewarding, punishing, and dialectical powers (and so of the possibility that their voting behavior and exercise of power would have an effect on the health of American political institutions) and their increasing participation in mainstream community activities (and so of the possibility that their actions would influence the quality of shared community living) would furnish additional reasons and more compelling motives for giving them access to public schooling.

Providing schooling for them was now dictated by the traditional arguments for universal, public, and free education. All children who would become members of the interdependent, interacting community should receive the schooling that would develop their abilities and talents to the fullest and enable them to contribute their share to the onward progress of society; all children should receive such schooling as would prevent them from becoming a threat to the community's safety, prosperity, and happiness.[24]

These were arguments that were now convincing to nearly all Republicans and many Democrats. But ahead lay questions of how access to public schooling should be translated into law and into concrete school policies, practices, and experiences. Thus Charles B. Steele, senator from central Coles County, a stalwart Republican, in a speech in the General Assembly, observed that "Negroes are everywhere." The black, he said, was in legislative halls, in the pulpit, at the legal bar, and part and parcel of the government. The question was "shall he be a curse or a help to our nation" and the answer would be decided "by the measure of education meted out to him."[25]

Down in deepest Egypt the same arguments were made and the same question raised in the antiblack *Cairo Bulletin* and none of its Democratic readers rushed forward to write letters of protest. The whites, the article in the *Bulletin* declared, should make certain that "the streams of intelligence that flow through our system of popular education" were poured into the minds of the blacks. "We must educate them, must use every possible effort to develop their faculties, and teach them to think for themselves." Ignorant voters could be manipulated by designing politicians; ignorance was dangerous to liberty and should not be tolerated in a republic. Granted therefore that blacks should have access to public schooling, what form should that schooling take?

How can these people be educated? . . . To attempt, by law, to throw open our public schools to them would, no doubt, result in a loud and angry outcry; and probably, in the present condition of the public mind, disorganize most of them. Nevertheless, the public weal, every consideration of philanthropy, the dictates of Christianity, all demand the education of these unfortunate people. How, then, shall we proceed to the performance of this important and imperative duty?[26]

8

Gaining Access to Public Schools

The question perplexing the writer of the editorial in the Democratic *Cairo Bulletin* quoted in the last chapter was this: What steps should be taken in performing the imperative and important duty of furnishing public schooling for blacks, now that there was general agreement that such schooling was necessary? Clearly, unless the whole issue were to be evaded entirely, the steps would involve a consideration of appropriate changes in the state constitution and school laws as well as in city and town ordinances, board of education rules, and much else pertaining to the institution of public education.

Already in 1870 a change had been made in the state constitution, with Article 8, Section 1, laying upon the General Assembly the obligation of providing free schools "whereby all children of this State may receive a good common school education." Insofar as the education of blacks might be concerned, the two operative words were the quantitative "all children" and the qualitative "good common school education." The "all" posed the question of whether now, contrary to what had been the habit previously, the children of the blacks were to be regarded as coming within the scope of the term. If the answer were in the affirmative and embodied in law, then further questions were bound to follow about the nature of enabling statutory provisions toward that end and their formulation in obedience to constitutional and statutory mandate.

If blacks were to have access to public schools, the constitution would require that their education be "good." As "good" as that for whites? Which was to ask, "equally" good for "all," blacks and whites alike? Was the "equally" good education to be offered in racially separate or mixed schools? Was the education to be equally good in respect to physical facilities? Organization? Instruction? Was it possible to provide equally good learning environments and experiences for blacks and whites if they were isolated from each other and made to attend schools reserved for each race alone? Were mixed schools necessary in order to achieve equality in the goodness of the education furnished the races? This last question may seem anachronistic, suggesting a hindsight recourse to the arguments in the decision of the United States Supreme Court in *Brown* v. *Board of Education*, of Topeka, May 17, 1954, but the question does not actually represent a deviation from a strict chronological standard. In the early 1870s it was a question raised in the Illinois courts on the issue of public schooling for blacks.

The next General Assembly to meet after the ratification of the Illinois constitution of 1870 was the 27th convening on January 4, 1871. Facing it were decisions to be made on the tasks enjoined by the new constitution, one of which was revision of the free-school laws to conform with the provisions of Article 8, Section 1. Should the Assembly have the courage to act on the issue of black school rights, there were at least three forms of legislative response possible.

At a minimum the Assembly could enact a law dropping "white" and Section 80 and assume that counting black children in the formula for allotting money from the state school fund would dissolve the obstacles to their public schooling. A second kind of law that could be enacted would drop "white" and Section 80 and put into the free-schools law or enact as a supplement to it a guarantee ensuring the inclusion of blacks within the "all children" and so of access to the public schools. A more sweeping law would drop "white" and Section 80, add a guarantee of access, and oblige black children to attend a "colored school" or permit them to enter their neighborhood school although that school might be attended by whites.

The premise for the last kind of enactment would be that the issue of racially mixed versus racially separate schools should be settled by state law and not by discretion of the individual school districts: this is to say that it was an issue of such far-reaching consequences for the society that it should not be decided miscellaneously according to the parochial feelings and opinions of local enclaves of black and white citizens.

Two of the schooling petitions from blacks to the 27th General Assembly dealt with the third kind of alternative. Petitions from "sundry" blacks of southern Alexander and Massac counties—and it could be that similar petitions from southern Saline County also included blacks within their vague "certain" and "sundry" citizens labels—called for laws requiring separate schools for the races. No petitions from northern or central county blacks were presented. Nor did black persons in any region of the state hold mass meetings or engage in drives, campaigns, or lobbying efforts intended to pressure or persuade the 27th General Assembly into taking certain kinds of action on school rights. Except for the petitioning of the "sundry colored citizens" from the southern counties, the blacks of the state seem to have decided to rest their trust in their political party, the Republican party, and let it be free to determine what kind of school-rights bills should be introduced and what strategy should be adopted.

One of the other factors that may have influenced the blacks' decision to limit the independent exercise of their own bargaining power and rely on that of the Republican party could have been produced by a partial diversion of their attention from remedies possible at the state level to those proposed at the federal level. Introduced in Congress on May 13, 1870, Charles Sumner's "A bill supplementary to an act entitled 'An Act to protect the citizens of the United States in their civil rights, and to furnish the means for their vindication,' passed April 9, 1866," contained a public-school rights clause. Pinning hopes on Sumner's bill made good sense, for the same sequence that had occurred with suffrage rights might be expected in the case of school rights: state law would follow upon superior federal law.[1]

At the fifth Illinois state convention of colored men at Springfield, December 2, 1873, delegates were elected to a national convention in Washington that was to urge Congress to pass the Sumner bill. Lewis B. White of Chicago represented Illinois at the Washington gathering of blacks from the states and he was one of the signers of the "Memorial of National Convention of Colored Persons, praying to be protected in their civil rights." The "Memorial" was devoted wholly to arguments for public schooling and jury-duty rights, yet when Sumner's bill came to the floor in 1875, the public-school rights clause was excised because of fears in the Senate and House that it would bring black and white children together in the same schools. "After the provision for enforced mixed schools had been eliminated from the [Sumner] bill," remarked the *Chicago Tribune*, "it became a comparatively insignificant measure." Nevertheless the deletion of the schooling provision had come only in the last stage of the legislative process in 1875, and during the years before there was reason for Illinois blacks to entertain hopes that the Sumner bill would pass intact and that then federal law might be imitated by state law.[2]

Thus at the state level in the early 1870s Illinois blacks were not exercising independently on school rights issues the enhanced bargaining powers they had derived from suffrage rights and increasing participation in community life. Nor did they have to. It was clear to themselves and to everyone else that they did possess latent rewarding, punishing, and dialectical power. They did not have to flex their muscle; they did not have to make a show of their bargaining power. The perception that they had it could furnish one of the motives for the Republican party to act for them. Manifestly the blacks could bestow their vote or withhold it; they could resort to physical militancy; they could apply dialectical power and argue in letters, addresses, and speeches that school rights for them were morally, religiously, and ethically justified, were part of the unfinished agenda of the war and of the mission of the Republican party, and were imperative for their own sake and for the sake of the progress and safety of the community. The perception of all this could elicit a response from the Republicans almost as surely as if the white members of the party were a target group at which overt black power was aimed and volleyed.

The person who did most to shape the kind of legislation for public-school rights for blacks that came out of the 27th and 28th General Assemblies in 1872 and 1874 was State Superintendent of Public Instruction Newton Bateman. To get his recommendations translated into law, he had available the power generated by his own personal prestige and by the advantages attached to his high office. He had been first elected state superintendent in 1858 and again in 1860. Defeated in the Democratic landslide of 1862, he had been re-elected in 1864 and would serve in that office until his retirement in January 1875. In his biennial reports from 1865 to 1875 he had vehemently protested discriminations against black children in the school laws and he had pleaded for enactments that would admit them to the public schools.

Bateman had been born on July 27, 1822, near Fairton, New Jersey, the youngest of five children of a weaver. His father, hoping for a better life in the West, took the family by covered wagon to central Morgan County, Illinois. Their fortunes did not mend and Newton had to find odd jobs to help the family survive. While employed as an errand boy by a judge in Jacksonville, he fell in love with the judge's daughter and wishing to make himself worthy of her he resolved to study for a degree from Illinois College in the city. He worked his way through college, graduating in 1843. In those years the president of Illinois College was Edward Beecher, a member of the famous Beecher family, a leader of the Illinois State Antislavery Society, and a fervent advocate of black rights. From college Bateman moved to another center of antislavery activity, Lane Theological Seminary in Cincinnati, where some of the most militant of the Ohio abolitionists had taught or studied. But illness and lack of money caused him to drop out within a year and he took a job as a book salesman.[3]

In 1845 Bateman began a career in the field of education continuing through the rest of his life. He opened a private English and Classical school in St. Louis; two years later he accepted a professorship of mathematics at St. Charles College, St. Charles, Missouri; then after four years he returned to Illinois to stay. He became principal of the Jacksonville public school and in succession superintendent of the Morgan County public school system, principal of Jacksonville Female Academy, and state superintendent of public instruction from 1859 to 1862 and from 1865 to 1875. Along the way before and through the war he had been a founder of the Illinois State Teachers' Association, associate editor and chief editor of *The Illinois Teacher*, the official journal of the association, and a corresponding secretary and state agent of the association and a member of its executive committee. In 1863 and 1864 when he was out of office as state superintendent, he was head clerk in the department of General Oakes, the United States recruiting officer for Illinois. A friend of Lincoln, Bateman was usually introduced by Lincoln as "Mr. Schoolmaster," though another version of the anecdote has Lincoln introducing

Bateman, a tiny man, as "My little friend, the big schoolmaster of Illinois."

(After resigning from the state superintendency in 1875, Bateman was appointed president of Knox College at Galesburg. In 1893 he became president emeritus and professor of mental and moral science. He also served on the Illinois state board of public health and as an assay commissioner during the Rutherford B. Hayes administration. At the time of his death, October 21, 1897, Bateman was editor-in-chief of the *Historical Encyclopedia of Illinois*, a multivolume source of valuable information on the state and especially rich in biographical information relating to the lives of Illinois worthies of the last century.)

Bateman was one of the great schoolmen of his era. He edited a volume of *School Laws and Common School Decisions of the State of Illinois*, published in 1865, with new editions and revisions in 1866, 1867, and 1871, and he wrote an immense number of official bulletins, circulars, and letters to interested citizens, school officers, and officials in the branches of state, county, and local government. Year after year he spoke before audiences in every corner of the state, beseeching them to support the measures he proposed for improving the public-school system.

His seven biennial reports were compared to those of Horace Mann. Nor was the comparison too farfetched. His biennial reports, like those of the secretary of the Massachusetts state board of education, were eloquent treatises on a wide range of topics, from advice on teaching the three R's to translations of American political philosophy into the idiom of arguments for universal, public, and free education. Like Mann, Bateman had a profound faith in the preventive and remedial powers of universal schooling and the public school. Like Mann, too, he wrote his reports in "high" style, preaching righteousness and summoning the citizens of the state to educational salvation in the imagery, diction, and sentence rhythms of the King James Version of the Bible.

Bateman denounced the exclusion of blacks from the public schools as unjust, the "opprobrium and shame of our otherwise noble system of free schools." In his biennial reports his constant refrain was that the restrictive "white" and Section 80 should be deleted from the school laws and that all the children of the state should have a legal guarantee of school rights. Although the issue of racial integration or segregation was an explosive one, he attempted to defuse it by telling nervous whites that no one should be frightened by the "phantom" of racial mixing in the classrooms. The issue of co-attendance of the races or their separation ought to be decided locally, he claimed. It should be left to the discretion of the citizens and school board of each district; it should not be regulated by statutes handed down from Springfield by the General Assembly. The Assembly should pass legislation removing all unjust distinctions from the school laws and "requiring equal provision to be made for the education of all, but leaving each school district or community free to adopt its own course as to the manner in which such provision shall be made—whether by one school for all, or by separate schools."

As for the decision to be made by the local authorities, he predicted that in districts where there were comparatively few blacks it would be the economic factor that would settle the matter in favor of integration: "When the continued indulgence of a mere prejudice is found to be expensive, it is not probable that it will be very long persisted in." Where the number of black children was sufficient to make separate schools possible without laying a financial burden on a district, separate schools for the races would be advisable until "wiser counsels" should prevail. He never did reveal what these wiser counsels should be and what principles and motives should give them shape.[4]

As a person and as the highest officer in the education branch of state government, Bateman was a public figure whose views and recommendations had best be treated with all due respect by the members of the legislature. He was widely known as a friend of the deified Lincoln. He had been the candidate of the dominant Republican party in recent elections for the state superintendency, almost all of which he had won by generous margins. His large and loyal following among the voters of the state would listen attentively to what he had to say. On his side he had the governor, and the popular Palmer could by virtue of his office reward or punish through the use of the veto and the temptations of patronage.

Bateman's own official position yielded advantages too. His reports, circulars, digests of school law, correspondence, lectures, and teacher seminars kept him in touch with educational affairs in every nook and cranny of the state and in communication with administrators, teachers, parents, and citizens in each of the 11,285 school districts. He had been solving problems in the field of education for more than a quarter of a century as they had come to him in the classroom and as they had crossed his desk in the state capitol in Springfield. His unrivaled knowledge, his broad experience, his seasoned judgment were further strengthened by his idealism and fervor, all conveyed in Old Testament rhythms and language that could stir pious hearts.

In his eighth biennial report, transmitted to the governor on December 15, 1870, and praised, quoted, and paraphrased by Palmer in his message to the 27th General Assembly in 1871, Bateman again expounded as he had in the past the moral and pragmatic arguments for the schooling of blacks. Under the heading, "Justice at Last," he hailed the first section of Article 8 of the 1870 constitution as embracing the children of blacks within its "all children." By the "wise and noble" provisions of that section they would be among those children to whom the public schools would dispense the priceless means of intellectual improvement and culture. God would "smile" upon the state for helping the children of a "poor and despised race." Let the blacks, on their part, make the most of a benefit that would enable them to become "an upright, intelligent, educated people."

These latter words would recall to his audience developmental and preventive arguments appealing to motives of hope that, educated, the blacks would share in advancing the well-being of society and to fear that, uneducated, they would be a threat to it. Continuing, Bateman told the members of the General Assembly that they should bring the law into compliance with the state constitution: they should omit "white" from the text of a revised free-schools law. Then there would be no ambiguity about the district school committees' obligation "to provide at once for the education of children of color, as efficiently and thoroughly in all respects, as for the education of white children." [5]

Bateman knew very well that a serious obstacle to the enactment of any school legislation for blacks had been the emotionalism surrounding the issue of whether there should be separate schools for blacks and whites or the same schools for all children regardless of color. There was the dread that any legislation opening the schools to blacks by even a crack would lead inevitably to the association of the races and to "amalgamation." In his eighth biennial report Bateman's strategy was designed to clear this obstruction out of the path of legislating access. He insisted that the separate versus mixed schools issue was "trivial," "one of those matters which involve no principle worth striving about, and which are best left to regulate themselves."

The regulatory mechanism he advised was, as in previous reports, that of "cost" in districts having few black children. Establishing and maintaining separate schools in those districts would be too expensive for taxpayers to tolerate. Where large enough numbers of blacks could be educated in separate schools without extra expense, the citizens should have the option of providing separate or mixed schooling at their discretion. In all districts, he said, the citizens and their school boards should be free to decide for themselves as local feelings, wishes, opinions, and circumstances would suggest. They should not be subjected to the dictates of state law on the issue. State law should be "silent" on the issue.

At odds with this strategy were two of the three measures relating to the schooling of blacks introduced in the 27th General Assembly. The two failed but a third, compatible with Bateman's recommendations, succeeded. The third bill, submitted by Willard C. Flagg, a Republican senator from southern Madison County, proposed a revision of the free-schools law that would among other changes eliminate the discriminatory "white" and Section 80, avoid explicit mention of the issue of separate or mixed schools, and contain a clause empowering school boards to "assign" pupils to the several schools of a district. Reported favorably by the Senate committee on education, the Flagg bill was passed by the Senate 32 to 1 with 24 Republicans and 8 Democrats voting for and one Democrat voting against and by the House 99 to 27 with 73 Republicans, 25 Democrats, and 1 member of an unknown political party voting for and 24 Democrats and 3 Republicans voting against. It was signed by Governor Palmer on April 1.[6]

"An act to establish and maintain a system of free schools," approved April 1, 1872, with some slight revisions, would control public education in Illinois through the rest of the century. The act did not contain the restrictive adjective "white" that since Illinois statehood had been a hindrance to the public schooling of blacks. From 1872 onward the district school officers were required to make public schooling accessible to all children, not just to white children.

Furthermore the act of April 1, 1872, gave to local school boards the freedom to decide for themselves whether the district should have separate "colored" schools or the same schools for both races. This discretion was invested in local boards by a sentence in Section 48 affirming that they had the authority to "assign" pupils to the several schools, a safeguard included for the express purpose of ensuring that the localities would have the option of deciding the issue without interference from prescriptive state law. (After 1950 they were deprived of the option by United States and Illinois law and the decrees of the courts.)

Another clause in Section 48 made school boards responsible for providing a sufficient number of free schools to secure to "all" children "the right and opportunity to an equal education in all such free schools." This was the first time that "equal" had appeared in a free-schools-law paragraph specifying the powers and duties of the district school boards. Now in 1872 there were in constitutional and statutory law the three terms, "all," a quantitative term, "good," a qualitative, and "equal," a comparative, on which future argumentation and rulings in and out of the courts would pivot during the nineteenth and twentieth centuries.[7]

Bateman's plan of isolating the "all" from the "good" and the "equal," that is, of obtaining the enactment of provisions for legalizing access to public schooling for blacks without having the law dictate the medium for delivering access, whether by racially separate or mixed schools, and his reliance upon financial incentives produced by dropping the "white" and counting black children within the formula for allocating money from the state school fund, was successful as strategy. Yet in the push and pull of everyday school life financial incentives did not outweigh prejudice in some districts or prevent an interplay among "all," "good," and "equal" in other districts that rendered the free-schools law of April 1, 1872, deficient as a solution to the problem of access.

In the autumn when the questionnaires Bateman had sent to the county superintendents for his biennial survey of Illinois education had been returned, he discovered that in certain districts the black children were still being denied admission to the schools and that in other districts the blacks were being admitted but shunted into a single classroom. They were being gathered together regardless of age and level of scholarship and were missing the advantages the white children were receiving in those districts where the favored race was grouped in classes and grades according to maturity and academic attainment. Black children were being deprived of a "good" and "equal" education. And some black parents were keeping their children at home because they were unwilling to accept the inferior schooling foisted on their children. Hence schooling for "all" children was not being achieved in some districts that were disobeying the law in every respect pertaining to blacks and in other districts where violations of the "good" and "equal" were precipitating black absences that led to a breaching of the "all."[8]

In his ninth biennial report Bateman spoke briefly about all three types of violation, but his recommendations did not deal much with the "good" and "equal." He concentrated chiefly on remedies for delinquencies relating to "all." The inadequacies of the law of April 1 he attributed to the "paltry" fines levied for disobedience and to the omission from it of any description of a procedure by which the blacks could resort to the courts for assistance against recalcitrant school boards. He asked the 28th General Assembly, convening on January 8, 1873, to amend the free-schools law or to pass supplementary legislation imposing larger fines and laying out surer and speedier procedures of redress when school boards failed to provide schooling for black children.

Spokesman for Bateman in the 28th General Assembly was George W. Henry, a Republican senator from southern Clay County. On February 13 Henry offered a resolution intended to begin the process of enacting into law the recommendations made by Bateman. The resolution quoted Section 1, Article 8, of the 1870 state constitution, Section 48 of the April 1, 1872, free-schools law, and the sentences in Bateman's biennial report disclosing the negligence of some school boards in the matter of schooling for black children. The Senate should resolve to instruct its committee on education to investigate further, Henry declared, and the committee should report a bill penalizing those guilty of the offense.[9]

Henry's resolution was tabled for the rest of the session, but when the 28th General Assembly reconvened, Henry introduced his resolution again. The ensuing debate revealed once more how hard it was to keep the issue of "access" to schooling isolated from the issue of racially mixed or separate schooling. Although Bateman's biennial report and Henry's resolution to implement it had clearly indicated a bill centering on access only, the old worries that access would bring mixing and that mixing would bring "intimacies" had quickly come to the fore, and an effort was then made to append a provision forbidding the intermingling of the races in schools. Nor were the arguments of the pro-access legislators of a kind that would quiet such worries.

The responses of the Progressive Democrats and the Republicans had included mention of gratitude owed Negroes for fighting in the Union army, the necessity of obeying the federal and state constitutions and the free-schools law, the need to complete the unfinished agenda of the war, and the urgency of schooling blacks now that they were participating more extensively in the community. The urgency argument was accompanied by talk of the damage that uneducated blacks could inflict upon the community and of the contributions educated blacks could make to its advancement.

These were arguments addressed to access. The only arguments directed to worries about the prospect of mixing were allusions to the expensiveness of separate schools in districts where few blacks were of school age, to the dangers of distinctions in schooling, and to "equality" in the abstract as an attribute of "our Government." None was likely to soothe the fears of people who were anti-access because they believed that a law silent on the issue of separate versus mixed schooling would certainly lead to the intermingling of the races.[10]

Still, a majority of the legislators were evidently of the opinion that Bateman's views could be translated into a law that would assure access and yet also assure the right of local option to decide the separate–mixed schools issue. Amendments by Thomas Sloo Casey and Alexander Starne, two Bourbon Democrats from southern Jefferson County and central Sangamon, respectively, that would have required or permitted separate schools for Negro children, were defeated 27 to 5 and 21 to 9, and the Henry resolution was adopted 22 to 10 and referred to the Senate committee on education.[11]

On February 7, Henry, a member of the committee, reported a bill for "An act to protect colored children in their rights to attend Public Schools." The proposed act had three sections:

*AN ACT to protect colored children in their rights
to attend Public Schools*

SECTION 1. *Be it enacted by the People of the State of Illinois, represented in the General Assembly,* That all directors of schools, boards of education, or other school officers, whose duty it now is, or may be hereafter, to provide, in their respective jurisdictions, schools for the education of all children between the ages of six and twenty-one years, are prohibited from excluding, directly or indirectly, any such child from such school on account of the color of such child.

SECTION 2. Any such school officer or officers as are mentioned in the foregoing section, or any other person, who shall exclude, or aid in the exclusion from the public schools any child who is entitled to the benefits of such school, on account of such child's color, shall be fined, upon conviction, in any sum not less than five nor more than one hundred dollars each, for every such offense.

SECTION 3. Any person who shall, by threats, menace or intimidation, prevent any colored child entitled to attend a public school in this State from attending such school, shall, upon conviction, be fined in any sum not exceeding twenty-five dollars.[12]

The anti-access legislators were not about to surrender, however. When the Senate took the Henry bill up for consideration, Samuel P. Cummings, Democrat from central Fulton County, moved to strike the words "on account of the color of such child." This dilution of the bill was defeated and the bill passed by a vote of 26 to 6. On March 19 it was sent to the House for concurrence. Already that chamber had disposed of a bill that would have meant separate schooling for the races. Spencer M. Kase, Democratic representative from southern St. Clair County, had introduced on January 20 a bill for "An act to provide for the better education of the colored children in the State of Illinois." The "better education" Kase visualized for blacks was to be in segregated schools. His bill was referred to the House committee on education and was reported out by Alson J. Streeter, a Democrat from northern Mercer County, with a recommendation that it be laid upon the table. Kase objected, but the report of the education committee was sustained and the Kase bill tabled. All this was done without a roll call vote. Later, on March 23, the House passed the Henry bill, 79 to 17, and it was signed by the governor on March 24.[13]

In the Senate and House the voting behavior on the Henry resolution and bill and the attempts to amend had displayed the now customary pattern of Republican unity and Democratic fragmentation on measures relating to public-school rights for blacks. If votes for the Casey and Starne motions and against the Henry resolution and bill are classified as "hostile" and the votes against the Casey and Starne motions and for the Henry resolution and bill classified as "friendly," then in both chambers 136 votes by Republicans were friendly and 3 hostile whereas 39 by Democrats were friendly and 44 hostile.

On March 24, the day Henry's bill had become law, he wrote to Bateman:

> I herewith send you letters etc. kindly afforded me by you. You have doubtless observed that the General Assembly has passed the "bill to protect colored children etc." I congratulate you on the concurrence of the Legislature in passing a law embodying your suggestions.[14]

It had been a genuine triumph for Bateman and his strategy. Henry had incorporated into the law the recommendations of the superintendent's ninth biennial report. The Henry law had increased the penalties for noncompliance with Section 48 of the free-schools act; it had laid out a definite mode of redress for aggrieved blacks; it had named blacks as the special beneficiaries of the March 24th law; it had made plain that they must be included in the "all children" wherever the term appeared in the educational clauses of the constitution and the statutes. Furthermore the Henry law was, or was supposed to be, drafted in accordance with Bateman's idea that Illinois law should have nothing to say on the issue of racially separate versus racially mixed schooling. The very title of the Henry law demonstrated that its purpose was to protect black children's rights to "attend" public schools, not their rights to a "good" or an "equal" education. Nowhere in the law was to be found any language denoting a concern with issues other than those relating to "access" and its antonym "exclusion."

But out in the state, as in the Assembly, there were whites who clung to suspicions about the Henry law's purported neutrality by omission. The experience of John H. Oberly, a Progressive Democrat, owner and editor of the *Cairo Bulletin*, and a House member of the Assembly who had voted for the Henry bill, is illuminating. When Bourbon Democrats in Cairo had taunted him with the accusation that his vote had indicated approval of the commingling of blacks and whites, he retorted that there was nothing in the Henry bill or law that "squints toward mixed schools." He had voted for the bill, he emphasized, because the best interests of the country demanded that the blacks be raised out of the "slough" of ignorance. This the Henry law would help to accomplish; he did not dream it would inaugurate mixed schools.

Extremist Democrats were not satisfied with his explanation, as he was to learn when he attended a party convention to nominate a candidate for Congress. He was denounced as a "hand-holding nigger man" and a delegate from southern Williamson County roamed the streets, pistol at the ready, threatening to shoot him on sight. A resolution was put forward charging that "the effect of the act of the general assembly of Illinois, at the last session thereof, entitled 'An act to protect the colored children in their rights to attend the public schools,' will be inimical to the interests of the negro and retrogressive to white civilization." Oberly, a brave man, stood up to criticize the resolution and was greeted with shouts of "Don't let him talk," "Dry up," "You are a liar," and "Damn you, you're no Democrat!" Undaunted, Oberly held his ground and defended the wisdom of the Henry law and his voting for it and repudiated the notion that it was conducive to mixed schooling. His speech succeeded to the extent that no further action was taken on the resolution, but he did not get nominated as the candidate for Congress.[15]

Skepticism about the professed neutrality of the Henry law

also surfaced in the 29th General Assembly convening on January 6, 1875. During the session six antiblack schooling measures were introduced. Four of the six in one way or another attempted to amend the Henry law so that it would require separate schools for the races. Two were attempts to repeal the Henry law. No roll call vote was taken on any of the six bills and it is impossible to tell how the individual members of the Assembly lined up. As all six bills were defeated, it is clear that a majority of legislators in a body composed of 24 Republicans, 18 Democrats, and 9 Independents in the Senate and of 69 Republicans, 42 Democrats, and 41 Independents in the House had been satisfied with the wording and content of the Henry law as it had been framed by the General Assembly of 1874.

Plain, too, was agreement by a majority of the legislators that the issue of access to public schooling for blacks was now settled while leaving the local districts at liberty to decide whether this schooling should be in racially segregated or integrated schools. The fact that the Democrats in the 29th General Assembly made only two attempts, and these from a single person, Lewis F. Plater, Democrat from southern Hardin County, to repeal the Henry law suggests as much. So does the derision heaped on Plater by the Democratic and Republican newspapers.

The papers saw in him foolish Bourbon fears that educated blacks might outdo the whites and prove themselves mentally superior. He was "idiotic," and a spokesman for "the backward philosophy espoused by the discredited Democratic party before the war" in an "epoch of prejudice and superstition." He imagined that the safety of the Republic "requires that the niggers be kept in ignorance, and knowing his rights and the rights of such as he, he wishes to preserve inalienable the right of a white man to knock down any d——d nigger who expressed a desire to become educated." He was devoted to saving the Republic "from the degredation of niggers who can read and write, use soap, and wear white shirts."[16]

Thus "An Act to protect colored children in their rights to attend Public Schools," March 24, 1874, Section 48 of the free-schools law of April 1, 1872, and Section1 of Article 8 of the Illinois constitution of 1870 brought to a triumphant legal conclusion the blacks' struggle for access to public schooling. As for a conclusion involving actual attendance at public schools, that, too, statistical and testimonial evidence shows was achieved by the end of the year 1874.

On October 19 Bateman sent to the county superintendents the forms on which they were to record and return to him for his tenth biennial report the customary data on school attendance, teachers' salaries, and the like. He also asked for answers to other questions, one of which was "If there are colored children of school age in your county, are they taught in separate schools, or in the same schools with white children? Give the facts and results in relation to this matter as fully as you can, together with your opinion of the best course to be pursued in the premises." [17]

Bateman did not seek from the superintendents the number of black children of school age. To fill this gap in his report necessitates extrapolating from returns over the previous eight years: 4,444 blacks of school age in 1865; 4,931 in 1866; 5,472 in 1867; 6,210 in 1868; 6,875 in 1869; 7,299 in 1870; 7,714 in 1871; 8,167 in 1872. Doing this yields a number of school-age black children of approximately 8,600 in 1873 and 9,000 in 1874. Without burdening the reader further with the calculations involved, it would be safe to say—on the basis of Bateman's statistics and the replies of the county superintendents—that some 98 percent of black children of school age had access to public schooling in the autumn following the passage of the Henry law.

These data showing the near disappearance of the problem of the exclusion of blacks from public schooling were corroborated by Bateman himself. In his tenth biennial report, after analyzing the returns from the county superintendents, he commented that although there had been some "deplorable" instances, "comparatively few cases of willful injustice and wrong to colored children, by peremptorily refusing to make any provision for their education," had been reported to his office. The improvement had been marked and justified "a hopeful view of the future." [18]

The Henry law had removed ambiguities in the constitution and the free-schools law by stipulating, in effect, that Negro children must be included in "all children" wherever that term was used in school legislation. It had given blacks a means of legal redress when they were barred from the schools; they were now able to invoke the authority of the courts and bring recalcitrant school officers to heel. It had explicitly placed the responsibility of schooling the blacks upon the local public school officials in both urban and rural districts. It had clinched the victory of access to public schooling for the blacks and guaranteed it. It was a law that has been retained, *mutatis mutandis*, in the statutes from that year to this. Today Section 2 of the original Henry law continues almost unchanged in the school code and refers, as it did in 1874, only to the exclusion of children on account of color. Section 1 has become elaborated to prohibit exclusion from and segregation in schools on account of color, race, nationality, or religion, and Section 3 now imposes penalties on persons preventing by threat, menace, and intimidation "any child" from attending a public school.[19]

Manifestly the Henry law was but the culmination of efforts made by blacks and sympathetic whites over many decades of struggle. The enacting of the bill had benefited from the favoring circumstances and attitudes that had developed during and after a war in which the blacks had taken part and a war in which a major objective had been the "freeing" of the blacks in the South and eventually, in a more comprehensive sense, those in the North. Among Republicans there was a resolve to complete the unfinished agenda of the war and among Independent and Progressive Democrats the hope of restoring the competitiveness of their party by conceding Negro rights and moving on to issues of fiscal accountability and honesty. The result was united voting on the part of the Republicans and a division of the Democrats, with the Independents and Progressives joining the Republicans in voting for black rights while the Bourbons persevered in voting against.

Concomitantly there had been an enormous strengthening of the bargaining power of the blacks when they came into possession of the vote, into affiliation with the powerful Republican party, and into participating membership in the interdependent, interacting community and hence into a position where they could help to improve the quality of shared life or do damage to it. Nonetheless during the 1870s the dialectical power exercised in the blacks' behalf was less by the blacks than by whites like Bateman, Palmer, Henry, Flagg, Youngblood, Steele, Oberly, the author of the editorial in the *Cairo Bulletin*, and others. The blacks did not have to exert their power overtly. The perception that they had it and could use it was a possibility to be reckoned with.

All these events, actions, and motives combined to make possible the victory of access to public schooling for blacks. Given the widespread fears of "amalgamation," the victory had been assisted, too, by Bateman's strategy of having the bill and law remain silent on the issue of segregated or integrated schooling for the races. Yet, as Chapter 9 will show, in the spring of 1874 a ruling was handed down by the Illinois Supreme Court that narrowed the independence of the districts.

While the Senate and House of the 28th General Assembly were debating the Henry bill, the Supreme Court was listening to arguments in *Chase v. Stephenson,* the first case on separate schooling for blacks heard by the highest court of the state. The decree of the court reduced the options available to the local districts in the matter of separate or mixed schooling; the reasoning of the court would furnish principles for later interpretations of Article 8, Section 1, of the 1870 constitution, Section 48 of the free-schools law of 1872, and the Henry law of 1874, constricting still more the freedom of the districts to decide issues erupting over insulating and isolating blacks and whites from each other in the local schools. It was in *Chase v. Stephenson* and the nineteenth-century cases following it that the justices of the Supreme Court and counsel for appellants and appellees began the process, continuing over the next hundred years, of unpacking the meanings of "equal," which with "all" and "good" was one of the triad of legal terms governing the conduct of public education in the state until a new constitution was ratified in 1970.

9

Illinois Supreme Court Opinions in School Segregation Cases

It will be of interest to learn what arguments and what decisions on the issue of public-school rights for blacks were offered in the courts, those sanctuaries created by the community to ensure that its disputes will be resolved by the application of dialectical power, not by rewarding or punishing power. The community intends that the participants in actions in the courts will exercise dialectical power as the sole means by which decisions are to be reached. The attorneys for the defense and prosecution are expected to rely upon persuasion, upon reason and rhetoric in the best sense of both terms.

This is to describe the ideal and not necessarily the actuality; everyone realizes that there is the possibility of bribery and intimidation. But we realize also that this would be a distortion of the ideal and a deviation from the high standards of integrity and professionalism we hold up for the courts. Neither rewarding power nor punishing power is supposed to influence the deliberations of the judges and juries who are to decide the issues and settle the conflicts. They are expected to be swayed by reason and logic and by no other stimuli than the cogency of the arguments directed to them. Only after they have fulfilled the role of arbiter surrogated to them by the community and have determined innocence or guilt, do they assume the role of enforcer and exert the rewarding and punishing powers with which they are endowed by general consent of the citizens. Such, at least, is the ideal.

Having supplied concise orientation through a description of the exercise of power in the courts and having used for it the terminology adopted in this study, let us now turn to the nineteenth-century Illinois Supreme Court cases on racial segregation in the schools. The first of these was *James A. Chase et al. v. David Stephenson et al.*, heard by the state's highest court, January term, 1874, opinion filed June 19, 1874. As might be expected, *Chase* v. *Stephenson* is cited and passages from it quoted in some of the later court decisions, in annotated editions of the statutes and school code, and in legal digests. It was the subject of contemporary articles in Illinois newspapers and the *New York Times*, and it was reproduced with brief comments by Bateman in a circular distributed by the Illinois Department of Public Instruction on August 12, 1874, and dissected by Bateman in his tenth biennial report transmitted to the governor on December 15, 1874.

But in twentieth-century nonlegal literature *Chase* v. *Stephenson* is either ignored or summarized superficially or inaccurately. The usual political, social, and educational histories and studies of the black experience in the state rarely mention it, though early in this century it got a paragraph in the report of the Chicago Commission on Race Relations' investigation of the Chicago race riots of July and August, 1919. The latest narrative of the case, in Tate's *The Way It Was In McLean County, 1972–1822*, is only nine pages long and is a confused jumbling of two different cases, *Chase* v. *Stephenson* and *Martha Crow, by her next friend* v. *Board of Education of Bloomington*, the latter a case decided locally and never appealed to the Illinois Supreme Court.

Long overdue are a full and accurate account of *Chase* v. *Stephenson* and an analysis of it in the context of nineteenth-century Illinois thinking on issues of schooling for blacks. As a caveat, however, it should be said that the attorneys and supreme court justices in *Chase* v. *Stephenson* showed no signs of being aware that a piece of relevant legislation, the Henry law, had been passed on March 24, 1874. Probably the case had been heard and decided before mid-March although the filing was delayed until June. At any rate the omission of the mandates of the Henry law from the grounds on which *Chase* v. *Stephenson* was argued and determined does limit, but not destroy, its value as a precedent-setting case.[1]

The essentials of *Chase* v. *Stephenson* are these. On January 25, 1872, David Stephenson, Thomas Shorthose, John T.

Gunnell, and William Paul, white residents and taxpayers in District 6, Danvers Township, McLean County, entered a bill of complaint in the court of the eighth judicial district of the state in Bloomington against the white District 6 school directors, James A. Chase, Ward P. Johnson, and Daniel Slaughbaugh. Stephenson and his fellow complainants said in their bill that some three years earlier a new and commodious schoolhouse had been built to accommodate all the children of the district. Yet in December 1871, when four Negro children living in the district had applied for admission, they had been "forcibly resisted" and threatened with violence by the teacher who, the complainants alleged, had been hired because of his known antagonism toward blacks. (Later this same teacher had not been able to qualify for the county teaching certificate and had been dismissed.)

On January 12 Chase and the other two school directors had published notice of a referendum to take the sense of the voters for or against building another school for the children of the district. In the voting place, however, the question put to the voters was different from that announced: they were asked to vote on whether a tax should be assessed to build a separate schoolhouse for the education of the Negro children of District 6. Sixteen votes were cast for and one against assessing such tax and erecting such school.

Now, wishing to prevent its erection, Stephenson and his fellow complainants prayed the court to grant an injunction against the school directors because the referendum was illegal, because building another school and hiring an additional teacher would be an extra financial burden on the taxpayers, and because the schoolhouse was intended for Negro children only. The school directors' actions were oppressive and harmful, the complainants charged, and done only to "gratify a prejudice and blind hatred" toward black children who desired to secure the benefits of the public schooling to which they were lawfully entitled. Unless stopped by the court, the school directors would begin erecting the colored school and this would cause great expense to the taxpayers. Therefore the complainants requested the court to enjoin the school directors from building the proposed school and from hiring a teacher for the sole purpose of teaching four black children who were being refused admission to the commodious regular district school.[2]

In answer to this plea Judge Thomas F. Tipton granted a temporary injunction. But, defending their actions, Chase and the other school directors brought before Judge Tipton a motion to have the temporary injunction dissolved. They denied the particulars asserted by the complainants in respect to the ampleness of the accommodations to be had at the regular district school, the racial prejudice of the former teacher, and the illegality of the referendum. While acknowledging that the black children had not been admitted to the district school, they insisted that it was not for reasons of prejudice but for the reason that the blacks were "so filthy as to make it improper to allow them to associate in school with decent children." The school directors had acted in good faith "with a view to promote the best interests of said District and in obedience to the vote of said District and in the discharge of the duties imposed on them by law." They were ready to receive the black children in the separate school, it having been virtually completed and a teacher hired before the injunction had been served upon them.[3]

Judge Tipton overruled the motion to dissolve the temporary injunction, yet the school directors went ahead and had the black children taught in the separate school. This resulted in a supplemental bill on August 23 from Stephenson and his fellow complainants accusing the school directors of opposing the law of the land by excluding blacks from "equal benefit" of the public schools. The complainants prayed that the injunction be made perpetual. Chase and the school directors replied by falling back on the routine argument that white parents would not continue sending their children to a school receiving blacks. Given this prospect, the school directors believed that the interests of "all" the children would be best met if the races were taught in separate schools. Their motive, they affirmed, was a sincere desire to furnish black children with such means of education as those children were entitled to by law but in such manner as would not interfere with the education of the white children.

Nearly a year elapsed before Judge Tipton handed down a decision. On May 22, 1873, he decreed that Chase and the school directors of District 6 were perpetually enjoined from occupying or using the separate schoolhouse on the district school lot for carrying on a "school for colored children exclusively at the expense of said District." His opinion was naked of any supporting reasoning or justification.

(It should be noted that the District 6 colored school was on the same lot as the regular school: the black children would have no farther to walk to the colored school than to the regular school. In *Chase* v. *Stephenson* the distance black children had to walk to the separate school was not a factor as it was in some cases to be discussed later in this chapter and in the earlier *Martha Crow* case.)

Immediately Chase and his fellow complainants prayed for and were granted permission to appeal to the state's supreme court. The case of *James A. Chase et al., appellants* v. *David Stephenson et al., appellees,* was heard in the January term, 1874, opinion filed June 19. The justices were Sidney Breese, chief justice, Democrat, and Pinkney H. Walker, Democrat, William K. McAllister, Democrat, John M. Scott, Republican, Benjamin R. Sheldon, probably a Republican, John Scholfield, Democrat, and Alfred M. Craig, Democrat. The Democrats outnumbered the Republicans five to two.[4]

Attorneys for the appellants were William E. Gapen and Henry A. Ewing, Republicans and partners in a Bloomington law firm. The brief they submitted to the supreme court paid major attention to arguments bearing on "all" and minor attention to arguments relating to "equal." They contended that a racially mixed school in District 6 would result in the withdrawal of white and black children and would bring the school board into violation of Section 48 of the free-schools law requiring district school boards to establish and keep in operation a sufficient number of free schools for the education of "all" the children in the district over age six and under twenty-one years.

Most of the white parents, Gapen and Ewing asserted, would refuse to allow their children to attend the district school if colored children were admitted as scholars into the same school with whites. Also, admitting blacks into the district school might interfere with their education as well. Separating the races was necessary and reasonable "because it preserved order and decorum, and prevented contacts and collisions in the school arising from well known repugnances." These were code words signifying that there would be harassment of black children and implying that under such circumstances the black parents would withdraw their children from the district school. A racially mixed school would deprive both races of schooling, so Gapen and Ewing concluded.[5]

Their arguments relating to "equal" were largely attempts to show that classification according to race for school purposes and the establishment of separate schools for the races did not contravene the 14th Amendment of the federal constitution by abridging the privileges and immunities of citizens of the United States. As authority the attorneys cited an Ohio case, *State of Ohio, ex rel. Garnes* v. *McCann et al.* (21 Ohio St. 198), in which the Ohio Supreme Court had ruled that equality of rights did not necessitate educating blacks and whites in the same school as long as the classification preserved "substantially equal school advantages." Gapen and Ewing did not define what the four words might mean, choosing to leave them as generalities unexplored.

For the appellees, attorneys Jonathan H. Rowell and John M. Hamilton, like Gapen and Ewing Republicans and partners in a Bloomington law firm, reversed the emphasis of the appellants' attorneys and devoted major attention to arguments derived from "equal" and minor attention to those from "all," and by also bringing into play the "good" as a source containing the specific characteristics and procedures of a good education. In doing so Rowell and Hamilton displayed a breadth of understanding and depth of insight amazingly sophisticated for a day when the nascent field of psychology had little to say about constructing attitudes and forging self-identities. Their operational definition of "good" as projected into "equal" was best expressed in the paragraph:

Here is a district with four colored children in it only. By law, they are entitled to an *equal education* with the other children of the district. We take it that this includes equal opportunities, equally good teachers, equal accommodation in the school house, equal facilities as to classes, and equal opportunities for improvement, by the associations of the class room. And that whenever a distinction is made between scholars of the same grade, either in the qualification of the teacher—in the school room—or in the arrangement of classes, that equal opportunity is not provided. It is useless to contend that a scholar has equal opportunities with another when he is told that he is not good enough to sit in the same room, to contend for the prizes in the same class, or to recite to a teacher paid to teach the favored scholars in the district, that he must be confined to a room too small for any school purpose; must be treated as an underling, and recite to a cheap teacher, willing to confine her labor to four children, in a 12 by 14 feet room, in a corner of the school house lot. It isn't equal opportunity, and no amount of protestation will make it so.[6]

This was an explication of policies, practices, and features that, in Rowell's and Hamilton's view, ought to be "equal" in a "good" education for "all." It specified intellectual and emotional influences and effects, promotive or retarding, that arose out of certain physical and human environments within the school and the classroom. It went beyond the "separate but equal" tangibles that were to be United States Supreme Court doctrine after *Plessy* v. *Ferguson* in 1896 and took into consideration the intangibles that were to be at the core of *Brown* v. *Board of Education* in 1954.

The rest of the brief consisted of arguments differentiating between public and private institutions and the social and personal rights appertaining to each, the commodiousness of the district schoolhouse and its ability to seat black children, and the financial burden laid upon the taxpayers of the district by separate schools for the races. On the last Rowell and Hamilton said that a colored school was unnecessary because the district school could accommodate all the children, black and white, who resided there. The colored school would occasion "large and unnecessary expense." Stephenson and the other appellees had already been forced to pay their portion of the expense of an additional schoolhouse and additional teacher and would be "continually" required to bear these unnecessary costs or, and here Rowell and Hamilton resorted to sarcasm, "be obliged to sell out and move away from this modern Egypt." It was the financial argument upon which the Illinois Supreme Court was to seize in rendering its decision.

The court found for the appellees. By a vote of six to one the justices affirmed the lower court's decree enjoining Chase and the District 6 school directors from requiring separate schooling for Negro children. Mr. Justice Craig delivered the majority opinion. He summarized the facts of the case, noting that the complaint was financial: four taxpayers had filed the bill to prevent the District 6 school directors from, it was charged, misappropriating public funds in which with other taxpayers the complainants had a direct interest. Craig noted further that on the other side the school directors' defense was that by law (here the reference was to Section 48 of the free-schools law of April 1, 1872, although it was not cited) school boards, committees, and directors were endowed with powers of adopting and enforcing all necessary rules and regulations for the management and government of the schools including the power of organizing separate schools for the races. Refuting this assumption of plenary powers by the directors, Craig argued that schools were public institutions and that the law contemplated that they be so managed as to give "all" children of school age in the district, irrespective of race or color, an "equal" right to the benefits of attendance. Therefore, Craig said, "while the directors, very properly, have large and discretionary powers in regard to the management and control of schools, in order to increase their usefulness, they have no power to make class distinctions, neither can they discriminate between scholars on account of their color, race or social position."[7]

To this point Craig was addressing the degree to which the powers of the school directors were limited by certain constraints imposed by the "all" and "equal" in Section 48 of the school law. It seemed as if he might move on to hand down a prohibition against all racially separate schooling. But he abruptly came to a halt on this line of logic and announced that in *Chase* v. *Stephenson* there were no questions of a kind that would be posed had the number of black children been sufficient for a separate school. Upon a case where the number of black children was sufficient the court was not expressing an opinion. He then reverted to the financial aspect of the case and rendered a judgment according to the cost principle. The local school directors' attempt to erect and continue a separate school for three or four black children when they could have been accommodated in the district school was, he maintained, to perpetrate a "fraud" on the taxpayers of the district. Any individual taxpayer had the right to interfere to prevent public funds "from being squandered in such a reckless, unauthorized manner." Citing no law or other authority, he wound up the case by concluding that the supreme court perceived no error in the decree of the circuit court and he affirmed that verdict.

Justice Pinkney H. Walker, the only member of the supreme court filing a dissent, addressed his objection, not to the financial elements of the case and his court's opinion, but to the limitations on the school directors' power for which Craig had argued. Walker declared that school directors possessed large discretion in selecting the means for providing facilities for the education of the district's children "so they [the school directors] furnished equal facilities to all the children." He did not elaborate on what "equal facilities" meant; rather he proceeded to indicate that he did not think the action of the school directors amounted to such an abuse of their powers as to call for the interposition of a court of equity. The decree of the lower court should be reversed.

The majority opinion of the court was hailed by State Superintendent Bateman in Circular No. 45 from his department on August 12, 1874, and in his tenth biennial report transmitted to the governor on December 15. Well might Bateman praise the opinion, for it had utilized the very financial principle he had long been advocating as the answer to the issue of racially separate or mixed schooling in districts where there were few black children. Too, the court had denied any intention of rendering an opinion that would be applicable in districts where the number of blacks was sufficient to avoid the extra costs of separation. Nor had the court in the financial paragraphs of the opinion said anything that would justify an intrusion upon the right of local option that Bateman wished to preserve for districts in which the number of blacks of school age exceeded a critical minimum. That minimum the court had put at three or four; Bateman put it at one to ten in his remarks on *Chase* v. *Stephenson*.[8]

Bateman was correct in thinking that a one to ten criterion in applying the cost principle would be viable for most of the school districts of the state. In 1872 there were 102 Illinois counties, with 11,231 school districts, and a black child population of school age of 8,167. If a county would have to have 111 school-age black children to have even a slight chance that one of its school districts would contain eleven or more such children to educate, then in 86 of the counties and 9,546 of the school districts, in which 2,594 blacks of school age resided, the financial principle as quantified by Craig and Bateman would apply and could furnish a reason and a motive for solving the separate–mixed school issue. Whether the school directors of these districts would choose to mix the races in the schools for the purpose of escaping extra costs and whether motives of economy would conquer motives of prejudice would be additional questions that would be posed. In any event there would remain 16 counties and 1,776 school districts with some 5,573 school-age blacks to which the financial principle would not, according to Craig's and Bateman's numerical standards, apply. What principles could the school boards or aggrieved blacks in those school districts apply?

They could turn to the pronouncements on black school rights in the dicta of the Craig opinion and the construction put on those dicta by Bateman in his biennial report. True, *Chase* v. *Stephenson* was a deviant school desegregation case. It had originated in protests against a separate colored school leveled by whites, not blacks. It had been brought into the circuit court by white taxpayers, not by black parents. The grounds of the state supreme court decision had been on financial injury done to taxpayers, almost all of whom were white not black, and the principle on which the decision hinged had been monetary not egalitarian. Yet in the course of his reasoning Craig had made statements of principles forbidding racial distinctions and discriminations. These were in the nature of dicta, apart from what he considered the essential financial complaint of the case, but these embodied principles that had now because of his opinion entered the stream of judicial precedent and thinking, becoming available to later plaintiffs, their counsel, and to judges.

Bateman had not been blind to the possibilities latent in Craig's dicta as they might arise in cases where the school districts would have more than ten black school-age children and where the cost criterion would not apply. In his tenth biennial report he discussed discriminations and distinctions in a context provided by the 14th Amendment of the United States Constitution. He saw that the amendment might be interpreted as divesting local school boards of options in responding to issues of racial separation. This interpretation he rejected. He quoted a New York Supreme Court decision and the Ohio Supreme Court ruling in *State of Ohio ex rel. William Garnes* v. *John W. McCann*, the same cited as authority by Gapen and Ewing, attorneys for Chase and the school directors of District 6, to prove that "equality of rights" as stipulated by the 14th Amendment did not confer upon blacks the right of being admitted to white schools.

What the 14th Amendme... guaranteed, Bateman insisted, was the right of the two races to have "equal" school "advantages." The races had the right of equal access to public schooling and this access could be in the form of separate or mixed schooling at the discretion of the district school board. When it was in the form of separate schooling, the schools must be equal in "facilities," by which Bateman apparently meant in physical features, and equal in "graded" classrooms and schools, by which he meant in schools organized by grades. All the blacks should not be collected together in a single room or grouped miscellaneously in a single school while whites were sorted out and put into grades corresponding to their mental and bodily maturity and their academic attainments. Blacks must be offered graded instruction if whites were. Nowhere in his discussion did Bateman betray any awareness of the intellectual, emotional, and psychological factors that Rowell and Hamilton had seen as precluding a genuinely equal education within separate arrangements.

Of these sources of principles to apply in cases arising in districts where many black children were to be educated, the justices of the state supreme court in later nineteenth-century school segregation cases drew mainly from the Henry law and Craig's dicta. They made no attempt to apply Bateman's definition of "equal" in facilities and grading or any other possible definitions of the term except in relation to walking distances between black children's homes and colored vis-à-vis regular district schools. One of the four subsequent cases, *The People ex rel. George Hunt, Attorney General v. Thomas W. McFall et al.*, in 1888 was decided on technicalities of quo warranto proceedings. The other cases were decided on substantive grounds. These were *The People ex rel. John Longress v. The Board of Education of the City of Quincy*, in 1882, *The People ex rel. John Peair v. The Board of Education of Upper Alton School District*, in 1889, and *The People ex rel. Scott Bibb v. The Mayor and Common Council of Alton*, in 1899.[9]

Longress, Peair, and Bibb were black parents who complained that their children were barred from the white schools and forced to attend "colored" schools. In reasoning on each case the court posed as salient the questions of whether the black children had been excluded from a school to which they had applied and whether this exclusion had been because of discrimination solely on account of race. "Yes" was the answer of the court to both questions and it found for the black parents in all three cases.

Longress deserves more than a word of mention. For the first time the supreme court took into consideration the full complement of relevant legislation and court rulings that had become available by the end of the year 1874: Article 8, Section 1, of the state constitution of 1870, Section 48 of the revised free-schools law of 1872, the Henry law of 1874, and the Craig opinion in 1874. *Longress* is interesting, too, in its resemblance to *Chase v. Stephenson*, for five of the seven justices of the 1874 bench were still sitting in 1882, the Democratic justices still outnumbered the Republicans, and again Alfred M. Craig, now chief justice, delivered the majority opinion and Pinkney H. Walker a dissenting opinion. Appropriately in view of his consistent espousal of black rights through the years ex-governor John M. Palmer was attorney for the Negro plaintiff.[10]

Known in Quincy as a reliable and competent blacksmith, John Longress had been born in Culpepper County, Virginia, and had come to Illinois in 1860. On September 17, 1879, he filed an affidavit in the circuit court of central Adams County swearing that he had resided for eighteen years in the Franklin school district of Quincy, living some five blocks from the district school. He had, he said, five children between the ages of six and twenty-one, "all of whom like himself are persons of African descent, commonly called colored persons." But under the regulations of the Quincy board of education the only school the Longress children were permitted to attend was the Lincoln school, about twenty blocks, one and one-half miles, away from home. There were more than 300 school-age persons of African descent who were, Longress testified, similarly situated. They were bona fide residents of the city living within the several districts near and convenient to district public schools, yet by the regulations of the board their "descent and color" excluded them from the schools of their home districts.[11]

On the same day James K. Edsall, attorney general of Illinois, presented on behalf of Longress a petition to the Adams County circuit court for leave to file information in the nature of a quo warranto. The information was that the Quincy board of education in the due and lawful exercise of its powers, granted by special act of the General Assembly, February 20, 1861, had divided the city into eight school districts and in each district had established and maintained a public school for the instruction of the persons of school age residing therein and otherwise qualified for admission under the laws of the state. But the board had unlawfully and without warrant in law, Edsall asserted, enforced the following rules: that the colored school of Quincy should be composed of colored pupils of the prescribed age and bona fide residents of the city, that no pupil of African descent should be permitted to attend any of the public schools of the city other than the colored school, and that all black pupils in the city should attend the Lincoln school and no other. Edsall prayed the court to summon before it the Quincy board of education to make answer.

The court did so. On November 12 the attorneys for the board appeared and filed pleas that in good faith the belief of the board was that the disputed rules and regulations were necessary and requisite for the good order, discipline, and efficiency of the schools and greatly promoted and enhanced the education of persons, white and black, entitled to instruction therein. A demurrer was filed on November 20 by the attorneys of the plaintiff contending that the pleas of the board's attorneys merely were matters of opinion and inference, not matters of fact. On December 6 John H. Williams, judge of the Adams County circuit court, ruled in favor of the school board. His reasoning is not disclosed in the record.

Judge Williams' decision was appealed and the state supreme court heard the case in the January term, 1882. The majority opinion, delivered by Chief Justice Craig, reversed the decree of the lower court. After summarizing the facts of the case, Craig began by presenting the question: Were the Quincy rules that excluded children of African descent from the district schools and forced them to attend a school reserved for their race alone authorized by state law? He then cited and interpreted the germane passages from the legislative and judicial corpus of authority that had accumulated from 1870 to 1875. Quoting Article 8, Section 1, of the Illinois constitution of 1870, "The General Assembly shall provide a thorough and efficient system of free schools, whereby *all* children of this State may receive a good common school education," and italicizing the "all" but not the "good," he declared that the section made no distinction in regard to the race or color of the children who were entitled to share in the benefits to be derived from public schooling.

He next quoted Section 48 of the free-schools law of April 1, 1872, to the effect that school boards should establish and keep in operation "a sufficient number of free schools for the proper accommodation of all children in the district, and shall secure to all such children the right and opportunity to an equal education in such free schools." This passage, he said, demonstrated the intent of the legislature to make all children, regardless of race or color, beneficiaries of the same rights and privileges of public schools.

His third quotation was from Section 1 of the Henry law stipulating that school boards whose duty it was to provide for the education of all school-age children in their jurisdictions were "prohibited from excluding, directly or indirectly, any such child from such school on account of the color of such child." He asserted that this statute was violated by the Quincy school board's rules preventing a colored child from attending the school in the district in which he or she lived and compelling him or her to travel several miles perhaps to a distant part of the city to a colored school. Finally from his own opinion in *Chase* v. *Stephenson* Craig quoted the dicta announcing that school boards had no power to make class distinctions or to discriminate between pupils on account of color, race, or social position.

In the course of his argument Craig also mentioned the 14th Amendment of the federal constitution, alluding not to "equal protection" or to "due process" but to the citizenship clauses by which, he said, persons of color were citizens of the United States and of the state in which they resided upon an equality with other citizens. Yet he declined to use the 14th Amendment as authority for prohibiting school boards from excluding Negro children from the public schools by such rules as those adopted by the Quincy officials. This was a question, according to Craig, that the Illinois Supreme Court did not deem it necessary to determine. Putting aside the 14th Amendment, it was clear from state law that school boards had no discretion "to deny a pupil of the proper age admission to the public schools on account of nationality, color or religion."

Having lined up and interpreted each of the pertinent texts,

Craig pushed on to a conclusion. He argued that the Illinois constitution and laws placed all children "upon a perfect equality" in regard to "admission" to the public schools. (Here obviously he was speaking of "equality" in the limited sense of "access.") Whether this was wise or unwise was a matter with which the court had no concern. The court was bound to declare the law as it found the law written. The Quincy school board had no authority to adopt and enforce the city regulations at issue; the judgment of the lower court was reversed and the cause remanded.[12]

In the later *Peair* and *Bibb* cases the central problem and the concepts on which the court's arguments and opinions focused were much the same as in *Longress*. Again black children were being denied admission into white schools, and again they were being subjected to pressures to induce or force them to attend a colored school. In *Peair* and *Bibb* as in *Longress* the court cited, quoted, or paraphrased the Henry law and the dicta from Craig's opinion forbidding school authorities from excluding black pupils or discriminating between pupils on account of color, race, or social position.

Had the court chosen to explore "discriminations" and "distinctions" beyond simple admission to schooling in *Longress*, *Peair*, and *Bibb*, it might have had something of lasting importance to say to the courts of the next century when school segregation cases revolved around the issues of "equal" and "separate." Instead the nineteenth-century court drew mainly from the first section of the Henry law of March 24, 1874, prohibiting school officers and school boards from "excluding" Negro children on account of color. The result was that opinions in the three cases hinged on "exclusion," "access," "admission," and "all" more than on "equal." Black children could not be denied admission to a school or be forced to attend a school solely because of their race. The district might organize a colored school, and if the black parents objected to having their children consigned to it or if the children had applied for admission to the district school and were barred from it, their parents could seek a remedy in the courts and the courts would undoubtedly uphold their cause. Or the parents might employ the punishing power of their vote and embark on a campaign to unseat the offending school board members and elect members more sympathetic to their plight. Alternatives offered by the Illinois Supreme Court thus placed the initiative and expense squarely on the blacks and exposed them likewise to the dangers of reprisals from the whites.

The nineteenth-century state supreme court decisions reinforced the emphasis upon right of access to public schooling mandated by the Henry law, and in doing this they contributed to progress in the field of education for blacks. But no nineteenth-century Illinois legislation or judicial verdict had forbidden separate schooling or schools for the races. In 1940–41 there were still 46 "colored schools" enrolling 9,180 black pupils in the state. Among these schools were still the Lincoln school in Quincy and the Lovejoy school in Alton, the schools that the supreme court of the previous century had declared the Longress and Bibb children could not be forced to attend. Yet those schools were still functioning as segregated schools with enrollments of 321 and 119 black pupils.[13]

The dialectics heard in the nineteenth-century Illinois Supreme Court (except in the argument of the Rowell and Hamilton brief) had centered mainly on "all" and to a much lesser degree upon "equal" and "good" in the triad of terms governing public education in Illinois. Such attention as the courts did pay to "equal" was in the sense of equality of access to the benefits of public schooling no matter how delivered, whether through racially separate or mixed schools, so long as the colored school did not lead to a squandering of public funds, did not require long and dangerous travel from home, and did not provide instruction in the midst of inferior physical facilities in an ungraded setting. This remained the situation until the post–World War II years when federal legislation and federal court decisions followed by state legislation and state court decisions began to focus on the task of extracting meanings and performance criteria from "equal."

10 ═══════════════════════════

Yesterday, Today, Tomorrow

By now it is hardly necessary to repeat that the larger question I have had in mind is "How have disadvantaged groups within our society tried to secure the benefits and rights the society has granted to others, not to them?" I have taken the struggle of Illinois blacks for public-school and other rights as my case for study, and I have turned to "bargaining power" and the nineteenth-century American partnership ideal of "community" for concepts in marshaling and interpreting data. The principal kinds of data I have used have been petitions to and measures presented in the Illinois General Assemblies, the voting behavior of state senators and House members as recorded in Assembly journals, and the information and views contained in newspaper articles, editorials, and letters, in minutes of conventions, committees, and meetings, and in documents in the files of historical societies and state and local archives. I have also suggested possible connections between biographical variables and attitudes, motives, and actions. Here in this final chapter are the conclusions I have drawn from the data and certain speculations I have ventured to offer on the basis of those data. Too, I have spoken out personally in a way I have avoided in the previous chapters of objective narration, exposition, and analysis.

As for the concept of "power" and what this study might contribute to thinking about it, one approach would be to take Galbraith's *Anatomy of Power* and see how it holds up when tested against my data and conclusions. In Chapter 1, I noted that Galbraith has divided power into the compensatory, condign, and conditioned, similar to the rewarding, punishing, and dialectical terms I have used. Where I depart from Galbraith is in his resort to pugnacious, domineering words like "submission," "imposition," and "enforcement" in his treatment of all aspects of power. Such machismo diction may be appropriate when referring to the application of condign (punishing) power but wide of the mark when employed to describe the intent and operation of the conditioned (dialectical) and the compensatory (rewarding). I think my own definition of power as the capacity to "elicit" a favorable response from a hostile or indifferent opposition is more faithful to the tone, attitudes, and behaviors that were active elements in situations in which before the war the Illinois blacks appealed to the religious and patriotic sentiments of the whites and in which after the war the blacks appealed in addition to the self-interest of the community by promising rewards that would follow upon their access to public schooling.

Under "organization" Galbraith talks of the need for unity among the members of a disadvantaged group. They must, he emphasizes, submit to the common purpose of the organization so that it achieves "bimodal symmetry." Internal discipline begets external power: "from this internal exercise of power comes the ability of an organization to impose its will externally." Here Galbraith is giving passing mention to what I have suggested at greater length is one of the dangers of public controversies within the disadvantaged group. It may break up into factions, each of which applies power in an attempt to extract concessions from a target group. The result may be that the power brought to bear is fragmented and the scattered application of power scores no bunched hits and falls short of maximum impact, as happened on occasion to Illinois blacks in their petitioning.

Another deficiency in Galbraith's analysis is his failure to recognize that latent power may be perceived as a reason for granting a right or benefit. To Galbraith power does not exist unless it is overtly exercised upon an opposing group. Yet, as we have discovered, Illinois blacks were given public school rights partly because the whites saw that the blacks possessed the power, potentially, of nurturing or blighting the best hopes of the community. Public-school rights were conferred on blacks so as to make certain that their power, if ever committed to use, would be applied in a fashion that would be promotive, not regressive, to the common welfare. The perception of power possessed may be as effective a motivating force as the actuality of power exerted.

Nor does Galbraith offer us a well-rounded picture of power as it operates in and by the courts. He treats courts only as agencies for dispensing penalties and regulating the powers of government; he admits to ignoring them as an "original source of power." But, as I have explained in Chapter 9, the idealized image we have of the courts is that they are sanctuaries created by the society in which its problems are solved by a process of applying dialectical power without contamination from greed or fear. It is through the courts that the best intelligence and purest wisdom of the community are presumed to deal with the issues and grievances that emerge when human beings live together in close proximity. The courts as a source of power and as a tribunal in which power is exercised deserve a lengthier treatment than Galbraith (or I) have given them.

As for the concept of "community," we have found that in nineteenth-century Illinois it had both positive and negative attributes. Perhaps its American origins lie in the covenantal, congregational nature of Massachusetts Bay Puritanism, defined by John Winthrop on the deck of the *Arbella* when he told the assembled company that "wee must delight in eache other, make others Condicions our owne reioice together, mourne together, labour, and suffer together, allwayes haueing before our eyes our Commission and Community in the worke, our Community as members of the same body." As most of Winthrop's audience were of the "same body" in religion, politics, and culture, he and they could assume that the lines of influence flowing from church, government, legislature, courts, schools, and family would be compatible and that these institutions would together instill the values needed for the perpetuation of the community. But even in the Massachusetts Bay Colony deviations from the common body of beliefs and failures by the shaping institutions were to occur and would be met by excommunication and exile. The historic American concept of community would carry within it ingredients of sharing and participation and ingredients of tribalism and exclusion.[1]

In the first half of the nineteenth century the tide of immigration into the United States bore on its current a variety of peoples who had lived under differing governments and who had differing religious, cultural, and ethnic backgrounds. Their children and the children of the old American families growing up in a new age would have to receive a stronger, more systematic inculcation of the traditional native values and allegiances if the "community" in the American sense were to survive. This inculcation, the leaders of the society agreed, should be one of the most important of the tasks performed by the public school. The common attitudes and common beliefs should be transmitted by the common school. So it was that the partnership attribute of community life, as it was described, for example, in the memorial to the General Assembly from the Illinois State School Convention in 1844, supplied the premise on which the arguments for universal, free, and public schooling were reared.

For the community's school to be attended by all, poor and rich alike, it must be tuitionless; for it to be free and for it to be successful in carrying out the task assigned to it, it must be sponsored, financed, and controlled by the community. It must be public. This was the logical argument made by the governors, legislators, state superintendents of public instruction, administrators, teachers, and lay friends of popular education. Psychologically these messages, reports, and speeches appealed to fear or hope. If allowed to go unschooled, the rising generation would become a threat to the safety, prosperity, and happiness of the community and lower the quality of shared living enjoyed by all. If rightly schooled, the rising generation would preserve and enhance the interacting, participating, and mutual character of the American community and would elevate the quality of community life to which all give, from which all receive.

But "all" in antebellum and bellum Illinois did not include everyone residing within the territorial boundaries of a community. The blacks were "pariahs." They were barred altogether from the voting booth and the courtroom and in large part from the social and civic sectors of society. They held the humblest of occupations. They were generally an inoffensive, law-abiding people. They would not be dangerous to the community; they could not improve the quality of community life. As they did not come within the embrace of the usual arguments for free, universal, and public schooling, the question of whether they were schooled or unschooled was not of much concern to most members of most Illinois communities. Because they were isolated and excluded, the blacks were not in a position to draw upon arguments directed to the self-interest of the community. Rather the arguments that they and their white friends made for their schooling were directed to the opposition's sense of piety, benevolence, and justice and reverence for the religious and patriotic precepts of the Bible and Declaration of Independence.[2] But in 1870, that year of wonders, their bargaining power underwent a transformation from weakness into comparative strength. Having the vote and sharing in the fruits of Republican dominance, they penetrated into other sectors of community life as well. Schooling for them was recognized as being in the self-interest of all citizens because the blacks' actions could have effects, salutary or injurious, upon the fortunes of the community. The blacks could be a "blessing" or a "curse." Which they would be depended upon their receiving the developmental or disciplinary acculturation offered by the school and the schooling environment. Now they did come within the embrace of the usual arguments for universal, free, and public education. The consequence was that the free-schools law was revised to eliminate the restrictive "white" and the Henry law was passed to "protect colored children in their rights to attend public schools." Responding, most local school boards admitted black children into district schools or separate "colored" schools.

One is led to wonder whether the decision to provide all-race district schools or "colored" schools and take sides on the issue of racially separate or mixed schooling was not related to adherence to a particular rationale for universal education. As we have seen, there were two rationales presented in the arguments. The first said that all children could become a "blessing" to the community if given an education that would cultivate their faculties and teach them to think for themselves. This was to take a "developmental" view, conceiving children to be human beings possessing talents and capacities that should be nursed and stimulated to their uppermost potential. It was a postulate that would support a belief that when black children grew up and participated in community life, they could do their part in furthering the happiness, security, and prosperity enjoyed in common by the citizens of town, city, county, state, and nation. Such a conception of the potentialities of children, of appropriate education for them, and of what their adult role might be would introduce standards of meliorism into the education planned for them. These were standards that would apply to both black and white children and would be best met, it might be argued, if the races were exposed together to the same instruction and school environments.

This was the reasoning of Professor Allison Davis of the University of Chicago, the most prominent black scholar in the state, when he declared in May 1954 that the United States Supreme Court ruling in *Brown* v. *Board of Education of Topeka* would result in "a tremendous increase in the fund of ability and skill available to our country" and that the survival of the United States depended "on its developing the ability of millions of our citizens whose capacities have been crippled by segregation." It was implied in the *Brown* decision itself by the statement about "the importance of education in our democratic society," because required in the performance of "our most basic public responsibilities" and providing the "very foundation of good citizenship." [3]

Conversely another rationale emphasized the "preventive" purpose of universal education. The persons holding this view saw some children—whether because of race, ethnicity, socioeconomic class, religious affiliation, or physical, mental, or emotional traits—as in need of schooling that would prevent them from growing up to be dangerous, a "curse," to the community. This rationale anticipated that they would be adults who, without schooling, might be a drag on the progress of society and even a factor tending toward its decline. A corollary would be that such children must be taught in a manner that would keep them from becoming disruptive of community life and a menace to its happiness, security, and prosperity. In school they must be trained in a disciplinary mode. A conception of this nature, that some children might become dangerous to society (or to the quality of life enjoyed by the ascendant groups in society), might introduce dominating standards of restrictiveness and control into their schooling, standards most effectively met, it might be argued, if specialized treatment were applied in schools reserved for them alone.

Speculation aside, one notices in this discussion certain lessons that other deprived groups might heed. The partnership nature of the American community to the extent that it is an ideal and an actuality has not lost its power to convince and inspire. It can still furnish a major premise that with minor premises can yield conclusions that sway and win. Nor have suffrage rights diminished in potency. The ballot can be used as an instrument to reward and punish. Possession of suffrage rights can be seen as evidence that those persons who have been excluded have come to occupy positions in the community that render them capable, if they so desire, of harming or improving the life shared in common by its citizens. Political power still affords the best pacific means of bringing about the enactment of laws that will provide a firm footing for those who are struggling to climb upward to equality. A renewed appreciation of the rewarding and punishing opportunities conferred by the ballot is the motivating impetus behind the registration and voting drives mounted by the black leaders in the 1970s and eighties and recently, in imitation of the blacks, by the leaders of the Hispanics.

Another message conveyed by this study has to do with the versatility and energy a disadvantaged group is able and willing to put forth in its own behalf. Its chances of succeeding may be proportionate to the number and kinds of levers of power available to it and to the amount of effort it is willing to expend in finding other groups that will collaborate with it in promoting its cause. The more instrumentalities such a group tries the more likely it may be that one instrument will succeed or that the cumulative effect of all will breach the confining barriers. Trying them all would permit, too, an assessment of each and guesses and predictions about the circumstances under which one or a combination of some or all of those available would have maximum impact. And the amount and kinds of effort exerted by the disadvantaged group might have a bearing on the amount and kinds of backing it would get from other groups. If the members of a group are vigorous and united in endeavors to obtain the right or benefit they proclaim they want, this may be taken as proof of their determination to strive together for a prize they agree is of first priority. Lacking proof, other groups may doubt the toughness of their resolve and become hesitant about entering into coalitions with them.

Some of the propositions laid down in the preceding paragraphs are postulates; some are anchored in the data of this study. The data show that Illinois blacks did not sit back idly and wait for sympathetic whites to run to their rescue. They sent delegates to national colored conventions where with their brethren they made addresses to the American public, drew up plans for national campaigns, and did their best to nurture an esprit de corps among their people throughout the country. At home they attempted to do as much, meeting in two state colored conventions before the war and three after. They established state organizations like the School Fund Association, the State Repeal Association, and the State Suffrage Association, with satellite councils, committees, auxiliary leagues, and local chapters. They gathered in rallies, meetings, and marches, wrote letters to the white newspapers and articles for the national Negro journals, and lobbied in the corridors of the state capitol, city and town halls, and offices of the district boards of education. By themselves or in conjunction with whites they sent petitions to the General Assemblies. They brought schooling suits into the lower courts and, beginning with *Longress,* fought these up into the Illinois Supreme Court. In Chicago they applied physical force to end the separate school policy. As soon as they had won suffrage rights, they became active in the Republican party and capitalized on the avenues of opportunity opening up to them.

A discussion like this of the Illinois blacks' use of power must not brake to a stop without speaking of the models they have bequeathed to later generations of their own people and to other deprived groups struggling for a share of the fruits of American community life. Of all the disadvantaged groups in American society the blacks had been the most disadvantaged. But in Illinois they did not surrender tamely to isolations, separations, and deprivations. Against heavy odds they battled to win the rights they believed should be theirs. They had been resourceful, employing methods of communicating grievances and for eliciting or forcing responses that could stock a depository of examples of strategies and tactics in the uses of power upon which in the future their own and other disadvantaged groups might draw. This is not to say that twentieth-century Illinois blacks in waging their own battles have been aware of equivalent efforts by their nineteenth-century forebears. Probably not. But this study can perform one of the traditional services of history: it can recover from obscurity the experiences of past humans and bring a knowledge of these experiences to present and future humans so that they may utilize that knowledge as it becomes relevant to their concerns.

Nevertheless warning flags should be flown here and there in this account of the experiences of nineteenth-century Illinois blacks. Lessons are to be learned from their mistakes. It would be logical to assume that a disadvantaged group that splits into factions, each with its own notions about appropriate means and ends, would become vulnerable to accusations from its enemies and complaints from its friends that its members do not know what they want (and do not much care), since they are unable to reach consensus on what should be first among their avowed goals. Illinois blacks did suffer from dissensions within the ranks. Fragmentation had ensued over the issue of colonization and over where acquiring political rights and gaining public-school rights should be placed, respectively, in their hierarchy of priorities. Within the field of school rights they differed on whether they wished to be exempted from the school tax, have it rebated to them for financing independent schools of their own, or continue to pay the tax and demand that their children, as children of taxpayers, should be admitted to the public schools. Having public-school rights, they differed on whether their children should go to schools attended by whites or by blacks only. These differences hurt them in their efforts to win favorable action from members of the General Assemblies and from delegates to the state constitutional convention.

It would be a mistake to blame on factionalism alone the failure of Illinois blacks to get organized support from whites before the war. The blacks had bad luck in timing; they were one of those disadvantaged groups that are victims of adverse circumstances arising out of the tempo and sequencing of events. Illinois was the last in the lower tier of states of the Old Northwest to be settled. In Ohio and Indiana the antislavery societies and religious denominations had a head start and could ride the crest of influence for a prolonged span of time. The Ohio Antislavery Society and the Indiana Committee on People of Color of the Antislavery Friends had a chance to recruit helpers and to mature plans for, among other objectives, enlarging educational opportunities for black children.

But in Illinois the antislavery societies had barely organized by 1840, and after peaking in a flurry of petitioning for the repeal of laws oppressive to blacks in the mid-1840s, they declined into purveyors of empty rhetoric at ceremonious annual meetings that were barren of concrete results. The ladies' branch did assist in arranging schooling for a few blacks, though the reform-minded women of the state soon became immersed instead in crusades for temperance and equal rights for their own sex. Meanwhile the antislavery men were shifting from methodologies of moral suasion to those of political action with no happier outcome for the state's blacks. The Liberty and Anti-Nebraska parties were feeble in Illinois and the Republican party in the antebellum period was preoccupied with national issues and not inclined to pay much attention to the plight of the Illinois black. Nor, for whatever reason, did any denominational or religious institution ally itself with the black cause before the war.

After the war and especially after the blacks had obtained suffrage rights from the state constitution of 1870 the situation became very different, obviously. Triumphant Republicanism, the white organization that was to dominate Illinois politics for decades, had pledged itself to the achievement of black rights. Its incentives were gratitude for black enlistments in the Northern army, a resolve to complete the unfinished agenda of the war, a desire to reap a full harvest from the blood and treasure sacrificed in preserving the Union and freeing the slave, and an appreciation of the opportunities and dangers brought by the blacks' participation in community life. Not entirely unfounded, too, was the Democrats' allegation that the Republicans saw the advantages of having loyal Negroes flock to the polls to cast their votes for the Grand Old Party.

Coincidental with the solidifying of Republican support was a rupturing of the front the Democrats had always maintained against measures for black rights. A splinter group of Democrats emerged, predicting that their party was fated to go down to defeat until it abandoned its traditional obsession with issues involving the Negro and substituted for those issues others relating to sound economic policy and honesty and efficiency in government. A coalition of unanimous Republicans and dissident Democrats outvoted the old, Negro-hating, Bourbon Democrats on the rights bills enacted between 1870 and 1875. No longer did the blacks have to engage in a lonely struggle for the right of sending their children to the public schools. They had achieved greater rewarding, punishing, and dialectical power themselves, and now had an ally, the Republican party, with overwhelming power in the political arena.

Has this study anything to tell us about the future course of the blacks' struggle for equal rights? It does give us some hints that the history of the Illinois blacks' struggle may be hypothesized as cyclical, as proceeding through stages.

The first stage, lasting from 1818 to 1875, the period on which this study has centered, may be described as one in which the blacks attempted to eliminate restrictive language in the laws and win enactments that would bestow on them the legal political, civil, economic, social, and schooling rights and benefits enjoyed by others. A second phase began in 1875 and extended over approximately the next seventy-five years. It was a period of local effort in which the legal victories at the state and federal levels in the previous stage were regarded as sufficient to enable blacks to progress within the local community. No more pro-black legislation was necessary unless, as in the instance of the Illinois civil rights act of 1885, rips in the fabric of legal rights woven earlier had to be mended. Concerted group effort was to be aimed at rewarding, punishing, or persuading local officialdom into compliance with the law. This tendency by individuals, ad hoc groups, organizations, and chapters of black leagues and societies to engage in local effort was reinforced by the state supreme court's verdicts in the *Longress, Peair,* and *Bibb* cases, saddling black parents with the responsibility of taking the initiative in seeking redress in the courts, if it were to be sought at all, when their children had been excluded from the district schools.

A third stage in the 1940s, 1950s, and early 1960s was like the first stage of struggle in that the blacks, frustrated at the local level, utilized their bargaining power in attempts to procure the amendment of existing federal and state laws, the enactment of fresh laws, and the reinterpretation of statutes and constitutional articles by the courts, all to demolish the barriers that still hemmed them in.

As in the aftermath of the Civil War so in the aftermath of World War II, another war in which racial philosophies and racial factors were involved, changes in the society and in the blacks' attitudes and expectations impelled them to make efforts to improve their condition. In these efforts they were assisted by the fact that their numbers in the state had increased to 645,980 in 1950 and 1,037,470 in 1960 and that one of the very few advantages of ghettoization was that being concentrated together residentially they could, if they would, attain political dominance in their voting districts. They could, if they would, elect persons of their own race to the General Assemblies and to Congress. They would then have their own representatives participating directly in the law-making process and occupying positions in the Senate and House to speak and act for them. This is what happened in Chicago and the Chicago example could encourage blacks elsewhere to do likewise.

Thus at the beginning of the third stage into which we have divided the history of the Ilinois blacks' struggle for equal school rights, there were five blacks serving in the 62nd General Assembly of 1941 while at the end of the period in 1965 there were eleven blacks serving in the 74th General Assembly. During that quarter of a century the two most important pieces of state legislation relating to black school rights, the Jenkins amendment of 1949 and the Armstrong act of 1963, were sponsored by black members of the house.

In the 66th General Assembly on June 21, 1949, Charles J. Jenkins, representing the third district of Cook County, Chicago, offered an amendment adding a fourth section to the annual school finance bill. His amendment prohibited the allotment of any portion of the state school fund to school districts in which students were excluded from or segregated in any public school because of race, color, or nationality. The amendment passed and became part of an appropriations bill approved by the governor on June 30, 1949.

Some fourteen years later in the 73rd General Assembly meeting on January 30, 1963, Charles F. Armstrong, from the twenty-second district of Cook County, and other legislators introduced a bill to amend certain sections of the school code. Among those proposed were several forbidding boards of education to exclude pupils from or segregate them in public schools on account of their color, race, or nationality. One of the proposed sections also charged boards of education with the responsibility of changing or revising school district boundaries or

creating new ones "in a manner which will take into consideration the prevention of segregation and the elimination of separation of children in public schools because of color, race or nationality." This, the so-called Armstrong bill, was adopted by the
House and Senate and was approved on June 13, 1963.[4]
Manifestly the Jenkins amendment and the Armstrong law
had linkages with events occurring in the first period ending in
1875, though neither man may have been aware of it. Both the
amendment and the law built on the Henry act of March 24,
1874, as it had continued in the statutes and as it had been
broadened by subsequent legislation. Both Jenkins and Armstrong carried the provisions of the Henry act a step further. To
the Henry act's penalty of fines for exclusion Jenkins had added
the additional penalty of denial of money from the state school
fund. Armstrong, too, had kept the prohibitions of the Henry
act, but his bill had required the positive remedial measure of
revising district boundaries to eliminate racial segregation and
separation in the schools. Jenkins had, moreover, displayed a
trust in the curative strength of the financial principle that was
similar to that expressed by Newton Bateman a century before.
Indeed when Jenkins had offered his amendment he had promised that it would wipe out "Jim Crowism" in the public schools of
the state: "by tying the antidiscrimination angle to the state's
purse strings we can eliminate the racial problem in Illinois in
another generation." This sounds much like Bateman's principle
that "when the continued indulgence of a mere prejudice is
found to be expensive, it is not probable that it will be very long
persisted in."[5]
Successful in having more favorable laws passed, the blacks
embarked in the period after 1965 on a fourth phase of effort re-
sembling that taken in the second phase. Once more the tendency was toward individual and group striving at the local level
in order to obtain compliance with state and federal enactments
and court rulings made in the previous period. In some localities
the blacks exerted punishing power through boycotts, sit-ins,
marches, and violence, but by the 1980s they had come to rely
on dialectical and rewarding powers that were exerted chiefly
through political channels. The black leaders recognized the
power inherent in suffrage rights, and they mobilized massive
voter registrations and voting drives as a means of rewarding

and punishing political parties and candidates and of electing members of their own race to legislative, executive, and other offices in city and town government. Having captured positions of power, they could employ the prerogatives of office to distribute patronage, give out coveted appointments, assign lucrative contracts, and compel obedience to federal and state civil rights and school legislation.

It is still too early to tell what the next stage will be in the Illinois blacks' struggle for equal rights and for an equal share in the benefits that accrue from community life. If, despite the overlappings and crudities that inevitably creep into any attempt to periodicize or establish a cycle motif, the pattern of stages postulated here has nonetheless some semblance of validity, we may expect that the black struggle will continue to alternate between, on the one hand, phases of effort directed at the state and federal levels and intended to elicit legislative and judicial responses and, on the other hand, phases of effort directed at the local level and intended to reward, force, or persuade local citizens and local officials to obey the laws and carry out the verdicts of the courts.

What did a group of disadvantaged persons do yesterday? What are they doing today? What will they do tomorrow? These are separate as questions but the answers to them needn't be.

References

Notes

Index

References

African Repository, The.

Alexander, Archibald. *A History of Colonization on the Western Coast of Africa.* Philadelphia: William S. Martien, 1846.

Andreas, A. T. *History of Chicago.* Vol. 1, Ending with the Year 1857; Vol. 2, From 1857 until the Fire of 1871; Vol. 3, From the Fire of 1871 until 1885. Chicago: A. T. Andreas, Publisher, 1884, 1885, 1886.

Angle, Paul M., ed. *Herndon's Life of Lincoln.* Greenwich, Conn.: Fawcett Publications, 1961.

Babeuf, Julius. *Babeuf's Directory of the City of Springfield and Sangamon County, Illinois, 1882–3.* Springfield: Compiled and Published by J. Babeuf, 1882.

Bailey, John C. W. *John C. Bailey's Chicago Directory for the Year 1864–5.* Chicago: John C. W. Bailey, Publisher, 1864.

Bailey, John C. W., and Edwards, Richard. *Bailey and Edwards' Chicago Directory, 1868.* Chicago: Edwards and Co., 1868.

Bateman, Newton. Official Correspondence. Illinois State Archives, Springfield.

———. Papers. Illinois State Historical Library, Springfield.

Bateman, Newton, and Selby, Paul. *Historical Encyclopedia of Illinois.* Vol. 1. Chicago: Munsell Publishing Co., 1900.

Bell, Howard H. "Chicago Negroes in the Reform Movement, 1847–1853." *Negro History Bulletin,* 21, no. 7 (Apr. 1958), 153–55.

———. *Minutes of the Proceedings of the National Negro Conventions, 1830–1864.* New York: Arno Press and New York Times, 1969.

Bellah, Robert N., Madsen, Richard, Sullivan, William M., Swidler, Ann, and Tipton, Steven M. *Habits of the Heart: Individualism and Commitment in American Life.* Berkeley: University of California Press, 1985.

Bench and Bar of Chicago, The. Chicago: American Biographical Publishing Co., 1883.

Bennett, Fremont O. *Politics and Politicians of Chicago, Cook County, and Illinois.* Memorial Volume, 1787–1887. Chicago: Blakely Printing Co., 1886.

References

Biographical Encyclopaedia of Illinois of the Nineteenth Century, The. Philadelphia: Galaxy Publishing Co., 1875.

Biographical Sketches of the Leading Men of Chicago. Chicago: Wilson and St. Clair, Publishers, 1868.

Bloomington Pantagraph.

Bradwell, James B. "The Colored Bar of Chicago." *Chicago Legal News,* 29, no. 10 (Oct. 31, 1896), 75–78.

Brigham, William B. *The Story of McLean County and Its Schools.* Bloomington: Published by the Author, 1951.

Brown, William W. *An Historical Sketch of the Early Movement in Illinois for the Legalization of Slavery.* Chicago: Press of Church, Goodman, and Donnelley, 1865.

Buck, Solon Justus. *Illinois in 1818.* Springfield: Illinois Centennial Commission, 1917.

Cairo Bulletin. Title varies from *Cairo Evening Bulletin* to *Cairo Daily Bulletin* to *Cairo Bulletin.* I use the last for all references.

Carter, Horace E. *Reports of Cases Argued and Determined in the Supreme Court of Judicature of the State of Indiana, May, 1850 to May, 1851, Inclusive.* Indianapolis: Austin H. Brown, Printer, 1853.

Chicago Board of Education. *First Annual Report of the Superintendent of Public Schools of the City of Chicago.* Chicago: Democrat Book and Job Office, 1854.

———. *Fourth Annual Report of the Superintendent of the Public Schools of the City of Chicago, for the Year Ending February 1, 1858.* Chicago: Chicago Daily Press, 1858.

———. *Report of the President of the Board of Education and the Fifth Annual Report of the Superintendent of Public Schools, for the Year Ending February 1, 1859.* Chicago: Scott and Co., 1859.

———. *Eighth Annual Report of the Board of Education, for the Year Ending December 31, 1861.* Chicago: Chicago Times Book and Job Printing Establishment, 1862.

———. *Tenth Annual Report of the Board of Education, for the Year Ending December 31, 1863.* Chicago: Chicago Times Book and Job Printing House, 1864.

———. *Sixteenth Annual Report of the Board of Education, for the Year Ending July 1, 1870.* Chicago: Rand, McNally and Co., 1870.

———. *Twenty-Fifth Annual Report of the Board of Education, for the Year Ending July 31, 1879.* Appendix: Historical Sketches of the Public School System of the City of Chicago. Chicago: Clark and Edwards. 1880.

Chicago City Council. "Proceedings, 1862–1864." Law Institute Vault, Law Library, Chicago Civic Center.

Chicago Commission on Race Relations. *The Negro in Chicago.* Chicago: University of Chicago Press, 1922.

Chicago Evening Journal.

Chicago Post.

Chicago Times. In the text and chapter notes I always cite the *Chicago Times* as *Times.* When the reference is to the *New York Times*, the citation reads *N.Y. Times.*

Chicago Tribune.

Clayton, John. *The Illinois Fact Book and Historical Almanac, 1673–1968.* Carbondale and Edwardsville: Southern Illinois University Press, 1970.

Cole, Arthur Charles. *The Constitutional Debates of 1847.* Springfield: Trustees of the Illinois State Historical Library, 1919.

———. *The Era of the Civil War, 1848–1870.* Springfield: Illinois Centennial Commission, 1919.

Decatur Board of Education. *Thirty-Fifth Annual Report of the Board of Education, Decatur, Illinois, 1900.* Decatur: Herald Printing and Stationery Co., 1900.

Dewey, John. *The Public and Its Problems.* Denver: Alan Swallow, 1957.

Dillon, Merton L. "The Antislavery Movement in Illinois, 1809–1844." Ph.D. diss., University of Michigan, 1951.

Donald, David. *Charles Sumner and the Rights of Man.* New York: Alfred A. Knopf, 1970.

Drake, St. Clair, and Cayton, Horace R. *Black Metropolis.* Revised and enlarged edition. 2 vols. New York: Harcourt, Brace and World, 1962.

Eames, Charles M. *Historic Morgan and Classic Jacksonville.* Jacksonville, Ill.: Daily Journal Steam Job Printing Office, 1885.

Edwards, Richard. *Merchants' Chicago Census Report and Statistical Review, Embracing a Complete Directory of the City.* Chicago: Richard Edwards Publisher, 1871.

Encyclopaedia of Biography of Illinois. 2 vols. Chicago: Century Publishing and Engraving Co., 1892, 1894.

Erickson, Leonard Ernest. "The Color Line in Ohio Public Schools, 1829–1890." Ph.D. diss., Ohio State University, 1959.

Fehrenbacher, Don E. *Chicago Giant: A Biography of "Long John" Wentworth.* Madison: American History Research Center, 1957.

Fitzpatrick, John C. *Journals of the Continental Congress, 1774–1789.* Vol. 28. Washington: Government Printing Office, 1933.

Fitzwilliam, Sarah Raymond. "History of the Public Schools of Bloomington." *Transactions of the McLean County Historical Society.* Vol. 2. Bloomington: Pantagraph Printing Co., 1903.

Flower, George. *History of the English Settlement in Edwards County, Illinois.* Chicago: Fergus Printing Co., 1882.

Frederick Douglass' Paper.

Freeman, Norman L. *Reports of Cases at Law and in Chancery Argued and*

Determined in the Supreme Court of Illinois. Vol. 71. Springfield: Printed for the Reporter, Journal Co., 1876.

————. *Reports of Cases at Law and in Chancery Argued and Determined in the Supreme Court of Illinois.* Vol. 101. Springfield: Printed for the Reporter, 1882.

————. *Reports of Cases at Law and in Chancery Argued and Determined in the Supreme Court of Illinois.* Vol. 124. Springfield: H. W. Rokker, Printer, 1889.

————. *Reports of Cases at Law and in Chancery Argued and Determined in the Supreme Court of Illinois.* Vol. 127. Springfield: H. W. Rokker, Printer, 1889.

Gager, John. *Gager's Chicago City Directory for the Year Ending June 1st 1857.* Chicago: John Gager and Co., 1856.

Galbraith, John Kenneth. *The Anatomy of Power.* Boston: Houghton Mifflin Co., 1983.

Gliozzo, Charles A. *John Jones and the Repeal of the Illinois Black Laws.* Duluth: Social Sciences Research Publications, University of Minnesota, Duluth, 1975.

Gosnell, Harold F. *Negro Politicians.* Chicago: University of Chicago Press, 1935.

Halpin, Thomas M. *Halpin's Chicago City Directory, 1865–6.* Eighth Annual Edition. Chicago: T. M. Halpin, Compiler and Publisher, 1865.

Harlow, George H. *Thirtieth General Assembly of the State of Illinois, Official Directory.* Springfield: D. W. Lusk, State Printer, 1877.

Harris, I. C. *The Colored Men's Professional and Business Directory of Chicago.* Chicago: I. C. Harris, Publisher, 1885–86.

Harris, N. Dwight. *A History of Negro Servitude in Illinois and of the Slavery Agitation in that State, 1719–1864.* Chicago: A. C. McClurg and Co., 1904.

Heller, Herbert L. "Negro Education in Indiana from 1816 to 1869." Ed.D. diss., Indiana University, 1951.

Herrick, Mary J. *The Chicago Schools: A Social and Political History.* Beverly Hills: Sage Publications, 1971.

Hicken, Victor. *Illinois in the Civil War.* Urbana: University of Illinois Press, 1966.

Hill, Roscoe R. *Journals of the Continental Congress, 1774–1789.* Vol. 32 (1787). Washington: Government Printing Office, 1936.

History of Adams County, Illinois. Chicago: Murray, Williamson and Phelps, 1879.

History of Jo Daviess County, Illinois. Chicago: H. F. Kett Co., 1878.

History of Knox County, Illinois. Chicago: Chas. C. Chapman and Co., 1878.

History of McLean County, Illinois. Chicago: Wm. LeBaron Jr. and Co., 1878.

History of Sangamon County, Illinois. Chicago: Inter-State Publishing Co., 1881.

Homel, Michael W. *Down from Equality: Black Chicagoans and the Public Schools, 1920–1941.* Urbana: University of Illinois Press, 1984.

Howlett, John R. *Manual of the Twenty-Fifth General Assembly of the State of Illinois.* Chicago: Chicago Printing Co., 1867.

———. *Manual of the Twenty-Sixth General Assembly of the State of Illinois.* Lanark, Ill.: Howlett and Adair, Publishers, 1869.

Hurd, Harvey B. *The Revised Statutes of the State of Illinois, A.D. 1874.* Springfield: Illinois Journal Co. 1874.

Illinois Colored Convention. *Proceedings of the First Convention of the Colored Citizens of the State of Illinois, Convened at the City of Chicago, Thursday, Friday, and Saturday, October 6th, 7th, and 8th, 1853.* Chicago: Langdon and Rounds, Printers, 1853.

———. *Proceedings of the [Second] State Convention of Colored Citizens of the State of Illinois, Held in the City of Alton, November 13th, 14th, and 15th, 1856.* Chicago: Hays and Thompson, 1856.

———. *Proceedings of the [Third] Illinois State Convention of Colored Men, Assembled at Galesburg, October 16th, 17th, and 18th [1866].* Chicago: Church, Goodman and Donnelley, Printers, 1867.

———. [Proceedings of the Fourth Illinois State Convention of Colored Men, Assembled at Springfield, January 4th, 5th, 6th, and 7th, 1869.] *Illinois State Journal,* Jan. 6, 9, 1869; *Illinois State Register,* Jan. 5, 1869; *Tribune,* Jan. 9, 1869.

———. [Proceedings of the Fifth Illinois State Convention of Colored Men, Assembled at Springfield, December 2nd, 1873.] *Illinois State Journal* and *Illinois State Register,* Dec. 3, 1873.

Illinois Constitutional Convention. *Journal of the Constitutional Convention Assembled at Springfield, June 7, 1847, for the Purpose of Altering, Amending, or Revising the Constitution of the State of Illinois.* Springfield: Lanphier and Walker, Printers, 1847.

———. *Journal of the Constitutional Convention of the State of Illinois, Convened at Springfield, January 7, 1862.* Springfield: Charles H. Lanphier, 1862.

———. *Journal of the Constitutional Convention of the State of Illinois, Convened at Springfield, December 13, 1869.* Springfield: State Journal Printing Office, 1870.

———. *Debates and Proceedings of the Constitutional Convention of the State of Illinois, Convened at the City of Springfield, Tuesday, December 13, 1869.* Vols. 1, 2. Springfield: E. L. Merritt and Brother, 1870.

Illinois Department of Public Instruction. "Report of the State Superintendent of Public Instruction, 1855." *Reports Made to the Nineteenth General Assembly of the State of Illinois, Convened January 1, 1855.* Springfield: Lanphier and Walker, Printers, 1855.

References

―――. *Fourth Biennial Report of the Superintendent of Public Instruction of the State of Illinois, 1861–1862.* N.p., n.d. The 5th, 6th, 7th, 8th, 9th, and 10th biennial reports have the same bibliographic form as the 4th, although, of course, the content varies. To save space, I list them here in this abbreviated manner.

―――. *Fourteenth Biennial Report of the Superintendent of Public Instruction of the State of Illinois, July 1, 1880–June 30, 1882.* Springfield: H. W. Rokker, State Printer, 1883.

―――. *School Directory, 1940–1941. Circular 327.* Springfield: Printed by Authority of the State of Illinois, [1941].

Illinois General Assembly, House. *Journal of the House of Representatives of the Twenty-Eighth General Assembly of the State of Illinois, at the Adjourned Regular Session, Begun and Held at Springfield, January 6, 1874.* Springfield: State Journal Printing Office, 1874.

Illinois General Assembly, Senate. *Journal of the Senate of the Twenty-Eighth General Assembly of the State of Illinois, Begun and Held at Springfield, January 6, 1874.* Springfield: State Journal Steam Print, 1874. Here as examples of the bibliographic format of the journals of the Illinois General Assemblies of the last century and this century, I give the full entries for the House and Senate journals of the 28th General Assembly. I have chosen these as examples because the 28th General Assembly passed the act, the Henry law of March 24, 1874, that was the culminating event in the blacks' struggle for public-school rights. These are good examples, I think, of all the other entries that could be made for the nineteenth- and twentieth-century Illinois General Assembly journals I have cited in my chapter notes. The most convenient list of the sessions of the Illinois General Assembly and of the names of the members is to be found in Clayton's *Illinois Fact Book,* pp. 197–323. See also the *Illinois Blue Book* for 1913–14 and subsequent volumes in the *Blue Book* series.

Illinois General Assembly, Laws and Statutes. *Illinois Revised Statutes, 1981.* St. Paul, Minn.: West Publishing Co., 1982.

―――. *Laws of the State of Illinois Passed by the Eighteenth General Assembly at the Second Session, Commencing February 9, 1854.* Springfield: Lanphier and Walker, 1854.

―――. *Laws of the State of Illinois Passed by the Nineteenth General Assembly, Convened January 1, 1855.* Springfield: Lanphier and Walker, Printers, 1855.

―――. *Laws of the State of Illinois Enacted by the Sixty-Sixth General Assembly at the Regular Biennial Session, Begun . . . on the Fifth Day of January A.D. 1949, and Adjourned on the Thirtieth Day of June A.D. 1949.* Printed by Authority of the General Assembly of the State of Illinois, n.p., n.d.

——. *Laws of the State of Illinois Enacted by the Seventy-Third General Assembly at the Regular Biennial Session, Begun . . . on the Ninth Day of January* A.D. *1963, and Adjourned on the Twenty-Ninth Day of June* A.D. *1963.* Printed by Authority of the General Assembly of the State of Illinois, n.p., n.d.

——. *Private Laws of the State of Illinois, Passed by the Twenty-Third General Assembly, Convened January 5, 1863.* Springfield: Baker and Phillips, Printers, 1863.

——. *Private Laws of the State of Illinois, Passed by the Twenty-Fourth General Assembly, Convened January 2, 1865.* Vol. 1. Springfield: Baker and Phillips, Printers, 1865.

——. *Private Laws of the State of Illinois, Passed by the Twenty-Sixth General Assembly, Convened January 4, 1869.* Springfield: Illinois Journal Printing Office, 1869.

——. *Public Laws of the State of Illinois, Passed by the Twenty-Fourth General Assembly, Convened January 2, 1865.* Springfield: Baker and Phillips, Printers, 1865.

——. *Revised Laws of Illinois.* Vandalia: Greiner and Sherman, Printers, 1833.

——. *School Law: An Act to Establish and Maintain a System of Free Schools in the State of Illinois, as Amended February 21, 1859.* Springfield: Bailhache and Baker, Printers, 1859.

——. *School Laws of Illinois, 1869: An Act to Establish and Maintain a System of Free Schools, Approved February 16, 1865; Together with the Amendatory Acts of 1867 and 1869.* Springfield: Illinois Journal Printing Office, 1869.

——. *The Illinois School Law, 1872–1877: An Act to Establish and Maintain a System of Free Schools, Approved April 1, 1872, with an Appendix Containing All Acts Relative to the Schools in Force, July 1, 1877.* Springfield: D. W. Lusk, State Printer, 1877.

Illinois General Assembly, Reports. *Reports Made to the Senate and House of Representatives of the State of Illinois at Their Session Begun and Held at Springfield, December 2, 1844.* Springfield: Walters and Weber, Public Printers, 1845.

——. *Reports Made to the Senate and House of Representatives of the State of Illinois at Their Session Begun and Held at Springfield, December 7, 1846.* Springfield: George R. Weber, Public Printer, 1846.

——. *Reports Made to the Eighteenth General Assembly of the State of Illinois, Convened January 3, 1853.* Springfield: Lanphier and Walker Printers, 1853. ("Biennial Report of the Superintendent of the Common Schools of Illinois.")

——. *Reports Made to the Nineteenth General Assembly of the State of Illinois, Convened January 1, 1855.* Springfield: Lanphier and Walker, Printers, 1855.

References

Illinois Legislative Manual for the 30th General Assembly, 1877 and 1878. Springfield: M. G. Tousley and Co., 1877.

Illinois Schoolmaster, The.

Illinois State Journal.

Illinois State Register.

Illinois Supreme Court, Office of the Clerk, Springfield. Briefs and other documents pertaining to *James A. Chase et al. v. David Stephenson et al.* (1874), *The People ex rel. John Longress v. The Board of Education of the City of Quincy* (1882), *The People ex rel. George Hunt, Attorney General v. Thomas W. McFall et al.* (1888), *The People ex rel. John Peair v. The Board of Education of Upper Alton School District* (1889), and *The People ex rel. Scott Bibb v. The Mayor and Common Council of Alton* (1899).

Illinois Teacher, The.

Indiana Department of Public Instruction. *Fourteenth Report of the Superintendent of Public Instruction for the State of Indiana, Being the Third Biennial Report, and for the Years Ending Respectively August 31, 1865 and August 31, 1866.* Indianapolis: Samuel M. Douglass, State Printer, 1866.

————. *Sixteenth Report of the Superintendent of Public Instruction for the State of Indiana, Being the Fourth Biennial Report, and for the Years Ending August 31, 1867 and August 31, 1868.* Indianapolis: Alexander H. Conner, State Printer, 1869.

Indiana General Assembly, Senate. *Journal of the Indiana State Senate, during the Called Session of the General Assembly, Commencing Monday, November 13, 1865.* Indianapolis: W. R. Holloway, State Printer, 1865.

Johnson, Allen, and Malone, Dumas. *Dictionary of American Biography.* 20 vols. Index. Supplements. New York: Charles Scribner's Sons, 1928–

Jones, John. *The Black Laws of Illinois, and a Few Reasons Why They Should be Repealed.* Chicago: Tribune Book and Job Office, 1864.

————. Papers. Chicago Historical Society.

Jones, John, Mrs. "Interview." In Rufus Blanchard, *Discovery and Conquest of the Northwest with the History of Chicago,* vol. 2, pp. 297–302. Chicago: R. Blanchard and Co., 1900.

Journal of the Illinois State Historical Society.

King, Willard L. *Melville Weston Fuller.* New York: Macmillan Co., 1950.

Lakeside Annual Directory of the City of Chicago, The. Thomas Hutchinson, Compiler, 1876–86, and Reuben Donnelley, Compiler, 1887–1900. Chicago: Printer varies.

Liberator, The.

Lockridge, Kenneth A. *A New England Town: The First Hundred Years.* New York: W. W. Norton and Co., 1970.

Lusk, D. W. *Eighty Years of Illinois: Politics and Politicians, Anecdotes and Incidents, 1809–1889.* Springfield: H. W. Rokker, Printer, 1889.

Magee, James Henry. *The Night of Affliction and Morning of Recovery: An Autobiography.* 2nd ed. Cincinnati: Published by the Author, 1873.

Manual for the Use of the Twenty-Fourth General Assembly of the State of Illinois. Springfield: Baker and Phillips, Printers, 1865.

Marquis, Albert Nelson. *The Book of Chicagoans, 1911.* Chicago: A. N. Marquis and Co., 1911.

————. *The Book of Chicagoans, 1917.* Chicago: A. N. Marquis and Co., 1917.

Marshall, Helen E. *Grandest of Enterprises: Illinois State Normal University, 1857–1957.* Normal, Ill.: n.p., 1956.

Moses, John. *Illinois, Historical and Statistical.* 2nd ed., rev. 2 vols. Chicago: Fergus Printing Co., 1895.

Muelder, Hermann R. *Fighters for Freedom.* New York: Columbia University Press, 1959.

National Colored Convention. *Minutes of the National Convention of Colored Citizens: Held at Buffalo, on the 15th, 16th, 17th, 18th, and 19th of August, 1843.* New York: Piercy and Reed Printers, 1843.

————. *Report of the Proceedings of the Colored National Convention, Held at Cleveland, Ohio, on Wednesday, September 6, 1848.* Rochester: Printed by John Dick, 1848.

————. *Proceedings of the Colored National Convention, Held in Rochester, July 6th, 7th, and 8th, 1853.* Rochester: Printed at the Office of Fredrick Douglass' Paper, 1853.

"Newton Bateman." *Illinois Teacher*, 12, no. 8 (Aug. 1866), 236–38.

New York Times.

Nisbet, Robert A. *The Quest for Community.* Rev. ed. New York: Oxford University Press, 1969.

Ohio Commissioner of Common Schools. *Annual Report of the State Commissioner of Common Schools to the Governor of the State of Ohio, for the Year 1854.* Columbus: Statesman Steam Press, 1855.

————. *Third Annual Report of the State Commissioner of Common Schools to the General Assembly of Ohio, for the Year Ending August 31, 1856.* Columbus: Richard Nevins, State Printer, 1857.

Ohio General Assembly, Laws and Statutes. *Acts of a General Nature, Passed by the Forty-Seventh General Assembly of the State of Ohio, Begun and Held in the City of Columbus, December 4, 1848.* Columbus: Chas. Scott, State Printer, 1849.

Owen, William D. *Constitutions of 1816 and 1851 of the State of Indiana and Amendments.* Indianapolis: Wm. B. Burford, Contractor for State Printing and Binding, 1895.

Palmer, George Thomas. *A Conscientious Turncoat: The Story of John M. Palmer, 1817–1900.* New Haven: Yale University Press, 1941.

Palmer, John M. *The Bench and Bar of Illinois*. 2 vols. Chicago: Lewis Publishing Co., 1899.

———. *Personal Recollections of John M. Palmer*. Cincinnati: Robert Clarke and Co., 1901.

Patterson, Isaac Franklin. *The Constitutions of Ohio*. Cleveland: Arthur H. Clark Co., 1912.

Pease, Theodore Calvin. *Illinois Election Returns, 1818–1848*. Collections of the Illinois State Historical Library. Vol. 18. Springfield: Trustees of the Illinois State Historical Library, 1923.

Phillips, Isaac Newton. *Reports of Cases in Law and in Chancery Argued and Determined in the Supreme Court of Illinois*. Vol. 179. Springfield: n.p., 1899.

Pierce, Bessie Louise. *A History of Chicago*. 3 vols. New York: Alfred A. Knopf, 1937, 1940, 1957.

Pillsbury, W. L. "Early Education in Illinois." *Sixteenth Biennial Report of the Superintendent of Public Instruction of the State of Illinois, July 1, 1884–June 30, 1886*. Springfield: H. W. Rokker, Printer, 1886.

Purple, Norman H. *A Compilation of the Statutes of the State of Illinois of a General Nature in Force January 1, 1857*. 2nd ed. Part 2. Chicago: Keen and Lee, 1857.

Reece, J. N., Brig. Gen. *Report of the Adjutant General of Illinois*. Vol. 8. Springfield: Journal Co., Printers and Binders, 1901.

Richardson, James D. *A Compilation of the Messages and Papers of the Presidents, 1789–1897*. Vol. 7, Washington: Government Printing Office, 1898.

Richmond, Mabel E. *Centennial History of Decatur and Macon County*. Decatur: Decatur Review, 1930.

Root, O. E. *Root's Peoria City Directory for 1872 and 1873*. Peoria: N. C. Nason, Printer, 1872.

Rummel, Edward. *The Illinois Handbook of Information for the Year 1870*. Springfield: F. Hudson Jr., Printer, 1870.

———. *Rummel's Illinois Handbook and Legislative Manual for 1871*. Springfield: Illinois State Register Printing Office, 1871.

Sabine, George W. *A History of Political Theory*. 4th ed., rev. by Thomas L. Thorson. New York: Dryden Press, 1973.

Sanders, James W. *The Education of an Urban Minority: Catholics in Chicago, 1833–1965*. New York: Oxford University Press, 1977.

Scott, Franklin W. *The Semi-Centennial Alumni Record of the University of Illinois*. Urbana: University of Illinois, 1918.

Solberg, Winton U. *The University of Illinois, 1867–1894*. Urbana: University of Illinois Press, 1968.

Spear, Allan H. *Black Chicago: The Making of a Negro Ghetto, 1890–1920*. Chicago: University of Chicago Press, 1967.

Springfield City Directory and Sangamon County Record, Biographical and

Historical, 1877–78. Springfield: M. G. Tousley and Co., Publishers, 1877.

Springfield Superintendent of Public Schools. *Seventh Annual Report of the Superintendent of Public Schools, of Springfield, Illinois, to the Board of Public Instruction, 1865.* Springfield: Johnson and Bradford, Printers, 1865.

————. *Eighth Annual Report of the Superintendent of Public Schools, of Springfield, Illinois, to the Board of Public Instruction, 1866.* Springfield: Johnson and Bradford, Printers, 1866.

————. *Ninth Annual Report of the Superintendent of Public Schools, of Springfield, Illinois, to the Board of Public Instruction, 1867.* Springfield: Johnson and Bradford, Printers, 1867.

————. *Eleventh Annual Report of the Superintendent of Public Schools, of Springfield, Illinois, to the Board of Public Instruction, 1869.* Springfield: Illinois State Register Book and Job Office, 1869.

Steele, William Lucas. *Galesburg Public Schools: Their History and Their Work, 1861–1911.* Galesburg: Published by the Board of Education, 1911.

Sumner, Charles. *The Works of Charles Sumner.* Vols. 2, 14, 15. Boston: Lee and Shepard, 1883.

Tate, H. Clay. *The Way It Was In McLean County, 1972–1822.* Bloomington: McLean County Historical Association, 1972.

Thornbrough, Emma Lou. *The Negro in Indiana.* [Indianapolis]: Indiana Historical Bureau, 1957.

The United States Biographical Dictionary and Portrait Gallery of Eminent and Self-Made Men. Illinois Volume. Chicago: American Biographical Co., 1876.

United States Bureau of the Census. *Statistics of Population* volumes, 8th, 9th, 10th, and 19th censuses. Washington: Government Printing Office, 1866, 1872, 1883, 1973.

————. *Negro Population, 1790–1915.* Washington: Government Printing Office, 1918.

————. *Statistical Abstract of the United States: 1984.* Washington: Government Printing Office, 1983.

United States Congress. *The Congressional Globe: Containing the Debates and Proceedings of the Second Session, Forty-First Congress.* Part 4. Washington: Office of the Congressional Globe, 1870.

————. *Congressional Record: Containing the Proceedings and Debates of the Forty-Third Congress, First Session.* Vol. 2, Parts 4 and 5. Washington: Government Printing Office, 1874.

————. *Miscellaneous Documents Printed by Order of the House of Representatives During the First Session of the Forty-Third Congress, 1873–74.* Washington: Government Printing Office, 1874.

United States Supreme Court. *United States Reports: Cases Adjudged in the*

Supreme Court at October Term, 1953. Vol. 347. Washington: Government Printing Office, 1954.

University of Chicago. *Twelfth Annual Catalog.* Chicago: The Globe Publishing Co., 1870.

Voegeli, V. Jacque. *Free But Not Equal: The Midwest and the Negro During the Civil War.* Chicago: University of Chicago Press, 1967.

Walsh, Justin E. *To Print the News and Raise Hell: A Biography of Wilbur F. Storey.* Chapel Hill: University of North Carolina Press, 1968.

Wells, H. W. *The Schools and Teachers of Early Peoria.* Peoria: Jacquin and Co., 1900.

Western Citizen and Chicago Weekly Times, The.

Willard, Samuel. "Newton Bateman." *Twenty-Second Biennial Report of the Superintendent of Public Instruction of the State of Illinois, 1896–1898,* pp. lxix–lxxiv. Springfield: Phillips Brothers, n.d.

Wilson, Edwin A. *Illinois Legislative Manual for 1875.* Springfield: Journal Co., Printers, 1875.

Winthrop, John. "A Model of Christian Charity." *Winthrop Papers,* vol. 2, p. 294. Boston: Massachusetts Historical Society, 1931.

Wright, John W. D. *A History of Early Carbondale, Illinois, 1852–1905.* Carbondale: Southern Illinois University Press, 1977.

Notes

Chapter 1. Coping with Exclusion

1. Fitzpatrick, *Journals, Cont. Cong.*, vol. 28, p. 378; Ill. Dept. Pub. Instruc., *14th Bien. Report, 1880–82*, pp. cxx–cxliii.

2. Hill, *Journals, Cont. Cong.*, vol. 32, pp. 340, 343.

3. Buck, *Ill. in 1818*, pp. 94–96; Harris, *Negro Serv.*, p. 48; Moses, *Ill.*, vol. 1, pp. 547–49, vol. 2, pp. 1137–39.

4. U.S. Census, *9th, Pop.*, *1870*, p. 24; *10th, Pop.*, *1880*, pp. 387–88.

5. Patterson, *Constitutions, Ohio*, pp. 118, 135; Owen, *Constitutions, Indiana*, pp. 22, 49–51; Ill. Const. Conv., *Journal, 1847*, pp. 352–53; Palmer, *Personal Recoll.*, pp. 51–53.

6. Ill. Dept. Pub. Instruc., *4th Bien. Report, 1861–62*, p. 105; Pillsbury, "Early Educ., Ill.," *16th Bien. Report, 1884–86*, pp. civ–cciii.

7. Ill. Dept. Pub. Instruc., "Report, 1855," in Ill. Gen. Assem., *Reports, Reports, 19th Gen. Assem., 1855*, pp. 69–72.

8. Ill. Gen. Assem., *Reports, Reports, 1844*, p. 101.

9. Ohio, Com. Common Schools, *Report, 1854*, pp. 16–18; *Report, 1856*, pp. 14–15.

10. Owen, *Constitutions, Indiana*, pp. 22, 49.

11. Jones, *Black Laws*, p. 8; *Tribune*, Nov. 12, 1863; Palmer, *Personal Recoll.*, p. 327; Ill. Gen. Assem., Senate, *Journal, 19th, 1855*, p. 13.

12. Ill. Gen. Assem., Laws and Statutes, *Revised Laws, 1833*, pp. 556–62; *School Law, 1859*; *School Laws, 1869*.

13. E.g., "An Act to Establish and form the Tuscola Union School District," Ill. Gen. Assem., Laws and Statutes, *Priv. Laws, 26th Gen Assem., 1869*, vol. 3, pp. 511–19; "Rules and Regulations of the Board of Education of the City of Springfield," Springfield Supt. Pub. Schools, *11th Report, 1869*, p. 72; Ill. Colored Conv., *Proceedings*, [3rd, 1866], pp. 6, 10.

14. Galbraith, *Power*, pp. 4–6.

15. The evidence for these statements is derived from an analysis of the occupations of persons whose "place from" is listed as "Ireland" in Gager, *Chicago Dir., 1857*. Also from an analysis of the occupations of persons with Irish surnames and of persons designated as "colored" in Bailey, *Chicago Dir., 1864–5*, and Halpin, *Chicago Dir., 1865–6*. It is interesting to note that in the *Tribune*, Feb. 2, 1983, Vernon Jarrett, a black columnist, tells blacks to learn lessons of unity and mobilized effort from the example of the "old-time Irish."

16. Purple, *Ill. Statutes, 1857*, pt. 2, pp. 361, 737, 776–83.

17. *Western Citizen*, Apr. 5, 1853. The information about Jews is from my analysis of the three Chicago directories cited in n. 15. I identified persons as Jewish if they were listed as officers in Jewish voluntary associations or religious congregations or were mentioned as Jewish in Andreas, *Chicago*, vol. 1, 2, 3. As for my statements about the occupations of the blacks, see the data presented in ch. 7 and the accompanying notes.

Chapter 2. Black Efforts at the State Level

1. *Tribune* and *Times*, Mar. 12, 1875, May 24, 29, 1879; Jones Papers, Chicago Historical Society; Mrs. John Jones, "Interview."

2. National Colored Conv., *Minutes, 1843*, p. 8; *Proceedings, 1848*, pp. 3, 12; *Proceedings, 1853*, pp. 6, 46. See Howard H. Bell, *Minutes, Proceedings, 1830–1864*.

3. *Tribune*, Jan. 2, 1874; *Douglass' Paper*, Jan. 14, June 10, Sept. 12, 1853, Jan. 13, Feb. 17, 1854.

4. *Douglass' Paper*, Sept. 3, 1852, May 13, June 10, Oct. 28, Nov. 15, 18, Dec. 2, 1853, Jan. 13, Feb. 17, Mar. 24, 1854, Feb. 9, May 18, Oct. 5, Dec. 14, 1855; *Liberator*, July 27, 1855; *Tribune*, Jan. 21, 1857; Gager, *Chicago Dir., 1857*; Ill. Colored Conv., *Proceedings, 1853*, pp. 5, 11, 12, 19; *Proceedings, 1856*, pp. 4–5, 10–13.

5. *Douglass' Paper*, Feb. 17, 1854.

6. Alexander, *Colonization*, p. 89; Dillon, "Antislavery Movement," pp. 142–43; *Ill. State Journal*, Aug. 15, 1849, Mar. 21, 1850, Jan. 17, 18, 1851, Jan. 26, 1857; *African Repository*, vol. 21, no. 3 (Mar. 1845), 94–95, vol. 22, no. 3 (Mar. 1846), 73–80, vol. 30, no. 2 (Feb. 1854), 45, vol. 34, no. 9 (Sept. 1858), 259–61, vol. 46, no. 8 (Aug. 1868), 248–49; *Western Citizen*, July 2, 1850; Ill. Gen. Assem., Senate, *Journal, 17th, 1851*, pp. 63, 86, 141, 246–47; Ill. Gen. Assem., House, *Journal, 17th, 1851*, p. 420; Manuscript petitions, Ill. State Archives.

7. *Western Citizen*, May 4, 1853; Ill. Colored Conv., *Proceedings, 1853*, pp. 6, 10, 13.

8. Ill. Gen. Assem., House, *Journal, 19th, 1855*, pp. 17–18; *Douglass' Paper*, Feb. 9, Mar. 2, 1855.

9. "Petition of P. L. Donegan and others to amend the School Law," presented in the Senate, 18th Gen. Assem., Jan. 11, 1853. Manuscript copy in Ill. State Archives.

10. Ill. Gen. Assem., Reports, *Reports, 1846,* vol. 2, pp. 305–6; Ill. Gen. Assem., House, *Journal, 15th, 1846,* pp. 115, 319–20.

11. "Petition of 52 Colored Citizens of Illinois asking a change of the School Law so as to permit them to receive the benefit of such taxes paid by them," presented in the Senate, 18th Gen. Assem., Jan. 14, 1853. Manuscript copy in Ill. State Archives.

12. *Douglass' Paper,* May 13, 1853; Ill. Gen. Assem., Senate, *Journal, 18th, 1853,* p. 73.

13. Ill. Colored Conv., *Proceedings, 1853,* pp. 11, 14–15.

14. *Douglass' Paper,* Feb. 3, 17, Mar. 31, Apr. 7, 21, 1854.

15. *Douglass' Paper,* Jan. 14, 1853; *Western Citizen,* Dec. 21, 1852; *Tribune,* Dec. 30, 1852; Ill. Gen. Assem., Senate, *Journal, 18th, 1853,* pp. 112–13, 206–7, 256–57.

16. Ill. Colored Conv., *Proceedings, 1856,* pp. 12, 13, 20.

17. Pillsbury, "Early Educ., Ill.," in Ill. Dept. Pub. Instruc., *16th Bien. Report, 1884–86,* p. cxci; Ill. Gen. Assem., Laws and Statutes, *Laws, 18th, 2nd Sess., 1854,* pp. 13–15.

18. Ill. Gen. Assem., Reports, *19th, 1855,* pp. 65–119; Ill. Gen. Assem., Laws and Statutes, *Laws, 19th, 1855,* p. 85.

19. Ill. Colored Conv., *Proceedings, 1866,* pp. 9–10; Ill. Dept. Pub. Instruc., *9th Bien. Report, 1871–72,* pp. 375, 376; *7th Bien. Report, 1867–68,* p. 409; *6th Bien. Report, 1865–66,* pp. 28–29.

Chapter 3. White Efforts at the State Level

1. Harris, *Negro Serv.,* pp. 124–45, 152; *Western Citizen,* Nov. 25, Dec. 9, 1842, Apr. 13, 1843, Oct. 20, 1846, Jan. 12, 1847, Dec. 24, 1850, Jan. 21, Oct. 28, 1851. The best secondary source for the "moral suasion" period of white Illinois antislavery activity is Dillon's "Antislavery Movement"; the best for the white "political power" phase is Harris' *Negro Serv.* None of these sources provides data on the extent to which, if at all, blacks enrolled as members of the white antislavery societies. My reading suggests that, for whatever reason, blacks did not join the white antislavery societies and that the societies made no effort to recruit blacks to membership. The subject deserves study.

2. *Western Citizen,* Dec. 5, 1844.

3. Ibid., June 20, Aug. 8, 15, Sept. 5, 19, 1844, June 10, Aug. 11, 1846, Aug. 3, 1847, May 23, 1848.

4. Ill. Gen. Assem., House, *Journal, 15th, 1846,* pp. 115, 319–20; Ill. Gen. Assem., Reports, *Reports, 1846,* vol. 2, pp. 305–6.

5. Erickson, "Color Line, Ohio Schools," pp. 51–52, 72–81; Thornbrough, *Negro, Indiana*, pp. 166–69; Heller, "Negro Education, Indiana," pp. 144–74; U.S. Census, *Statistics, 8th, 1860*, pp. 377, 386.

6. Information about the political party of the members 1st–15th General Assemblies and the constitutional convention of 1847 is in Pease's *Ill. Elect. Returns*, pp. 467–594. After 1847 see for the 16th–18th and 20th–22nd General Assemblies the *Ill. State Journal*, Jan. 2, 1849, Nov. 26, 1850, Jan. 4, 1853, Nov. 17, 1856, Jan. 1, 1859, Jan. 7, 1861. For the 19th and 23rd General Assemblies see Moses, *Ill.*, vol. 2, pp. 591–92, 667–68. For the 24th General Assembly see *Manual, 24th Gen. Assem.*, 1865, pp. 63–67. The *Manual* for the 24th General Assembly also gives the state of birth and the occupation of the members, as do most of the legislative manuals from 1865 through 1875 and later. I have not found a *Manual* for the 28th General Assembly, 1873–74. For members of the General Assemblies up to 1847 the best biographical source is Cole's *Const. Debates*, pp. 949–83, containing biographies of the delegates to the 1847 constitutional convention, many of whom were members of previous or later General Assemblies. For biographical information about members of the 16th–23rd General Assemblies and of later ones I have found the most helpful, besides *Manuals* when available, to be Bateman, *Hist. Encyc*, vol. 1; Palmer, *Bench and Bar; U.S. Biog. Dict. and Port. Gall., Ill.;* and *Biog. Encyc., Ill., 19th Cent.* Histories of Illinois counties often contain short biographies, and occasionally city directories will give capsule biographies, while others may give place of birth in addition to address, occupation, and, sometimes, race of residents.

7. Ill. Gen. Assem., House, *Journal, 4th, 1824*, p. 218. For McGahey see Bateman, *Hist. Encyc.*, vol. 1, p. 363, and Pease, *Ill. Elect. Returns*, p. 539. On the Ames motion see Ill. Gen. Assem., Senate, *Journal, 16th, 1849*, pp. 173–74; for Ames' political party see Pease, *Ill. Elect Returns*, p. 469. I have not been able to find Ames' birthplace. The political party of the members of the 16th General Assembly is listed in the *Ill. State Journal*, Jan. 2, 1849.

8. Ill. Gen. Assem., Senate, *Journal, 19th, 1855*, pp. 259–60; Ill. Gen. Assem., House, *Journal, 20th, 1857*, pp. 500–501. Political party of the 19th Gen. Assem. members is given in Moses, *Ill.*, vol. 2, pp. 591–92; of 20th Gen. Assem. members in *Ill. State Journal*, Nov. 17, 1856. Biographies of Talcott and Moulton are in Bateman, *Hist. Encyc.*, vol. 1, pp. 517, 388. I could find no biographical information about Wheeler.

9. Jones, *Black Laws*, pp. 14–16.

10. Ill. Gen. Assem., Senate, *Journal, 24th, 1865*, pp. 30–32, 67, 72, 80, 131, 260–62; Ill. Gen. Assem., House, *Journal, 24th, 1865*, pp. 76–79, 401, 463, 549; *Tribune*, Jan. 20, 1865.

11. Ill. Gen. Assem., Senate, *Journal, 24th, 1865*, pp. 260–62, 420; Ill. Gen. Assem., House, *Journal, 24th, 1865*, pp. 551–52; Ill. Gen. As-

sem., Laws and Statutes, *Public Laws, 24th, 1865*, p. 105. For biographical information see *Manual, 24th Gen. Assem.*, 1865, pp. 63–67; for political party, *Times*, Nov. 26, 1864.

Chapter 4. Exclusion at the Local Level

1. Ill. Colored Conv., *Proceedings, 1866*, pp. 2, 5–6.
2. Ill. Dept. Pub. Instruc., *6th Biennial Report, 1865–66*, pp. 27–29.
3. *Times*, Feb. 1, Mar. 1, Apr. 5, 1865; *Ill. Teach.*, vol. 13, no. 5 (May 1867), 184, vol. 8, no. 5 (May 1862), 222; Springfield Supt. Pub. Schools, *8th Report, 1866*, p. 9.
4. *History Sangamon Co.*, pp. 533–34.
5. *Times*, May 3, 1867, Feb. 22, 1868; Marshall, *Grandest of Enterprises*, pp. 131–33.
6. Muelder, *Fighters for Freedom*, pp. 219–20; *History Knox Co.*, pp. 713–15; Ill. Dept. Pub. Instruc., *10th Bien. Report, 1873–74*, p. 300; Steele, *Galesburg Pub. Schools*, pp. 41–42.
7. Flower, *English Settlement*, pp. 339–40.
8. Lusk, *Eighty Years of Illinois*, p. 350; *History Jo Daviess Co.*, pp. 362–63.
9. *History Adams Co.*, pp. 481, 484; Ill. Dept. Pub. Instruc., *4th Bien. Report, 1861–62*, p. 238.
10. *Ill. State Journal*, Dec. 23, 1858; *Ill. State Register*, Dec. 24, 1858; Nov. 10, 1863; *History Sangamon Co.*, pp. 588–89; Springfield Supt. Pub. Schools, *7th Report, 1865*, pp. 22–23; *9th Report, 1867*, pp. 18–19.
11. Decatur Bd. of Educ., *35th Report, 1900*, p. 58; Richmond, *History Decatur*, p. 333; Fitzwilliam, *History Pub. Schools, Bloomington*, vol. 2, pp. 58–61; Ill. Gen. Assem., Reports, "Biennial Report of the Superintendent of the Common Schools of Illinois, 1851–52," *Reports to the 18th Gen. Assem., 1853*, p. 71; Eames, *Hist. Morgan*, p. 221; Wells, *Schools and Teachers Early Peoria*, pp. 100–102; *Ill. Teach.*, vol. 8, no. 5 (May 1862), 222.

Chapter 5. Segregation in Chicago

1. Pierce, *Chicago*, vol. 1, pp. 413–18, vol. 2, pp. 481–82, vol. 3, pp. 515–21; *Times*, Aug. 2, 1861, Apr. 8, 12, 15, June 14, 1862; Walsh, *Print News*, pp. 163 ff.; *Tribune*, Jan. 11, 13, 20, Mar. 2, 3, 17, 18, 20, Apr. 8, May 7, Sept. 28, Oct. 2, 13, 26, 29, Nov. 1, Dec. 1, 28, 1858, Aug. 6, 1863; *Post*, Sept. 11, 1861, July 16, 1862.
2. Chicago Bd. Educ., *4th Report, 1858*, pp. 18–22, 38; *5th Report, 1859*, pp. 18–19; *8th Report, 1861*, pp. 3, 8–9; *16th Report, 1870*, pp. 12, 27.

3. *Times*, Feb. 2, Mar. 6, 1858; *Tribune*, Feb. 2, Mar. 2, 1858. For biographical information about Higginson see Gager, *Chicago Dir., 1857*, pp. xxi, 149, and Bateman, *Hist. Encyc.*, vol. 1, p. 232; for Foster see Andreas, *Chicago*, vol. 2, p. 104; for Dore see *U.S. Biog. Dict.*, pp. 50–52; for Bass see Gager, *Chicago Dir., 1857*, p. 16, and *Post*, Oct. 22, 1853.

4. *Tribune*, July 28, 1861; *Times*, July 29, 1861; *Post*, July 28, Aug. 1, 1861.

5. Voting for Wentworth's resolution on July 27, 1861, were Philo Carpenter (Mass., Prot., Repub.), John C. Dore (N.H., Prot., Repub.), Henry T. Steele (N.Y., Prot., Repub.), Levi B. Taft (Mass., Prot., Repub.), Christian Wahl (Germany, probably Prot., Repub.), and John Wentworth. Joining Sheahan were Samuel Hoard (Mass., Prot., Repub.) and Flavel Moseley (Conn., Prot., Repub.). For biographial information about Carpenter see Andreas, *Chicago*, vol. 1, p. 340; about Dore, note 3 above; about Steele, Andreas, *Chicago*, vol. 3, p. 808, and *Bench and Bar*, pp. 320–21; abput Taft, Andreas, *Chicago*, vol. 2, p. 449, and *Times*, Mar. 18, 1864; about Wahl, Gager, *Chicago Dir., 1857*, p. 339, and *Times*, Mar. 18, 1864; about Wentworth, Fehrenbacher, *Chicago Giant*. For Sheahan see Andreas, *Chicago*, vol. 2, p. 494, and *Tribune*, June 18, 19, 1883; for Hoard, *Biog. Sketches*, pp. 401–5, and *Tribune*, Nov. 27, 1881; for Moseley, Andreas, *Chicago*, vol. 2, pp. 104–5.

6. Editorials defending Mary E. Mann's admission were published in the *Tribune*, July 28, 31, 1861; editorials opposing her admission were published in the *Journal*, July 30, 1861, *Post*, Aug. 1, 1861, and *Times*, Aug. 2, 1861. A letter opposing her admission appeared in the *Journal*, July 30; letters favoring her admission appeared in the *Tribune*, July 30, Aug. 1, and the *Journal*, July 31. At least one of the letters favoring her admission was written by a black, "J. W. M. (Colored)," *Tribune*, Aug. 1.

7. "Proceedings," June 2, 1862, p. 4, in "Chicago City Council Proceedings, 1862–64," Law Institute Vault, Law Library, Civic Center, Chicago. Newspaper accounts and letters to the editor on Sheridan's proposed ordinance are in the *Tribune*, June 3, 7, 1862, and the *Times*, June 4, 1862. A letter denouncing the proposed ordinance from Joseph Stanley, a black, is in the *Tribune*, June 7, 1862. For biographical information about Redmond Sheridan see *Times*, Oct. 22, 1885, and Bennett, *Politics*, p. 502.

8. *Times*, Dec. 18, 22, 1862.

9. Ill. Gen. Assem., House, *Journal, 23rd, 1863*, pp. 78, 83, 157, 372–74, 375–78, 387–89, 499–500, 526–29; Ill. Gen. Assem., Senate, *Journal, 23rd, 1863*, pp. 218, 284–85; King, *Fuller*; Ill. Gen. Assem., Laws and Statutes, *Priv. Laws, 23rd Gen. Assem., 1863*, p. 129.

10. *Tribune*, Feb. 18, 19, 1863.

11. *Journal*, Feb. 17, 26, 1863. For biographical information about Duggan see Andreas, *Chicago*, vol. 2, pp. 397–98. Relations between

the Catholics and the city board of public education are described in Sanders, *Educ. Urban Minority*, pp. 18–39. See also *Times*, July 2, Aug. 10, Sept. 3, 1863, May 9, 1865. The Chicago members of the 23rd Gen. Assem. were, in the Senate, William B. Ogden (N.Y., Prot., Repub.), and Jasper D. Ward (N.Y., probably Prot., Repub.), and, in the House, Michael Brandt [Brand] (Germany, Prot., Dem.), Melville W. Fuller (Me., Prot., Dem.), Lorenz Brentano (Germany, Prot., Repub.), Ansel B. Cook (Conn., probably Prot., Repub.), Francis A. Eastman (N.H., Prot., Repub.), William E. Ginther (unknown but probably Germany, unknown, Repub.), and Amos G. Throop (N.Y., Prot., Repub.). For biographical information on Ogden and Brandt see Andreas, *Chicago*, vol. 1, p. 619, vol. 2, p. 449, vol. 3, p. 579; for Ward, *Biog. Encyc., 19th Cent.*, pp. 477–78; for Brentano, Bateman, *Hist. Encyc.*, vol. 1, p. 60; for Cook, Howlett, *Manual, 26th*, pp. 56–61; for Eastman, Marquis, *Bk. Chicagoans, 1917*, p. 204; for Ginther, Moses, *Ill.*, vol. 2, p. 668; for Throop, Edwards, *Merch. Chicago Census Report*, p. 1104, and Pierce, *Chicago*, vol. 2, p. 437.

12. *Times*, Mar. 26, 1863.

13. Ibid., May 9, 12, 13, 1863; *Tribune*, May 9, 1863. For eleven of the fifteen members of the Chicago board of education—Brentano, Carpenter, Foster, Haven, Moseley, Sheahan, Steele, Taft, Wahl, James Ward, and Wentworth—place of birth, religion, and political party, together with sources of biographical information, have been given in the text or in the previous notes for this chapter. For Charles N. Holden (N.Y., Prot., Repub.) see *Biog. Encyc., 19th Century*, pp. 461–62; for Walter L. Newberry (Conn., Prot., Repub.), *Encyc. Biog. Ill.*, vol. 2, pp. 402–4; for Redmond Prindiville (Ill., Cath., Dem.), Edwards, *Merch. Chicago Census Report*, p. 551, and *Times*, Mar. 19, 1864, Feb. 7, 1867; for Ryder (Mass., Prot., Repub.), Andreas, *Chicago*, vol. 2, p. 441, and *Times*, Mar. 19, 1864. Voting for Wentworth's motion were Carpenter, Haven, Wahl, and Wentworth; voting against were Foster, Holden, Newberry, Ryder, Taft, Ward, and Brentano. Four members were absent.

14. *Tribune*, June 10, July 1, 1863; *Times*, June 10, 12, July 1, 2, 1863.

15. *Times*, Sept. 20, Nov. 4, Dec. 5, 30, 31, 1863; *Ill. State Journal*, Sept. 30, 1863; Chicago Bd. Educ., *10th Report, 1863*, pp. 24, 52–53.

16. *Ill. State Journal*, Oct. 5, 1864; *Tribune*, Sept. 18, Oct. 5, 1864; *Times*, Oct. 12, Dec. 3, 1864; *Post*, Oct. 5, 1864.

17. Ill. Gen. Assem., Senate, *Journal, 24th, 1865*, pp. 255, 579, 607; Ill. Gen. Assem., House, *Journal, 24th, 1865*, p. 1052; Ill. Gen. Assem., Laws and Statutes, *Priv. Laws, 24th Gen. Assem., 1865*, vol. 1, p. 285.

18. *Times*, Feb. 15, 21, 1865.

19. *Journal*, Oct. 5, 1864; *Post*, Oct. 6, 1864; *Times*, Oct. 5, 1864; *Tribune*, Oct. 6, 1864.

20. *Tribune*, Apr. 15, 30, Oct. 1, 3, 6, 31, Nov. 12, 13, Dec. 23, 30,

1863, Jan. 6, 9, 18, 27, Apr. 28, 1864; *Times*, Apr. 18, 1863, Jan. 6, 1864; Reece, *Report*, vol. 8, pp. 775–810; Hicken, *Ill.*, *Civil War*, pp. 334–43.
    21. Indiana Dept. Pub. Instruc., *16th Report*, *1867*, pp. 23–27; Drake and Cayton, *Black Metropolis*, vol. 1, p. 44.

Chapter 6. Winning Suffrage

    1. *Tribune*, Jan. 20, 1865; Ill. Gen. Assem., Senate, *Journal*, *24th*, *1865*, p. 157.
    2. Ill. Gen. Assem., Senate, *Journal*, *25th*, *1867*, pp. 764, 964, 1033, 1059–60; Howlett, *Manual*, *25th*, pp. 49–52.
    3. Ill. Gen. Assem., Senate, *Journal*, *25th*, *1867*, pp. 88, 105, 117, 147, 157, 224, 911; Ill. Gen. Assem., House, *Journal*, *25th*, *1867*, vol. 2, p. 861.
    4. *Tribune*, Feb. 26, 1867; *Times*, Feb. 4, 1867; *Ill. State Journal*, Feb. 26, 1867, Feb. 2, 1869.
    5. Palmer, *Personal Recoll.*, pp. 51–53, 324–32; Palmer, *Consc. Turn.*, pp. 225–26; Johnson and Malone, DAB, vol. 14, pp. 187–88; Ill. Gen. Assem., Senate, *Journal*, *18th*, *2nd sess.*, *1854*, p. 29; *Journal*, *19th*, *1855*, p. 19; Ill. Const. Conv., *Journal*, *1847*, pp. 352–53; *Ill. State Journal*, Sept. 27, 1869.
    6. Ill. Gen. Assem., Senate, *Journal*, *26th*, *1869*, vol. 1, pp. 163, 187, 347, vol. 2, pp. 260–62; Ill. Dept. Pub. Instruc., *7th Bien. Report*, *1867–68*, pp. 18–21, 145; *Ill. State Register*, Jan. 9, 1869; *Ill. State Journal*, Jan. 6, 9, Feb. 2, 1869; *Times*, Jan. 5, 9, 29, 1869.
    7. *Tribune*, *Times*, and *Post*, Sept. 28, 1869; *Ill. State Journal*, Jan. 6, 9, 1869.
    8. *Tribune*, Jan. 18, Feb. 4, 1870; *Times*, Feb. 4, 1870.
    9. Bradwell, "Colored Bar", p. 75; *Times*, Feb. 4, 5, 1870; *Post*, Feb. 4, 1870; Bailey and Edwards, *Chicago Dir.*, *1868*, pp. 231, 719; Edwards, *Merch. Chicago Census Report*, *1871*, p. 271.
    10. Ill. Const. Conv., *Journal*, *1869–70*, pp. 429, 431, 860–61; *Debates and Proceedings*, *1869–70*, vol. 1, pp. 679–80, 703; Rummel, *Handbook*, *1870*, pp. 176–78.
    11. Ill. Const. Conv., *Journal*, *1869–70*, pp. 30, 234, 246, 638–39, 1008; *Debates and Proceedings*, *1869–70*, vol. 2, pp. 1732–35.
    12. Ill. Const. Conv., *Debates and Proceedings*, *1869–70*, vol. 1, pp. 320–21; *Times*, Jan. 26, 1870; *Cairo Bulletin*, Oct. 2, 26, 1869.
    13. Ill. Gen. Assem., Senate, *Journal*, *26th*, *1869*, vol. 2, pp. 260–62; Ill. Gen. Assem., House, *Journal*, *26th*, *1869*, vol. 2, pp. 733–34, 741–42.
    14. Ill. Const. Conv., *Journal*, *1869–70*, pp. 27, 71–72, 106–9, 110–11, 176–77; *Debates and Proceedings*, *1869–70*, I, 82.

15. Ill. Const. Conv., *Journal, 1869–70,* pp. 472–74; *Debates and Proceedings, 1869–70,* vol. 2, pp. 855–57.
16. Ill. Const. Conv., *Journal, 1869–70,* pp. 603–5; *Debates and Proceedings, 1869–70,* vol. 2, pp. 1281–1309.
17. *Ill. State Journal,* Sept. 27, 1869.

Chapter 7. Participating in Mainstream Community Life

1. *Times,* Apr. 1, 2, 6, 13, 14, 22, 1870; *Tribune,* Apr. 8, 14, 1870; *Cairo Bulletin,* Apr. 13, 1870.
2. *Ill. State Journal,* Apr. 14, 1870; *Ill. State Register,* Apr. 13, 14, 1870.
3. *Tribune* and *Times,* Apr. 8, 1870.
4. Richardson, *Messages,* vol. 7, pp. 55–56; *Ill. State Journal,* Apr. 14, 1870, *Tribune,* Apr. 8, 1870.
5. *Times,* July 20, 27, 29, 30, Aug. 3, 11, 13, 19, 1869, Dec. 3, 1871.
6. *Times,* Apr. 6, 7, 13, 19, June 14, 15, July 8, Oct. 28, Nov. 9, 1870; *Tribune,* Apr. 6, 7, 8, July 1, 2, 3, 4, Nov. 6, 9, 1870; *Cairo Bulletin,* Apr. 19, 1870.
7. *Times,* May 17, 20, July 26, Aug. 26, 30, Oct. 7, 14, 29, Nov. 1, 9, 1870, Nov. 23, 1871, Apr. 24, Aug. 4, 9, Sept. 21, 24, Oct. 17, Nov. 1, 6, 17, 1872, July 3, Oct. 7, 10, 1873, Apr. 3, 4, 1874; *Tribune,* Nov. 1, 1870, June 16, Aug. 23, Oct. 2, 15, 16, 17, 26, 27, 1874; *Bloomington Pantagraph,* July 3, Aug. 14, 1872; *Cairo Bulletin,* Apr. 1, 26, May 21, 1870, Apr. 19, Nov. 8, 1873; *Ill. State Journal,* Sept. 3, 29, 1870; *Ill. State Register,* Apr. 7, Sept. 3, 1870; Eames, *Hist. Morgan,* pp. 181, 202; Gosnell, *Negro Polits.,* pp. 66, 81–82; Bradwell, "Colored Bar," p. 76; Harlow, *Direct.,* *30th,* *1877,* p. 89; *Ill. Legis. Manual, 30th, 1877–78,* p. 131.
8. Ill. Gen. Assem., Senate, *Journal, 27th, 1871,* pp. 127, 136, 216, 318, 437; Ill. Gen. Assem., House, *Journal, 27th, 1871,* pp. 273, 408, 501, 614; *Bloomington Pantagraph,* Jan. 27, 30, 1871; Rummel, *Ill. Handbk., 1871,* p. 175; Babeuf, *Direct. Springfield,* pp. 16, 43, 129.
9. *Cairo Bulletin,* Feb. 16, Apr. 13, 1870, Sept. 5, 1871, Apr. 19, 1873; *Ill. State Journal,* Feb. 19, 1874; Ill. Gen. Assem., Senate, *Journal, 28th, 1874,* pp. 70, 260; Scott, *Semi-Cent. Alumni Record,* p. 970; Solberg, *U. of Ill.,* p. 120.
10. *Cairo Bulletin,* July 2, 3, 7, 1874.
11. *History Sangamon Co.,* pp. 737, 738, 739, 742–43; *Times,* Apr. 1, 1870; Palmer, *Consc. Turn.,* p. 225; *Ill. State Journal,* Mar. 31, 1870, Jan. 14, 16, 19, 1871; Babeuf, *Direct. Springfield,* p. 125; Bateman, *Hist. Encyc.,* vol. 1, pp. 489–90, 476; *Ill. Legis. Manual, 30th, 1877–78,* p. 178.
12. My principal sources here are Harris, *Colored Men's Prof. and Bus. Direct.* and the volumes of the *Lakeside Annual Directory, Chicago.*

13. *Cairo Bulletin*, Sept. 2, 8, 13, 14, 28, 1871, Mar. 12, 14, 1872; *Ill. State Journal*, Mar. 2, 1875; Root, *Peoria Direct.*, p. 129; Harris, *Colored Men's Prof. and Bus. Direct.*, pp. 15, 25, 31, 36, 42; *Lakeside Direct.*, *1885*, p. 812.

14. *Times*, Oct. 27, 1870, Sept. 17, 1871, May 14, Aug. 27, Sept. 5, 1872; *Lakeside Directories, 1876–86*; Harris, *Colored Men's Prof. and Bus. Direct.*, pp. 20, 46, 52; Andreas, *Chicago*, vol. 3, pp. 107, 108; Babeuf, *Direct. Springfield*, pp. 9, 229.

15. *Times*, Oct. 25, 26, Dec. 23, 1872, Apr. 30, July 2, 1873, Nov. 12, 1874; Harris, *Colored Men's Prof. and Bus. Direct.*, p. 27; Andreas, *Chicago*, vol. 3, p. 121. As usual I have obtained the previous occupations of the blacks mentioned from the city directories of the time.

16. *History Sangamon Co.*, p. 738; Harris, *Colored Men's Prof. and Bus. Direct.*, pp. 17, 25, 26, 46; *Times*, May 30, 1869, July 2, 1870, Jan. 3, 1871; Andreas, *Chicago*, vol. 3, p. 556.

17. *Tribune*, June 7, 1869, Apr. 21, May 4, 12, 1870; *Times*, July 7, 1869, Apr. 21, May 4, July 26, Dec. 9, 1870; *Ill. State Journal*, Apr. 15, 1870. Perhaps the first school case brought by blacks into a court was *Martha Crow, by her next friend v. The Board of Education of Bloomington*, 1871. See ch. 9, n. 1.

18. Bradwell, "Colored Bar," p. 75; Univ. of Chicago, *12th Catalog*, p. 48; Bailey and Edwards, *Chicago Direct.*, p. 231; Edwards, *Merch. Chicago Census Report*, p. 271; Spear, *Black Chicago*, pp. 60– 61; Chicago Bd. Educ., *25th Report, 1879*, Appendix, p. 54. The first black woman to qualify for the Illinois bar was Ida Platt. She was the daughter of Jacob F. Platt, the owner of a Chicago lumber business, and like her older sister, Amelia, and her brother, Jacob F., Jr., attended the Chicago public schools. Graduating from the four-year Academic program of the high school in June 1879, she studied music and then became successively a private secretary, stenographer, head of the claims department of an insurance company, a general stenographer and law reporter, and a student in the Chicago College of Law, earning her LL.B. and passing the bar in June 1894.

19. *Tribune* and *Times*, Mar. 12, 1875.

20. *History Sangamon Co.*, pp. 533–34; *Springfield City Direct.*, *1877–78*, p. 108.

21. *Times*, Aug. 24, Sept. 10, Oct. 22, 1870, Sept. 22, 24, 1871, May 14, Nov. 24, 1872, Apr. 1, Aug. 22, 1873, Feb. 7, 8, 12, 27, June 13, 14, 17, 18, 1874, May 24, 1879; *Cairo Bulletin*, Nov. 5, 1869, Mar. 30, 1872, Apr. 18, 1875; *Bloomington Pantagraph*, July 18, 1872, May 9, June 24, Aug. 11, 12, 1874.

22. *Times*, July 18, Aug. 24, Sept. 5, 17, 20, 23, Oct. 7, 8, 1870, Jan. 29, June 3, July 11, Aug. 11, 1871, May 9, 1873, Aug. 13, 15, 16,

Sept. 20, 1874; *Bloomington Pantagraph,* May 18, 27, 1874; *Cairo Bulletin,* Oct. 7, 1874; *Tribune,* Aug. 24, 1874.

23. *Times,* July 18, 20, Sept. 12, 13, Nov. 19, 21, 1870, Mar. 15, May 15, 30, July 31, Aug. 1, 28, Sept. 6, 13, Dec. 3, 1871, Feb. 23, Apr. 5, Sept. 9, 1872, Mar. 16, 1875; *Ill. State Register,* Oct. 21, 1873; *Cairo Bulletin,* Sept. 21, 1871, Mar. 18, 1872.

24. *Times,* Jan. 2, 1874, Mar. 14, 1875.

25. Ill. Gen. Assem., Senate, *Journal, 28th, 1874,* pp. 177–78; *Ill. State Journal,* Feb. 3, 4, 1874; *Tribune,* Feb. 3, 1874; *Times,* Feb. 3, 4, 1874.

26. *Cairo Bulletin,* Sept. 2, 1869.

Chapter 8. Gaining Access to Public Schools

1. U.S. Congress, *Globe, 41st, 2nd Sess.,* pt. 4, p. 3434; Sumner, *Works,* vol. 14, pp. 365–66, 370; Donald, *Sumner,* p. 531.

2. *Ill. State Journal,* Dec. 3, 1873; U.S. Congress, *Misc. Docs., 43rd, 1st Sess, 1873–74,* no. 44; U.S. Congress, *Record, 43rd, 1st Sess.,* vol. 2, pt. 4, pp. 3451–52, pt. 5, pp. 4088–89, 4153, 4170, 4175–76; U.S. Congress, *Record, 43rd, 2nd Sess.,* vol. 3, pt. 2, pp. 1010, 1011, pt. 3, p. 1870; *Tribune,* Mar. 1, 1875.

3. Bateman, *Hist. Encyc.,* vol. 1, pp. 37–38; Johnson and Malone, *DAB,* vol. 2, pp. 44–45; Willard, "Bateman"; "Newton Bateman"; Angle, *Herndon's Lincoln,* p. 368. Copies of some of Bateman's private and public correspondence are in the Bateman Collection, Illinois State Historical Library. Copies of his official correspondence are on file at the State Archives Building.

4. Ill. Dept. Pub. Instruc., *6th Bien. Report, 1865–66,* pp. 27–29; *7th Bien. Report, 1867–68,* pp. 18–21, 145; *8th Bien. Report, 1869–70,* pp. 23–29, 166.

5. Ill. Dept. Pub. Instruc., *8th Bien. Report, 1869–70,* pp. 25–29, 166–67; Ill. Gen. Assem., Senate, *Journal, 27th, 1st Sess., 1871,* pp. 28–29.

6. Ill. Gen. Assem., Senate, *Journal, 27th, 1st Sess., 1871,* pp. 89, 487; *Journal, 27th, Adj. Reg. Sess., 1871,* pp. 314, 500, 567; Ill. Gen. Assem., House, *Journal, 27th, Adj. Reg. Sess., 1871,* pp. 394–95.

7. Ill. Gen. Assem., Laws and Statutes, *School Law, 1872–77,* pp. 25–26.

8. Ill. Dept. Pub. Instruc., *9th Bien. Report, 1871–72,* pp. 116–18, 230–31.

9. Ill. Gen. Assem., Senate, *Journal, 28th, 1873,* pp. 196–97.

10. Ill. Gen. Assem., Senate, *Journal, 28th, Adj. Reg. Sess., 1874,* pp. 177–78; *Ill. State Journal,* Feb. 3, 4, 1874; *Tribune,* Feb. 3, 1874; *Times,* Feb. 3, 4, 1874.

11. Ill. Gen. Assem., Senate, *Journal, 28th, Adj. Reg. Sess., 1874,*

pp. 177–78. Biographies of Thomas S. Casey and Alexander Starne are in Bateman, *Hist. Encyc.*, vol. 1, pp. 84, 502.

12. Ill. Gen. Assem., Senate, *Journal, 28th, Adj. Reg. Sess.*, 1874, pp. 231, 477–78; Ill. Gen. Assem., Laws and Statutes, *School Law, 1872–77*, Appendix, pp. v, vi; *Ill. State Journal*, Feb. 10, 1874.

13. Ill. Gen. Assem., Senate, *Journal, 28th, Adj. Reg. Sess.*, 1874, p. 398; Ill. Gen. Assem., House, *Journal, 28th, Adj. Reg. Sess.*, 1874, pp. 175, 197, 526, 528, 556, 562, 575; Hurd, *Rev. Statutes*, p. 983; *Ill. State Journal*, Feb. 3, 1874.

14. Henry to Bateman, Mar. 24, 1874, Bateman Papers, Folder, Jan. 1874–June 1874, Illinois State Historical Library. In 1875 George W. Henry was forty-seven years old. He had been a resident of Illinois for more than twenty years, having been born in Ohio. He was said to be one of the "earnest friends of popular education" in the 28th General Assembly, and on March 28, 1874, he gave a strong speech in favor of a compulsory education bill, declaring that universal, public, free education was the only reliable safeguard for republican institutions (*Ill. State Journal*, Mar. 30, 1874). The skimpy biographical information about him here is from Wilson, *Ill. Leg. Manual, 1875*, p. 82. I have searched all the standard biographical sources and Clay County histories without finding more than I have presented in this note and in my text.

15. *Cairo Bulletin*, Aug. 22, Sept. 6, 1874; *Times*, Sept. 9, 10, 1874.

16. *Times*, Jan. 12, 13, 15, 1875; *Tribune*, Jan. 12, 1875; *Ill. State Journal*, Jan. 18, Feb. 17, 22, 1875; *Cairo Bulletin*, Jan. 14, 1875.

17. Ill. Dept. Pub. Instruc., *10th Bien. Report, 1873–74*, p. 353; *6th, 7th, 8th, 9th Bien. Reports, 1865–72*, pp. 21, 5, 2, and 1, respectively.

18. Ill. Dept. Pub. Instruc., *10th Bien. Report, 1873–74*, pp. 50, 258–351.

19. Ill. Gen. Assem., Laws and Statutes, *Rev. Statutes, 1981*, vol. 3, pp. 6810, 6811.

Chapter 9. Illinois Supreme Court Opinions in School Segregation Cases

1. *Ill. State Journal*, June 20, 1874; *Bloomington Pantagraph*, June 22, 1874; *Times*, Aug. 28, 1874; *N.Y. Times*, Aug. 29, 1874; *Tribune*, Aug. 29, Sept. 28, Oct. 14, 1874; Ill. Dept. Pub. Instruc., *Circular 45*, Aug. 12, 1874; *10th Bien. Report, 1873–74*, pp. 46–49; Chicago Com. on Race Relations, *Negro in Chicago*, p. 234; Tate, *McLean Co.*, pp. 41–48. For the *Crow* case, *Bloomington Pantagraph*, Jan. 12, 13, 14, 21, 23, June 13, 23, 1871.

2. I have used copies of the circuit court and Illinois Supreme Court documents on file in the office of the clerk of the court in Springfield and furnished to me by Clell L. Woods. I have checked what is said against the content of relevant articles in the Bloomington and Spring-

field papers. I have been unable to find biographical information about the principals in *Stephenson et al.* v. *Chase et al.* and *Chase et al.* v. *Stephenson et al.* beyond learning that Chase was a Presbyterian minister and Stephenson, Shorthose, Paul, and Gunnell were farmers. Brigham, *McLean Co.*, p. 154; *History McLean Co.*, pp. 576, 1038, 1040, 1042.

3. For biographies of Judge Tipton see Bateman, *Hist. Encyc.*, vol. 1, p. 524; *History McLean Co.*, pp. 823–24; Palmer, *Bench and Bar*, vol. 2, pp. 721–23.

4. Biographies of Breese, Walker, McAllister, Scott, Sheldon, Scholfield, and Craig are in Bateman, *Hist. Encyc.*, vol. 1, pp. 59–60, 548, 357, 471–72, 477, 469, 123.

5. Biographies of Gapen and Ewing are in *History McLean Co.*, pp. 786, 780.

6. Biographies of Rowell and Hamilton are in *History McLean Co.*, pp. 813, 791–92, and Bateman, *Hist. Encyc.*, vol. 1, pp. 460, 217.

7. Freeman, *Cases Sup. Court, Ill.*, vol. 71, pp. 383–86 (71 Ill. 383).

8. *Tribune*, Aug. 29, Sept. 28, 1874; Ill. Dept. Pub. Instruc., *Circular 45; 10th Bien. Report, 1873–74*, pp. 43–49; *9th Bien. Report, 1871–72*, pp. 363–65.

9. Freeman, *Cases Sup. Court, Ill.*, vol. 101, pp. 308–19 (101 Ill. 308); vol. 124, pp. 642–45 (124 Ill. 642); vol. 127, pp. 613–26 (127 Ill. 613); Phillips, *Cases Sup. Court, Ill.*, vol. 179, pp. 615–33 (179 Ill. 615).

10. My account of the *Longress* case draws on copies of documents filed in the office of the clerk of the Supreme Court in Springfield and furnished to me by Clell L. Woods.

11. For a biography of Longress see *History Adams Co.*, pp. 656–57. The reader will note that there were, according to Longress, some 300 black children of school age in Quincy, more than enough to organize an economical, efficient, graded school. Whether the Lincoln school was graded or ungraded is not shown in the record. At any rate the question of whether the Lincoln school and the district schools were "equal" in facilities and instruction did not become a functional issue in the *Longress* case. Nor did it in the *Peair* and *Bibb* cases where the record shows that the colored schools were graded.

12. Pinkney H. Walker's dissenting opinion was concerned mainly with technicalities of writs of quo warranto and of the powers of the court vis-à-vis those of the legislature in abolishing or curbing corporations under special charters.

13. Ill. Dept. Pub. Instruc., *School Direct.*, 1940–41, pp. 11–70.

Chapter 10. Yesterday, Today, Tomorrow

1. The Winthrop quotation is from his "Modell of Christian Charity." A good discussion of the Massachusetts Bay idea of "community" is in Lockridge's *A New England Town*. Twentieth-century ideas of "com-

munity" are discussed in, for example, Dewey's *Public and Its Problems*, Nisbet's *Quest for Community*, and Bellah's *Habits of the Heart*. The concept has been a subject of philosophic scrutiny since antiquity, of course. See any of the standard histories of political thought such as Sabine's *History of Political Theory*.

2. On the law-abiding nature of the blacks see *Times*, Apr. 7, 1864; *Tribune*, May 1, 1864, Dec. 12, 1874. Official reports from the Chicago Department of Police for eleven of the twelve years from February 1861 to March 1873 show a total of 227,558 arrests, of which 6,900 (3 percent) were of blacks. Of the total arrests, 94,214 (41 percent) were of persons of Irish nativity, the most of any group. *Chicago Post*, Jan. 14, 1863, Jan. 5, 1864, Nov. 5, 1864; *Tribune*, Jan. 5, 1864, Apr. 6, 1865; *Times*, Apr. 7, July 14, Oct. 6, 1863, July 30, Aug. 10, 1864, Feb. 6, July 15, 1865, Apr. 3, 1867, Apr. 3, 1868, Apr. 2, 1869, Apr. 12, 1870, Apr. 11, 1871, Apr. 30, 1872, June 24, 1873.

3. *N.Y. Times*, May 18, 1954.

4. Ill. Gen Assem., House, *Journal, 66th, 1949*, pp. 1582, 1680; *Journal, 73rd, 1963*, vol. 2, 99, 295–96; Ill. Gen. Assem., Laws and Statutes, *Laws, 1949*, pp. 53–54; *Laws, 1963*, vol. 1, pp. 1107–10. Jenkins was the chairman of a House committee of the 67th General Assembly that investigated the extent of compliance with his amendment. See his report in Ill. Gen. Assem., House, *Journal, 67th, 1951*, vol. 2, pp. 2434–38.

5. *Tribune*, June 22, 1949; Ill. Dept. Pub. Instruc., *8th Bien. Report, 1869–70*, pp. 28–29.

Index

Abram (husband of servant America), 77
"Act to establish and maintain a system of free schools, An" (1872), 116–17
"Act to protect colored children in their rights to attend Public Schools, An" (Henry law, 1874), 120, 122, 123, 124–25, 128, 137, 140, 141, 142, 155
"Act to provide for the better education of the colored children of the state of Illinois, An" (1874), 121
"Address of the Colored State Convention to the People of the State of Illinois," 32
African Baptist College, 48
Allan, Mrs. Irene B., 35
Allan, Rev. William T., 35
Allyn, Robert, 96
Alton, black schooling in, 36, 45, 48, 142
Alton (Shurtleff) College, 77
Amalgamation, whites' fear of, 76, 116, 126
America (servant of Palmer family), 77
Ames, Alfred E., 39
Anatomy of Power (Galbraith), 12, 143
Andrews, Col. Robert, 102
Anis, Thomas E., 66
"Appeal to the Christian—to the Patriot—and the Philanthropist, An," 25, 29

Armstrong, Charles F., 154–55
Armstrong act (1963), 154–55

Baker, William, 97
Bargaining power: blacks' use of, 13–16, 19–20, 31, 32, 42, 68, 70, 71–72, 79, 88, 105, 111, 125–26, 143, 147, 149–50, 153, 155; compensatory, 12, 143–44, condign, 12, 143–44; conditioned, 12, 143–44; defined, 11–12, dialectical, 11–12, 15, 19–20, 32, 42, 68, 71, 72, 88, 105, 125, 127, 144; Galbraith's definitions of, 12, 143–45; organizing to use, 12–13, 43, 144; political, 34; punishing, 11, 13, 20, 32, 68, 70, 71, 72, 79, 88, 105, 144; rewarding, 11, 13, 20, 32, 79, 105, 144
Barnard, Henry, 5
Barnett, Ferdinand L., Jr., 101
Barney, Hiram H., 7
Baseball, black teams for, 103–4
Bass, Perkins, 57, 58
Bateman, Newton: experience of, 112–13; on numbers of black children excluded from public school system, 45, 118, 124; on Section 84 (80), 30–31, 80, 113; views on *Chase* v. *Stephenson*, 135–37; views on public education for blacks, 5, 76, 80, 111–12, 113–16, 117–18, 119, 121, 125
Beard, George, 97

Beecher, Edward, 112
Beecher, Roxanna F., 65
Bellows, George W., 100
Beveridge (governor of Illinois),
95, 96
Bibb, Scott, 137
Bird, John J., 94, 95–96, 100
Black code: defined, 9, 13–14; repeal of, 21, 27, 34, 36, 41–43,
69, 72, 73, 75, 83
Black laws. *See* Black code
*Black Laws of Illinois and a Few Rea-
sons Why They Should Be Repealed, The* (Jones), 41, 43, 72
Black Metropolis (Drake and
Cayton), 71
Blacks, in Illinois: bargaining
power of, 13–16, 19–20, 31, 32,
42, 68, 70, 71, 72, 88, 105, 111,
125–26, 143, 147, 149–50, 153,
155; in Chicago, 14–15, 27, 28;
as Civil War Volunteers, 43,
69–70, 119; court testimony
from, 21, 27, 100; in entertainment, 102–3; excluded from
public school system, 8–11,
38–39, 44–46, 51, 118, 129,
137–38, 146–47; inability to organize effectively, 31–32; included in public school system,
21, 23, 27, 35, 108–9; as law-
abiding citizens, 146, 184n.2;
motivation for education
among, 50; occupations of,
14–15, 96–101; petitions to Illinois General Assembly from,
20–25, 27–28, 73–76, 86–88,
110; population figures for, 4,
153; in Republican party, 91,
94; and school taxes, 23, 24, 25,
28, 29–30, 36–37, 38–39; sectional differences among, 4, 19,
80, 151; separate "colored"
schools for, 10, 23, 25–26, 27,
28, 29, 31, 51–54, 57, 59–68,
71, 109, 110, 117, 123, 129,
130–31, 142; social relations
with whites, 101–2, 104–5; in

sports, 103–4; suffrage for, 10,
13, 21, 44, 74, 75, 78, 79,
86–88, 90, 91, 93–95, 149, 152;
white assistance to, 15, 18, 32,
125. *See also* Black code;
Colonization
"Blind Tom," 103
Bloomington: black baseball
teams in, 103; education for
blacks in, 36, 53; first blacks
voting in, 94
Blue Stockings baseball team, 104
Bonner, James D., 17, 19
Bradley, Andrew F., 97
Brandt (Brand), Michael,
176–77n.11
Breese, Sidney, 131
Brentano, Lorenz, 176–77n.11
Brents (or Brentz), Rev. George,
95
"Brick," letter from, 27
Bross, William, 92
Brown, George, 46, 48–49, 50
Brown, Rev. Henry, 19
Brown, John, 18
Brown v. *Board of Education of To-
peka* (1954), 109, 133, 148

Cain, Rev. R. H., 19
Cairo: black baseball team in, 104;
blacks hired in, 97
Cairo Bulletin, 106–7, 108, 122
Cameron, Daniel, 86
Canada, education available for
blacks in, 47–48
Capital City Guards (of Spring-
field), 103
Carey, Adam, 13
Carpenter, Philo, 59, 176n.5
Cary, William, 87
Casey, Thomas Sloo, 119, 121
Cayton, Horace R., 71
Champaign, black fire company
in, 98
Chase, James A., 129. *See also*
Chase v. *Stephenson*
Chase v. *Stephenson* (*James A.
Chase et al.* v. *David Stephenson*

et al., 1874), 126, 128–36
Chase et al., appellants v. *Stephenson et al., appellees* (1874), 131
Chicago: black baseball team in, 104; black employment in, 97–98; black leaders in, 17, 19; black schoolteacher in, 47, 59; blacks in, 14–15, 27, 28, 55–56, 68–69, 80–83, 184n.2; celebration of new state constitution in, 90–91; education for blacks in, 45, 53–54, 55, 58, 59–68; ethnic populations of, 55; first blacks voting in, 94; Irish in, 4, 13, 55–56, 172n.15, 184n.2; Jews in, 14, 172n.17; population growth in, 55, 56. *See also* Cook County
Chicago Evening Journal, 63, 104
Chicago Evening Post, 82
Chicago Observer, 97
Chicago Post, 56
Chicago Repeal Association, 41
Chicago Socials baseball team, 104
Chicago Times, 56, 61, 68, 70, 82, 92, 93, 99, 103, 104, 105
Chicago Tribune, 56, 62, 69, 70, 94, 104, 111
Christopher, Hannah, 51
Civil War: black participation as tool to argue for blacks' rights, 69, 76, 119; black volunteers, 43, 69–70
Clere (or Clare), Richard, 17
Colonization: black opposition to, 22; charter for society in Illinois, 9; petitions for, 21–23. *See also* Illinois State Colonization Society
Colored Manual Training School, 18
Committee on People of Color of the Antislavery Friends, 37, 151. *See also* Quakers
Community, concept of: American sense of, 145–46; blacks

isolated from, 9, 93; importance of educated citizenry in, 5, 6–8, 106, 119, 148; in Indiana constitution, 8; partnership concept of, 6–7, 81, 143, 146, 148; Puritan definition of, 145
Conservator, 101
Constitution of the United States: arguments for blacks' rights based on, 32, 33, 75; 14th Amendment to, 132, 136, 137, 140; 15th Amendment to, 78, 84, 86, 88, 90, 91, 93
Cook, Ansel B., 176–77n.11
Cook, John Williston, 48
Cook County: blacks in patronage positions in, 97; Irish in, 4; population growth in, 56. *See also* Chicago
Craig, Alfred M., 131, 133–35, 136, 138, 139–41
Crow, Martha, by her next friend v. *Board of Education of Bloomington*, 128, 131
Crusaders baseball team, 103
Cummings, Samuel P., 120
Curtis, Sarah, 51

Davis, Allison, 148
Dawson, John B., 82
Dawson, Richard A., 82, 101
Decatur, education for blacks in, 45, 53
Declaration of Independence, arguments for blacks' rights based on, 32, 33, 75, 147
Dexters baseball team, 103
Donegan, Presley L., 23, 24–25
Donegan, Spencer, 19
Dore, John C., 57, 58, 176n.5
Douglas, Stephen A., 77
Douglass, Frederick, 18, 19, 26
Douglass, H. Ford, 69
Drake, St. Clair, 71
Duff, Andrew D., 96
Duggan, Rt. Rev. James (bishop of Chicago), 62, 63

Dunn, Edmund, 100
Dunn, Mrs. Teney, 100

Easley, David, 98
Eastman, Francis A., 74–75, 98–99, 176–77n.11
Eastman, Zebina, 14
Edsall, James K., 138
"Education of the Colored Race, The" (Bird speech), 96
Edwards, Ninian W.: appointment of, 29; on separate "colored" schools, 29, 71; support for property tax to fund school system, 6; views on public education, 5–6
Edwards, Richard, 96
Edwardsville: first black jurors in, 100; first blacks voting in, 94; interaction between whites and blacks in, 105
Elliott, Miss Rebecca, 53
"Emerald, John," in *Chicago Times*, 93
Ender, John, 98
Ewing, Henry A., 131

1st Regiment Illinois Colored Volunteers, 69
Fisk, Jim, 102
Flagg, Willard C., 80, 116, 125
Foster, Dr. John H., 57, 58
Fowler, Rev. Charles H., 96
Frederick Douglass' Paper, 27
"Free Frank," 21
Freeman, Elam C., 81, 82
Free school system. *See* Public school system
Free West (newspaper), 14
French, Martin V. (or F., or M.), 98
Fuller, Melville Weston, 61, 62, 63, 176–77n.11

Galbraith, John Kenneth, 12, 143–45
Galena, education for blacks in, 51

Galesburg: celebration of new state constitution in (1870), 90; public school open to black children in, 35, 36, 45, 49–50; racial tolerance in, 49
Gapen, William E., 131
Genius of Liberty (newspaper), 14, 33
Ginther, William E., 176–77n.11
Gladney, John, 94, 97
Golden Rule, arguments for blacks' rights based on, 32
Grant, Ulysses S., 78, 91, 93, 102
Gunnell, John T., 128–29. *See also Chase* v. *Stephenson*

Haines, Elijah M., 84–85
Hale, Dr. Morris, 100
Hamilton, John M., 103, 132–33
Hampton Singers, 103
Hannibal Zouaves (of Chicago), 103
Harris, William Torrey, 96
Hayes (Hays), Leroy, 97
Hayes, Rutherford B., 113
Hayes, Samuel Snowden, 24, 37, 60–61, 65
Henry, George W., 118–22, 125, 182n.14
Henry law. *See* "Act to protect colored children in their rights to attend Public Schools, An"
Higginson, George M., 57, 58, 65
Historical Encyclopedia of Illinois, 113
Hoard, Samuel, 176n.5
Holden, Charles N., 64, 177n.13
Homes baseball team, 104
Howard, Mrs. (schoolteacher in Bloomington), 53
Hoyt, John Q., 63
Hyers sisters, 103
Hynes, Thomas W., 30

Illinois: antislavery victory in, 3; balance of representation in, 3; black code in, 9, 13–14; black population of, 4, 153; constitu-

tional conventions in, 76, 77, 78, 80, 81, 83–88, 90; first constitution of (1818), 2; local school ordinances in, 44, 109, 114; pattern of immigration into, 2–3, 4; public education legislation in, 4–5, 9–10, 28–29, 38–40, 78, 116–17, 120–22, 123, 124–25, 128, 134, 139–40, 142, 154–55; revised constitution of (1870), 87–88, 90, 91, 93, 108, 109, 115, 123, 139, 152; school-age population of, 29; sectional conflict in, 3, 19, 80; slavery debate in, 2, 3
Illinois Civil Rights Act (1885), 153
Illinois College, 112
Illinois Female Antislavery Society, 35–37, 151–52
Illinois General Assembly: anti-black sentiment in, 61, 75, 79, 121, 123; antislavery society's petitions to, 33–35, 38; blacks in, 154; blacks' petitions to, 20–25, 27–28, 73–76, 86–88, 110; implementing 1870 revised constitution, 109–10, 116–17, 118–22; measures other than petitions introduced to, 38–41, 74, 116, 118, 123; political divisions within, 40; ruling on separate "colored" schools, 61–62; sympathy toward blacks in, 30, 75, 121. *See also* Illinois, public education legislation in
Illinois State Antislavery Society: assistance to blacks from, 33–35, 36, 37, 151–52; political power of, 34. *See also* Illinois Female Antislavery Society
Illinois State Central Suffrage Committee, 74
Illinois State Colonization Society, 9, 22
Illinois State Conventions of Colored Men: first (1853), 22, 25, 32; second (1856), 28; third

(1866), 44, 46, 53, 74; fourth (1869), 80, fifth (1873), 110
Illinois State Council, first meeting of (Chicago, 1854), 26–27, 32
Illinois State Normal University, 48–49
Illinois State Repeal Association, 32, 150
Illinois State School Convention, 7
Illinois State Suffrage Association, 150
Illinois State Teachers' Association, 112
Illinois Supreme Court cases: *Bibb*, 137, 141; *Chase* v. *Stephenson*, 126, 128–36; *Hunt* v. *McFall*, 137; *Longress*, 137, 138–41, 150; *Peair*, 137, 141
Illinois Teacher, The, 112
Indiana: first constitution of, 2, 4; legislation against slavery in, 2; public education legislation in, 4, 8; white assistance to blacks in, 37–38
Indiana Committee on People of Color of the Antislavery Friends, 37, 151. *See also* Quakers
Isbell, Lewis, 69

Jackson, Rev. Andrew W., 19, 94
Jackson, James I. (or T.), 94
Jackson, Rev. James W. H., 97
Jacksonville: black baseball team in, 104; education for blacks in, 45, 53, 112; first blacks voting in, 94
Jenkins, Charles J., 154, 184n.4
Jenkins amendment (1949), 154, 155
Jewish history, as parallel for black experience, 14
Johnson, Joseph G., 82
Johnson, Ward P., 129. *See also* *Chase* v. *Stephenson*
Johnson, William, 17, 19, 28

Joiner, Rev. Edward C., 95
Jones, John: appointed notary
  public, 79; as black leader,
  17–19, 22, 81; on blacks as
  "outlaws," 9; on blacks' social
  relations with whites, 105; in
  campaign to repeal black laws,
  41–43, 72; as Cook County
  commissioner, 94, 100; death
  of, 101; in favor of white assistance to blacks, 18; as first
  Negro on a grand jury, 100; as
  General Agent for State Central
  Suffrage Committee, 74; as lob-
  byist, 80, 81–82, 84, 85–86;
  party to celebrate thirtieth anniversary in Chicago, 102; priorities of, 18–19; recruiting of
  blacks for Civil War by, 69, in
  support of Republican party, 94
Jones, John P., 82
Jones, Nimrod W., 18
Jubilee Singers, 103

Kase, Spencer M., 120–21
Kellogg, Laura A., 65
King, Harrison D., 81
Knox, John, 49
Knox College, 113
Knox Seminary, 50

LaBough, Julia, 97
LaBough, Louis, 97
LaBough, Mrs. Mary J., 97
Lane Theological Seminary, Cin-
  cinnati, 112
Lee, J. Theodore, 99
Lee, Lavinia (née Jones), 99
Lincoln, Abraham, 78, 112–13,
  114
Lindsay, Thomas, 97
Longress, John, 137, 138

McAllister, William K., 131
McDowell, Charles E., 83
McGahey, David, 39
McLean County Guards (of
  Bloomington), 103

"McWorter," "Free Frank," 21
Magee, Alfred, 47
Magee, James Henry, 46–48, 50
Magee, Samuel, 47
Mann, Horace, 5, 113
Mann, Mary E., 47, 58–59, 65,
  176n.6
Matteson, Joel A., 9, 22
Metropolis, first blacks voting in,
  94
Metropolitan Tabernacle College
  (London), 48
Mission Sabbath School, Chicago,
  64, 65, 66
Mitchell, Robert M., 97
Morris, first blacks voting in, 94
Morrison, first black jurors in,
  100
Moseley, Flavel, 65, 176n.5
Moulton, Samuel W., 40
Mt. Emery African Baptist
  Church, Jacksonville, 53

National Council of the Colored
  People, 18
National Convention of Colored
  Citizens (Buffalo, 1843), 18
National Convention of Colored
  Freemen (Cleveland, 1848), 18
National Convention of Colored
  Freemen (Rochester, 1853), 18
National Convention of Colored
  People (Washington, 1868), 81
Natural rights philosophy, 6–7
Night of Affliction (Magee), 46
Northwest Ordinance of 1785, 1
Northwest Ordinance of 1787: Ar-
  ticle 3 of, 2, 4, 5, 8; Article 6 of,
  2

Oakes, General, 112
Oberly, John H., 122, 125
Ogden, William B., 63,
  176–77n.11
Ohio: first constituion of, 2, 4;
  legislation against slavery in, 2,
  oldest black church in, 48; public education legislation in, 4,

37; support for public schooling in, 4, 7–8, 37; Supreme Court rulings in, 132, 136; white assistance to blacks in, 37–38
Ohio Antislavery Society, 151
Ohio Ladies Society for the Education of Free People of Color, 37
Old Northwest Territory, sale of townships in, 1
"Old Settler," interviewed by Drake and Cayton, 71
Ottawa, first blacks voting in, 94

Palmer, John McAuley: as governor, 9, 76–79, 86, 88, 90, 92, 97, 114, 115, 125; as lawyer, 138
Palmer, Louis, 77
Parker, Rev. Byrd, 17, 19, 27
Paul, William, 129. *See also Chase v. Stephenson*
Peair, John, 137
Pekin, first blacks voting in, 94
People ex rel. Scott Bibb, The, v. *The Mayor and Common Council of Alton* (1899), 137, 141
People ex rel. George Hunt, Attorney General, The, v. *Thomas W. McFall et al.* (1888), 137
People ex rel. John Longress, The, v. *The Board of Education of the City of Quincy* (1882), 137, 138–41, 150
People ex rel. John Peair, The, v. *The Board of Education of Upper Alton School District* (1889), 137, 141
Peoria: education for blacks in, 45, 53; employment of blacks in, 97
Phillips, Nellie S., 65
Phillips, William C., 82, 97
Phoenix Band (of Cairo), 103
Pickard, Josiah L., 66, 71
Pinckney, Daniel J., 80
Pink Stockings baseball team, 103, 104
Plater, Lewis F., 123
Platt, Amelia, 180n.18

Platt, Ida, 180n.18
Platt, Jacob F., Jr., 82, 180n.18
Platt, Jacob F., Sr., 180n.18
Plessy v. *Ferguson* (1896), 133
Porter, James E., 98
Power. *See* Bargaining power
Princeton, first blacks voting in, 94
"Progressive Democrat, A," in *Chicago Times,* 92
"Progressive Democrat, Another," in *Chicago Times,* 93
Property tax, for funding public school system, 6, 7, 10, 23–25, 28, 29–30, 36–37, 38–39, 129
Prostitution, 105
Public school system, in Illinois: "colored" schools in, 10, 23, 25–26, 27, 28, 29, 31, 51–54, 57, 59–68, 71, 109, 110, 117, 123, 129, 130–31, 142; community control of, 146; exclusion of blacks from, 8–11, 38–39, 44–46, 51, 118, 129, 137–38, 146–47; funding of, 1–2, 6, 7, 10, 23–25, 28, 29–30, 36–37, 38–39, 129, 133, 146, 154; goals of, 8; importance of, 5–8, 148; inclusion of blacks in, 21, 23, 27, 35, 108–9; legislation for, 2, 4–5, 9–10, 28–29, 38–40, 78, 116–17, 120–22, 123, 124–25, 128, 134, 139–40, 154–55; religion in, 62–63; and school-age population, 29, 45–46, 66–67, 124, 135; superintendent appointed for, 29; Supreme Court decisions on, 126, 128–42

Quakers, assistance to blacks from, 37–38, 151
Quicksteps baseball team, 104
Quincy: education for blacks in, 45, 51–52, 137–41, 142, 183n.11; first blacks voting in, 94

Racine, Wis., education available for blacks in, 47
Republican party of Illinois: black loyalty to, 91, 94, 110; founded, 77; support for blacks from, 152
Richardson, Larkhill, 98
Richardson, Mary, 17–18
Ridge Prairie (Madison Co.), racially mixed school in, 47
Ridgway, Thomas S., 96
Robinson, Rev. Robert J., 19, 25, 26
Rockford, black baseball team in, 103, 104
Rogers Cornet Band (of Springfield), 103
Rollins, Reuben H., 17, 19
Ross, David, 97
Rowell, Jonathan H., 132–33
Ryder, Rev. William H., 62, 177n.13

St. Charles College, Missouri, 112
St. Paul's African Methodist Episcopal Church, Springfield, 52
St. Paul's Universalist Church, Chicago, 62
St. Peter's African Methodist Episcopal Church, Decatur, 53
Scholfield, John, 131
School Fund Association, 25–26, 27, 28, 31, 32, 150
School Laws and Common School Decisions of the State of Illinois (Bateman, ed.), 113
Scott, John, 98
Scott, John M., 131
Scott, Samuel Walter, 97
Second Presbyterian Church, Chicago, 64
Sectional conflict: differences in priorities for blacks due to, 19; and Negro public education, 3–4
Section 16 lands: acreage of in Illinois, 1; ordinance creating, 1; school funding from, 1–2, 10

Section 48, of Illinois free-schools law, 117, 123, 134, 140
Section 84 (80), of Illinois school law, 29–31, 72, 109, 116
Separatism, black: John Jones' opposition to, 18
Shaughbaugh, Daniel, 129. *See also Chase* v. *Stephenson*
Shawneetown, education for blacks in, 51
Sheahan, James W., 56, 58, 59, 66, 67, 70
Sheldon, Benjamin R., 131
Shelton, James P., 97–98
Sheridan, Redmond, 60
Shorthose, Thomas, 128. *See also Chase* v. *Stephenson*
Shreve, John H., 98
Shufeldt, William T., 63
Slavery: antislavery societies in Ohio and Indiana, 37–38, 151; debate over in Illinois, 2, 3; legislation against, 2. *See also* Black code; Illinois Female Antislavery Society; Illinois State Antislavery Society
Smith, Jerry M., 98
Smith, Reuben, 97
Smith, William F., 98
Smith, William M., 97
Southern Illinois Normal University, 96
Springfield: celebration of new state constitution in (1870), 90, 92; education for blacks in, 36, 45, 52; first blacks voting in, 94
Stanley, Joseph, 69
Starne, Alexander, 119, 121
State of Ohio, ex. rel. William Garnes v. *John W. McCann et al.* (21 Ohio St. 198), 132, 136
Steele, Charles B., 106, 125
Steele, Henry T., 176n.5
Stephenson, David, 128. *See also Chase* v. *Stephenson*
Stevens, Emily C., 65
Storey, Wilbur F., 56
Strain, James, 74

Streeter, Alson J., 121
Suffrage: for blacks, 10, 13, 21, 44, 74, 75, 78, 79, 86–88, 90, 91, 93–95, 149, 152; for women, 36, 152
Sumner, Charles, 110
Sumner bill (1866), 110–11
Surplus Revenue Act of 1836, 10
Sutphon, Thomas, 98

Taft, Levi B., 65, 176n.5
Talcott, Wait, 40
Taxes, for funding public school system. *See* Property tax
Temperance, in Illinois, 36, 152
Tennesseeans, 103
Terry, Frank S., 98
Thomas, Horace H., 103
Thomas, John W. E., 94–95, 100
Thomas W. H., 96
Throop, Amos G., 176–77n.11
Tipton, Thomas F., 130
Toronto, Canada: education available for blacks in, 47–48
29th Regiment United States Colored Infantry, 69

Union Baptist Church (Cincinnati, Ohio), 48
Uniques baseball team, 104
Universal schooling. *See* Public school system
University of Illinois, 95

Vantrece, Henry, 98, 100

Wagner, David C., 83, 84
Wagoner, Henry O., 17, 19, 27
Wahl, Christian, 176n.5
Walker, Pinkney H., 131, 134–35, 138
Ward, James, 64, 67
Ward, Jasper D., 63, 67, 176–77n.11
Waring, Robert C., 97
Washburn, James M., 83, 87
Washington, G., 39

Washington, Isaiah, 98
Washington, James, 100
Way It Was In McLean County, 1972–1822, The (Tate), 128
Weims, Warren, 97
Wells, William H., 56, 65
Wells-Barnett, Ida, 101
Wentworth, John, 27, 58–59, 64, 176n.5
West, Mary Allen, 50
Western Citizen (newspaper), 33, 34
Western Yearly Meeting of Friends of Southern and Western Indiana and Eastern Illinois, 38
Wheeler, Lloyd G., 82, 100–101
Wheeler, Rollin, 40
White, Lewis B., 80, 81, 84, 85–86, 98, 110
Whites, assistance to blacks: from antislavery groups, 33–38; bargaining power of, 15; failure of, 68; John Jones in favor of, 18; need for, 32; in passing legislation, 125. *See also* Illinois Female Antislavery Society; Illinois State Antislavery Society
Williams, Dennis, 46, 50, 102–3
Williams, Henry C., 98
Williams, John H., 139
Winthrop, John, 145
Wisconsin, education available for blacks in, 47
Wood River Colored Baptist Association of Illinois: activities for black schooling by, 25–26, 29; James Henry Magee ordained to, 47

York, Thomas, 52
Young, Andrew, 89

"Zeta" (*Chicago Tribune's* Springfield correspondent), 62
Zouaves (of Springfield), 103

Robert L. McCaul is Associate Professor of Education Emeritus, University of Chicago. He received his A.B. and Ed.M. degrees from Harvard and his Ph.D. degree from the University of Chicago. In addition to contributing chapters to various books, he has published approximately fifty articles in such journals as *Georgia Historical Quarterly, School Review, History of Education Quarterly,* and *Illinois Schools Journal.*